A Trip to the Museums in Korea

Copyright © 2021 by Dragon and Phoenix Publishing

All rights reserved.
Published in the United States by Dragon and Phoenix Publishing.
No part of this publication may be reproduced, distributed, or transmitted in any form or by any means,
including photocopying, recording, or other electronic or mechanical methods,
without the prior written permission of the publisher, except in the case of brief quotations embodied in
critical reviews and certain other noncommercial uses permitted by copyright law.

For permission requests, write to the publisher, addressed "Attention: Permissions Coordinator,"
at the contact information below.

Dragon & Phoenix Publishing
132 Brookside Avenue
Cresskill, NJ 07626

Publisher's Cataloging-in-Publication data

Written by Oh, Dong Suk and Kim, Yong Ho
Translated by Kim, Seok and Dr. Kim, Teayoun, Ph.D.

A Trip to the Museums in Korea
Volume 1; Foundation of Korea

A must have book when touring Korea.
A must read book if interested in Korean history, culture and philosophy.

ISBN: 978-0-578-75343-0
1. History 2. Travel 3. South Korea

First Edition

A must have book when touring Korea.
A must read book if interested in Korean history, culture and philosophy.

By Oh, Dong Suk and Kim, Yong Ho
Translated by Kim, Seok and Dr. Kim, Teayoun

Volume One; Foundation of Korea

Dragon & Phoenix Publishing

| Translator's Note |

It is not often that I come across a project that is significant both historically and culturally. I am grateful to have been given this opportunity to work on the translation of "A Trip to the Museums in Korea."

As you will encounter in the book, the authors successfully provide a glimpse into the rich and profound cultural and historical assets of Korea in an engaging and informative way. I took it as my duty and mission to assign appropriate translations for every word so that the original message is not lost.

Translating this book required an extensive research on the origins of the traditional terms in Korean - from the Lindenbaum tree, which directly connects to the Shindansu tree culture of Korea, to the metal stir-up of the Gaemamusa warriors. There was not a single page that has not fascinated and captivated me. This book shows you; Korea's magnificent gold crowns along with Korea's movable metal printing press prowess that was passed on to the West to give a spark to the age of enlightenment.

I tried to convey even the most difficult concepts naturally to the readers in hopes of delivering the same excitement I felt as I was reading this amazing book in Korean.

I want to thank Ms. Jamie Forgacs for the final edits of the English translation as well as Dr. Teayeon Kim for working hard with me in translating this book. Huge thanks go to Director Jaenam Kim for coordinating this project from start to finish.

Some would argue that there is a "war on history" going on in Northeast Asia as China and Japan look to increase its dominance in the region. While China is distorting the histories of the Uighurs, Mongolia, Tibet, and Korea to lay claims on those territories; Japan is falsely claiming ownership of the islands belonging to China, Korea, and Russia. They are rewriting their history textbooks to lay claims on those places.

The main reason why we must continue our research to seek an unadulterated version of Korean history is not only to ensure we do not lose the culture of Korea that we hold dear, but also to actually defend Korean identity and territory. So, my wish for this book is to be an entertaining resource for the English readership who are studying Korean history, as well as be an enjoyable companion for those with a general curiosity on Korean culture.

Seok Kim (Sean)
August 2020

Preface

I have spent many years connecting with people who are interested in Korean history, and taking them on tours of significant heritage exhibits and sites like the National Museum or Gyeongbokgung Palace.

Every time I go to a museum, I see small groups of young students on field trips with their teachers. It is no surprise that the dull and boring explanations of different eras make these children rapidly lose interest—so much is missing from those explanations. Throughout my years of museum tours, I wrestled with the question of how to better communicate this information in an easy and engaging way. How could I pass on the stories of the past so that they feel alive and relevant to people in the present? After a long process of trial and error, I decided that I could address this issue by introducing people to the world-class artifacts in Korea's museums that represent the Korean civilization through a story telling.

There is a seemingly endless supply of interesting stories of Korea's remarkable cultural heritage, which dates back almost 10,000 years. This book focuses on a selection of the oldest and greatest cultural heritage in the world as found in Korea, but there are many other artifacts not mentioned here that are preserved in Korean museums.

The world's oldest whale hunting petroglyphs can be found in Ulsan, a southeastern city in South Korea. Around the same time that these petroglyphs were made, the ancestors of modern Korea were also building ships and making comb-pattern pottery that would survive to become the oldest relics of their respective kinds in the world. This ancient society also left behind the vestiges of a farm from the world's oldest agricultural society and the world's oldest rice.*

Dolmens are another fascinating aspect of this heritage. There are 60,000 major dolmens—prehistoric megalithic tombs built with massive stones—in the world, and 40,000 of them are located in Korea. It wouldn't be an exaggeration to call prehistoric Koreans "the civilization of the dolmens" since they left behind such a wide variety of these megalithic structures, including pyramid-shaped tombs. Bronze daggers fashioned into the shapes of flames (the Gojoseon or Ancient Joseon type of Mandolin-shaped bronze dagger) have been found in these tombs, along with a bronze mirror that only reveals its hidden beauty if you look carefully. The fine, subtle patterns of the Danyu-semungyeong bronze mirror are a true work of art, deemed by experts to be difficult to replicate even with modern technology. And no book on amazing artifacts from ancient Korean history would be complete without an explanation of the Paljuryeong with its eight attached bells.** These excavated relics reveal important cultural aspects of the civilization of ancient Korea, which was known in its heyday for its splendor.

While the patterns of the Danyu-semungyeong mirror were carved into bronze, there are also carvings on the tops of Korean dolmens. These depictions of constellations are at least several thousand years old. Not only are they the world's oldest drawings of celestial bodies, but they also have been verified as astronomical observations that were stunningly accurate at the time of their making.

---

* Read [Ch 13. Rice Farming, the World's Oldest Agriculture Sec. 5. 17,000-year-old rice seeds]

** Read Ch. 10 The Unsolved Mysteries of the Ancient Danyusemungyeong Mirror, Sect. 7 The bronze mirror and the eight bells

The Seven Stars of the Northern Dipper (Ursa Major) constellation is an ever-present protagonist in these depictions. Centuries of this tradition of revering the Seven Stars of the Northern Dipper continued throughout the Goguryeo (37 BCE~ 668 CE), Goryeo (918-1392), and Joseon (1391-1897) dynasties and led to the invention of the Cheon-sang-yeol-cha-bun-ya-ji-do diagram.*

This diagram, which was crafted during the Goguryeo Dynasty, is a drawing of all the constellations that could be observed with the naked eye in Goguryeo at the time. It is the oldest astronomical chart in the world. The center of the diagram is the most auspicious spot in the heavens, a sacred site called the Jamiwon or Jamigoong. The Jamiwon was believed to be the place where the Heavenly Emperor (also called Sangje, a shortened form of a title that means Jade Emperor) resided and governed the universe.

Traditionally, the Jade Emperor was said to have ridden on the Seven Stars of the Northern Dipper, which were his heavenly chariot, and he governed the universe while traveling on the chariot throughout the four seasons. This was known as the Chil-jeong, or the seven governances.** The "Heavenly Son" who received divine orders from the Jade Emperor and implemented these commands in the earthly realm was called by many titles that included Heavenly Son, emperor, and king. These emperors of the land built their palaces on auspicious sites on Earth and governed the earthly realm

---

* Read Ch. 5 Mapping the Cosmos with Cheon-sang-yeol-cha-bun-ya-ji-do , Sect. 2 The troubled travels of the Cheon-sang-yeol-cha-bun-ya-ji-do.

** Shiji 史記 Tianguanshu 天官書 – [Shiji], written by Sima Qian 司馬遷(BCE 145 - BCE 86), also known as [Records of the Grand Historian]. There's a chapter in the Shiji called [Tianguanshu] which is solely dedicated to the observation of the celestial body. Here, it is written that the role of the Northern Dipper(referred to as the 'Seon-gi-ok-hyeong') is "to oversee the seven governances." Also, the chapter [Scriptures of Yao堯典] in the [Book of Documents 尙書] states that "through the Seon-gi-ok-hyeong(Northern Dipper), the Seven Governances are set right."

on behalf of the Jade Emperor, an act which we now call "politics" in the modern world.

Of the many palaces in the history of Korean civilization, Gyeongbokgung Palace of the Joseon Dynasty (1392-1897) is a classic example of architecture where the Korean people tried to recreate the auspicious site of Heaven on Earth. It was designed according to the Cheon-sang-yeol-cha-bun-ya-ji-do. In other words, the palace was built based on the principles of yin-yang and the five elements.* This is why Geongbokgung Palace is full of paintings of mysterious creatures that seem to have come down from the heavens. Among the most famous of these are the Five Gods: Blue Dragon of the East, White Tiger of the West, Red Phoenix of the South, and Black Tortoise of the North; the Golden Dragon takes the central position.

The ancestors of Korea also created a fascinating cultural footprint that spans many different fields like metallurgy and textiles, an impact seen in innovations like Goguryeo Dynasty stirrups and armored cavalry, the Goryeo movable metal type printing press (the oldest movable metal printing press technology in the world), and silk.** These spread throughout the world long ago, but you can still find traces of their effects in the modern era. Koreans also invented Hangul, the Korean alphabet that has become the envy of linguists worldwide.

Not long ago, the hit Korean TV drama "Dokkaebi (The Goblin)" shed new light on the historical context and cultural manifestations

---

* Yin-yang and five elements. Also known as the Yin-yang and Five Phases. A widely accepted philosophy throughout East Asia originating from the diagrams of Hado(Bokhee) and Nakseo(King Wen of Zhou). Yin-yang and five elements are the foundation of the Eastern Civilization as it is applied in numerous fields including politics, medicine, war strategies, education, and fengshui.

** Read Ch. 2 Conquering the Continent: The Stirrup and the Gaemamusa Sect. 3 The rise of the stirrup.

of its famous character.* "Dokkaebi" can be seen throughout Korean culture, appearing as a name, motif, or identifier of a variety of figures. It even functions as the nickname of Jaoji Hwanung, the fourteenth Hwanung of the state of Baedal.** Jaoji Hwanung never lost a battle and was venerated as the god of war in ancient times. The spread of Dokkaebi's cultural influence can be tracked to places as far away as Europe and South America.

Korea boasts more ancient gold crowns than any other country, retaining 10 of the world's 12 surviving gold crowns. Goguryeo, Shilla (57 BCE - 935 CE), and Gaya (42 – 562 CE)'s dynasties were all established as successors to Ancient Joseon (2333 BCE – 295 BCE), which is why the designs of their gold crowns are based on shared ideologies. The gold crown from the Shilla Dynasty in particular is a treasure among these other magnificent crowns; it is famous for being strung with numerous curved jades, and its design is a cultural code that renders various intrepretations.

Since antiquity, Korean societies prized jade to the extent that anything considered to be of the highest quality was attributed with the affix "ok"—a single syllable word pronounced like "oak" in oak tree and meaning jade. There are many examples of this, such as that a child born into a family without other children was called ok-dong-ja (the jade child); the hands of beautiful women were called seom-seom-ok-soo (delicate and precious jade hands); the king's body was known as the ok-chae (the jade body); the throne where the king sat was ok-jwa (the jade throne); the king's seal was known as the ok-

---

* Dokkaebi (South Korean TV drama, 2017). International hit known as 'The Goblin - Guardian: The Lonely and Great God'. Read Ch 16 Dokkaebi, the God of War Section 1 A familiar god passed down in folktale and legend
** State of Baedal, Baedal Shinshi, or Baedal Dynasty - An ancient Korean dynasty found in BCE 3897 and lasted until BCE 2333. 18 Heavenly Emperors ruled throughout the dynasty.

swae (jade seal); the highest god of all of the heavens was the Okhwang Sangje (the Jade Emperor), and the capital city of the heavens was known as the Ok-gyeong (Jade Capital).

These tales and treasures are just a taste of the countless fascinating stories found in Korean museums.

Once you start exploring different museums, you will quickly learn that Korea's ancestors revered the radiance and splendor of the cosmos. They tried to live by the heavenly rule of the Jade Emperor who governed the universe, and this gave rise to the culture of the Seven Stars of the Northern Dipper. There is also evidence that these people of long ago lived according to the principles of yin-yang and the five elements: the governing laws of the universe. Classic examples of this culture are represented in mirrors and potteries and show up in graves bearing the Drawing of the Five Deities (Oshindo), the Irworobongdo paintings, and the Taegukgi—the national flag of the Republic of Korea. Almost every aspect of the way Koreans today eat, dress, and make a home has a connection to the five elements, and Koreans even apply the principle of the five elements to medicinal practices to treat and heal internal organs (also known as the five viscera and six entrails).*

Essentially, these artifacts tell us a rich range of cultural stories—stories about the Heavenly Emperor, the Heavenly Son, yin-yang, the five elements, and a civilization of radiance and splendor.

Modern society tends to differentiate the ancient past into the

---

* (1) *Five dieties* - Read Ch.6 The Fantastic Beasts, the Five Elements, and the Drawing of the Five Deities
(2) *I-wol-oh-bong-do* - Read Ch 5 Mapping the Cosmos with Cheon-sang-yeol-cha-bun-ya-ji-do Sect. Governing the land in the image of the heavenly realm
** Five viscera and six entrails – Five of the main human organs (liver, heart, spleen, lungs, and the kidneys) and six supporting organs (stomach, small intestine, large intestine, gallbladder, urinary bladder, and the triple energizer) according to Eastern Medicine.

Neolithic, Bronze, and Iron Ages. But was humankind's level of culture actually barbaric and primitive during the Neolithic and Bronze Ages? Are we living in an era of high sophistication and culture now that we've started traveling by airplanes? Although the ancient people who lived in what is now modern-day Korea didn't have internet or smartphones, they did have a systematic ideology and philosophy. They didn't encounter major inconveniences in their day-to-day life. Their time-honored spiritual and cultural traditions form the foundation of Korean culture today, a culture that displays the unique characteristics of Korean civilization and is known to the world as Hallyu: the Korean Wave.

I once heard that the top one percent of first class travelers commonly read about history. If this is true, perhaps one reason for this is that studying history opens doors to immense opportunities for learning; another might be that you have to know your target country's culture if you want to successfully sell company products there. I think it is safe to say that culture is all but synonymous with history. The ways that people eat, sleep, dress themselves, behave, and enjoy life are the result of their respective cultural histories. This is why you can understand a certain country much better if you engage with its history.

It is clear that international tourists think this way, too. The most popular hotspots for international tourists in Korea are museums and palaces like the National Folk Museum, National Central Museum, National Gyeongju Museum, National Ancient Palace Museum, War Memorial of Korea, Gyeongbokgung Palace, Changdeokgung Palace, Deoksugung Palace, and Jongmyo Shrine.

In an era of global competition, intercultural competence has become the cornerstone to the development and prosperity of individuals and businesses. It is vital to learn about history so that we can deduce its impact on various cultures and understand the many strands that weave together into a global tapestry. All of this leads to developing a deeper understanding of the world as a whole.

While books are the most common approach to learning history, visiting museums in person will help you understand history more clearly and look back at history in more fun and engaging ways.

This is why I seek to extract the marvelous stories hidden deep within Korean relics and artifacts—and furthermore, why I seek to forge a path to share these stories with the rest of the world.

I would like to end with a special thanks to Mr. Chanhwa Park, who runs Hallyu Wave Love, for his significant contributions in gathering resources for this book. Also, I would like to offer my gratitude to my co-author Mr. Yong Ho Kim's spouse, Ms. Hyeseon Han, for providing us with many of the designs used to make this book easily accessible and understandable.

Dong Suk Oh
March 2018

contents

Preface

Part 01
The Glorious Nation of the Golden Crown 19

01 The nation that crafted the 10 of the 12 surviving golden crowns in the world 20
02 Gyeongju, the city of gold 24
03 Shilla's gold crowns take the form of the Shin-dan-su tree 30
04 Outfits and ornaments as class and status symbols 40
05 The splendid golden ages of the Four Kingdoms Period 43
06 Curved jade, the great mystery of the gold crowns 48
07 The origins of the ancient gold crowns 56
08 How did Shilla become the nation of gold crowns? 61

Part 02
Conquering the Continent: The Stirrup and the Gaemamusa 65

01 The nomadic people who conquered Eurasia on horseback 66
02 The Parthian shot and the art of mounted archery 72
03 The rise of the stirrup 79
04 The development of horse riding skills and stirrups 81
05 The military might of the Gaemamusa 86
06 The horse-revering nomadic people 95
07 The heavenly horse as a sovereign symbol 98
08 The bronze pot: a must-have for nomadic life 104
09 The introduction and impact of stirrups in the West 106

Part 03
The first metal printing of humanity that flipped the world upside down 113

01 The paradox of the Gutenberg Bible in film 114
02 Eastern paper and printing technologies in Europe's cultural awakening 117
03 Goryeo, the land of advanced wood and metal printing technologies 124
04 Did Gutenberg copy Goryeo's movable metal type printing press? 127
05 Meeting Iran's Gutenberg 130
06 Jeungdoga, predecessor of Jikji by 138 years 133
07 Korea's metal-refining and manufacturing technology gives birth to movable metal type 136

Part 04
The dream of all languages, Hangul 147

01 The beautiful design of the Korean alphabet 148
02 An alphabet to rival all others 151
03 King of communication and debate: Great King Sejong and his secret project 155
04 Great King Sejong's dream lives on in UNESCO award 160
05 Traditional lifestyle philosophy within Hangul's consonants and vowels 161
06 Hangul was not made in a day 164
07 The future of the Korean language 167

Part 05
My dear, if you see a shining star The cheonsangyeolchabunyajido 171

01 The universe within the 10,000 won bill 172
02 The troubled travels of the Cheon-sang-yeol-cha-bun-ya-ji-do 175
03 Depicting the vast majority of Northern Hemisphere constellations 179
04 Gyeongbokgung Palace, the auspicious site of Heaven on Earth 182
05 Guardians of the auspicious sites: Blue Dragon, White Tiger, Red Phoenix, and Black Tortoise 190
06 The heavenly guardians of Gyeongbokgung Palace 196
07 Governing the land in the image of the heavenly realm 201
08 Goguryeo astronomers draw the world's oldest constellation 207
09 Goguryeo's conception of the cosmos through astronomy 212
10 Astronomy in Shilla, Baekjae, and Goryeo 215
11 Astronomy inherited from Ancient Joseon 220

Part 06
The Fantastic Beasts, the Five Elements, and the Drawing of the Five Deities 225

01 Creating the turtle ship 227
02 The sacred beast that rules the water 233
03 The many tales of the turtle ship 240
04 Everyday life long ago with the Four Gods 242
05 The greatest of the fantastic beasts 246
06 The central figures of the Golden Dragon, the Golden Bear, and the Dokkaebi 251

Part 07
Taegeukgi: the Universe Spread on Cloth 255

01 Glory and agony in recent Korean history 256
02 The first Taegeukgi 260
03 The many forms of the Taegeukgi 266
04 The Taegeuk alive within the history of the Korean people 269
05 Contextualizing the Taegeukgi's white background 272
06 The geon, gon, gam, and ri trigrams 275
07 The universal principles of the Eight Trigrams 281
08 Four, not eight: the trigrams of the Taegeukgi 284
09 The Taegeuk as the "Great People of Korea" 286

Part 08
The dolmen, an evidence of a systematic society 291

    01 UNESCO World Heritage at the Ganghwa Dolmen Sites 292
    02 Megalithic culture around the world 297
    03 The era of stone tombs 301
    04 Ancient civilization as told by Korean dolmens 305
    05 The mystery of the Seven Stars on dolmen capstones 310

Part 09
A design of flame, the bronze daggar 315

    01 The Bronze Age: antiquity's Industrial Revolution 316
    02 The Ancient Joseon bronze dagger that predates the mandolin-shaped dagger 320
    03 Discoveries from the territories of the Dongyi people 323
    04 The flame of the Ancient Joseon bronze dagger 327
    05 A beautiful and lethal weapon for active combat 329
    06 The ingenious design of the ssembly-type dagger 335
    07 Ancient Joseon bronzeware's copper, tin, and zinc alloys 338
    08 Lightning, symbol of the divine 341

Part 10
The unsolved questions about an ancient Corean bronze mirror, Danyu-Semungyeong, which is engraved with many fine lines that is virtually unreproducible with modern technology. 349

    01 The taffy seller and the Danyu-semungyeong mirror 350
    02 Ancient technology turned modern marvel:
        the mystery of the Danyu-semungyeong mirror 355
    03 Symbolizing the sun and its brilliance 357
    04 The divine representative becomes both shaman and warrior 360
    05 The sophisticated metallurgy of ancient Korea's alloys 365
    06 Bronze mirrors in Ancient Joseon and China 370
    07 The bronze mirror and the eight bells 374

Part 11
Silk and Sil-Kkury 377

    01 Why did ancient Rome import silk thread? 378
    02 Parthia, the intermediary trading empire 382
    03 Nothing but purple silk for the top brass 386
    04 The portable and precise weight of sil-kkury trade 390
    05 Goguryeo invents sil-kkury 392
    06 Ancient Korean silk outshines Chinese textiles 394
    07 The bronze mirror and the eight bells 397

Part 12
Whale Hunting 7,000 Years Ago in the Bangudae Petroglyphs 403

- 01 The world's oldest depiction of whale hunting 404
- 02 Estimating when the Bangudae Amgakhwa was created 406
- 03 A prehistoric superstar makes waves 409
- 04 Prehistoric cinema 416
- 05 Secrets of successful whale hunting: sturdy nets and skilled shipbuilding 419
- 06 The power of organized community 425
- 07 The Bangudae Petroglyphs' Russian cousin: the Zalavruga Petroglyphs 428
- 08 A shaman's hunting song 433

Part 13
Rice, The Oldest Farming Culture in the World 441

- 01 Why prehistoric people began settling down 442
- 02 Ancient agricultural remains in Goseong-gun County 445
- 03 A 5,000-year-old diet 448
- 04 Growing rice 5,000 years ago 450
- 05 17,000-year-old rice seeds 456

Part 14
A Beginning of Korean Wave, Comb-Pattern Pottery 461

- 01 Korea's Oldest Earthenware: Gosan-li pottery from Jeju Island 462
- 02 Osan-li's comb-pattern pottery predates Siberian ware 465
- 03 Comb-pattern pottery spreads through East Asia and Europe 468
- 04 The anti-breakage science of comb-pattern pottery 472
- 05 A better name for comb-pattern: sunshine-pattern pottery 474

Part 15
The Ancient Fashion "It-Item", Jade 487

- 01 A people bedecked with precious jade 488
- 02 A jewel guiding the way to heaven 494
- 03 "Ok" as a modifier of beauty and greatness 498
- 04 Reconstructing ancient jade accessories 502
- 05 Banishing ghosts and bolstering health: the mystical powers of jade 506
- 06 Embracing divine vitality and bestowing virtue 508
- 07 The ancient state system evidenced by jade artifacts 510

Part 16
The God of War, Dokkaebi 515

- 01 A familiar god passed down in folktale and legend 516
- 02 Ttukseom Island, Emperor Chi-u's former shrine in Seoul 522
- 03 Dukje rites for the god of war 526
- 04 The Dokkaebi as a symbol of Emperor Chi-u 528
- 05 Emperor Chi-u: ancestor of the Korean Dongyi or Chinese Zhonghua? 534
- 06 The power of the Dokkaebi design 538
- 07 The Dokkaebi's journey to Europe and America 544

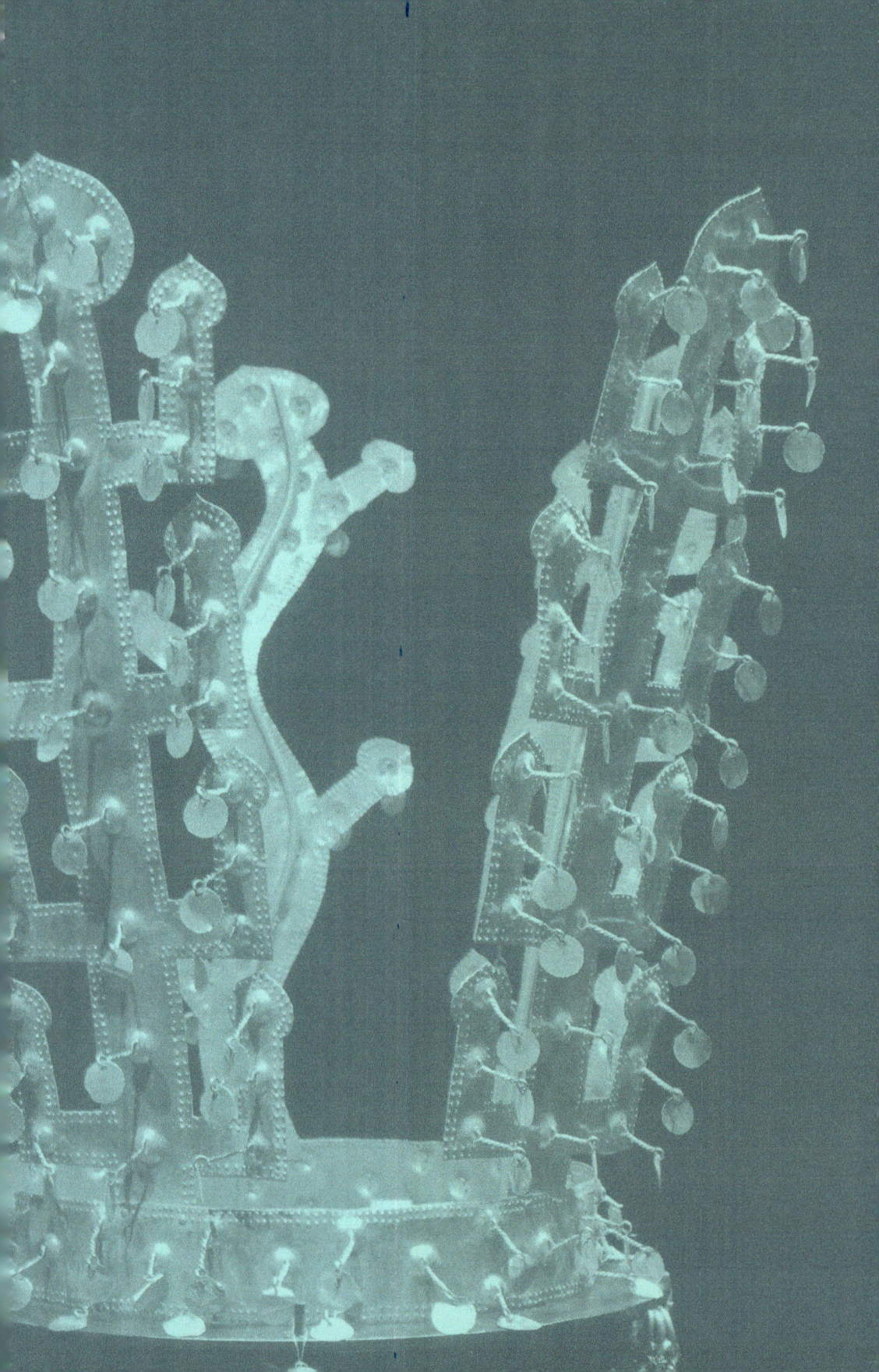

PART 01

A Trip to the Museums in Korea

The Glorious Nation of the Gold Crowns

01 The nation that crafted the 10 of the 12 surviving golden crowns in the world
02 Gyeongju, the city of gold
03 Shilla's gold crowns take the form of the Shin-dan-su tree
04 Outfits and ornaments as class and status symbols
05 The splendid golden ages of the Four Kingdoms Period
06 Curved jade, the great mystery of the gold crowns
07 The origins of the ancient gold crowns
08 How did Shilla become the nation of gold crowns?

01

The nation that crafted the 10 of the 12 surviving gold crowns in the world

If you who walk around the exhibits in the National Central Museums, you'll face the Shilla dynasty gold crowns displayed under a deem light. Almost everyone stops in astonishment and stay for a few minutes. The fanciness of gold and it's unique design has a charming affect that mesmerizes anyone who sees it.

I ask this question everytime to the visitors when talking about the golden crown.

"There are only twelve ancient Gold Crowns found in the world. Can you guess how many crowns were excavated in Korea?"

Everybody has a different answer for this questions. And when I tell them 10 of them are from Korea they get really surprised. Of the ten crowns, seven are from Shilla, two are from Gaya, and one is

Figure 1-1 The gold crown excavated from the Northern tomb of Hwangnamdaechong Tombs (the large tomb in Hwangnam) in Gyeong-ju / shaped standing ornaments are layered in three, and curved jades pieces in green color are hung to add a touch of splendor. (National Museum of Korea)

Figure 1-2 Side view of Hwangnamdaechong Tombs in Gyeongju (National Museum of Korea)

from Goguryeo. The fact that 10 of the 12 existing gold crowns are Korean tells us that Korea is a very special country, the suzerain state of the gold crowns.

There are many crown in the world decorated with gold. Austria Wien's crowns from the Holy Roman Empire, crown of Denmark, crown of Swden, crown of England and etc., which were made much later than our crown. But our crown is different in many aspects. Korean crowns were crafted with pure gold and when the kings passed away, they were buried together with the king whereas western crown, made with different metals including gold and gems, and were passed down when the king passed away.

Figure 1-3 Emperor's Coffin of the Holy Roman Empire from the 10th~~11th century currently preserved in the Shatskhammer Museum in Vienna, Austria.

Ancient crowns around the world

- Shilla(7) – Hwangnamedae-chong crown, Geumgwan-chong crown, Cheonma-chong crown, Geumryeong-chong crown, Jeon Gyodong crown, Horim crown
- Gaya(2) – Jeon-Goryeong crown, Jeon-Changnyeong crown (Ogura crown)
- Goguryeo(1) – Jeon-Gangseo-gun crown
- Outside Korea(2) – Tillya Tepe crown of Central Afghanistan, North of Black Sea region Sarmat crown from the Rostov region

02

Gyeongju, the city of gold

The gold crowns of Shilla were found in the following royal tombs in Gyeongju: Geumgwan-chong, Geumryeong-chong, Hwangnan-dae-chong, Cheonma-chong, Seobong-chong, and Gyo-dong tomb. But there is still one more gold crown: the gold crown currently preserved in Horim Art Museum. Because there is some ongoing debate as to whether this crown is from Shilla or Gaya, it is generally referred to as the Horim gold crown.

The Horim crown's outer design shares characteristics with the Gyodong gold crown*, so the two crowns are widely believed to have been made in the early Shilla Dynasty. This book classifies the Horim crown as a crown from Shilla.

Each of Shilla's and Gaya's gold crowns was discovered in a tomb. Additionally, ornaments for a gold crown have been found in the

---

* The description of the Gyodong gold crown, currently displayed in the Shilla History Exibition at the National Gyeongju Museum, points the origin of the gold crown to the early Marip-gan Period(356~540 CE) of Shilla Dynasty. From the 17th Emperor to the 23rd Emperor of Shilla Dynasty used the title Marip-gan.

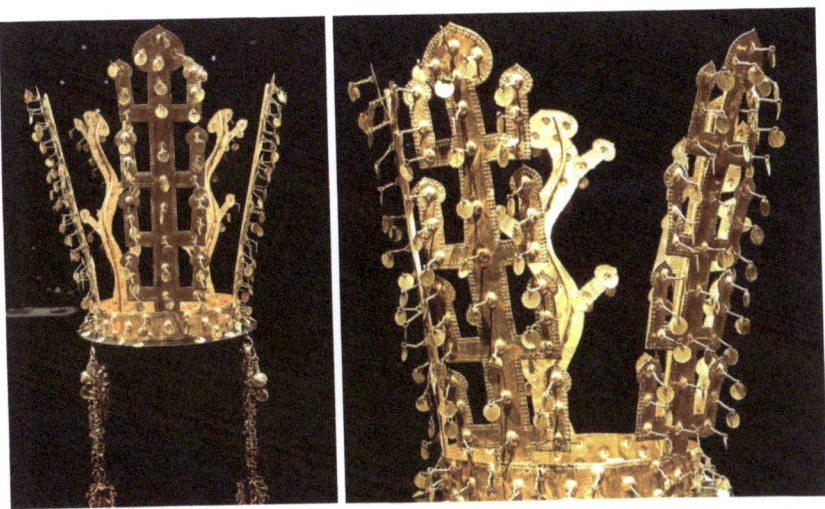

Figure 1-4 Geumryeongchong Tomb Gold Crown / 山-shaped standing ornaments have four layers, and there is no curved jade. (National Museum of Korea)

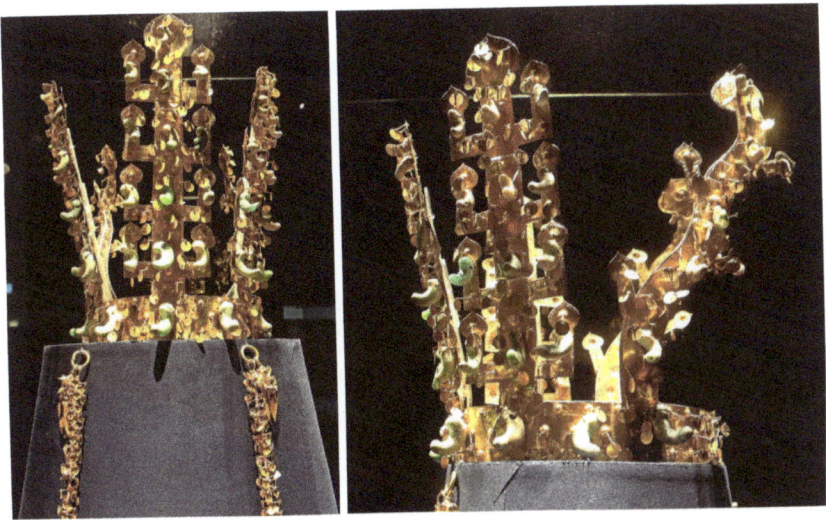

Figure 1-5 The gold crown of Cheonmachong Tomb/ 山-shaped standing ornaments are in four layers." (Gyeongju National Museum)

Tomb of King Muryeong of Baekjae, and there is one surviving gold crown from the Goguryeo Dynasty.

There are numerous tombs in Gyeongju that have not yet been excavated, making it safe to assume that more gold crowns will be found once further recovery efforts take place. Moreover, there have

Figure 1-6 Gold Crown of Geumgwanchong Tomb / 山-shaped standing ornaments are three layers. (Gyeongju National Museum)

Figures 1-7 Pre-Gyodong gold crown / leaf-shaped spangles are silimar to the gold crown of Silla, (Gyeongju National Museum)

Figure 1-8 The gold crown of Seobongchong Tomb / 山-shaped standing ornaments are three layers with bright curved jade and a phoenix at the tip of the ornament. (National Museum of Korea)

been multiple reports on the repatriation of Korean crowns stolen and taken to Japan during the Japanese colonial period. The number of crowns in Korea could increase in the future once these missing crowns are brought to light.

Besides the seven Shilla Dynasty crowns, two of the remaining three gold crowns are from Gaya, and one is from Goguryeo. Gaya's gold crowns are the Jeon-Goryeong crown in the Samsung Museum of Art and the Jeon-Changnyeong crown, which previously was kept by a Japanese collector. The Changnyeong crown is also called the Ogura crown after the last name of the Japanese person who bought the crown, a well-known collector of Korean cultural treasures that were stolen from royal graves. All of these stolen cultural treasures were donated to the Tokyo National Museum by Ogura's son and are known as the Ogura collection. A replica of the Changnyeong crown is currently on display at the National Central Museum.

It does seem significant that the character Jeon (傳) appears in front of the names of the Goryeong gold crown, Changnyeong gold crown, and Gangseogun gold crown. Scholars customarily use this character to mark when it is impossible to know the exact excavation location of a stolen artifact. Since these three gold crowns are believed to have been excavated from Changnyeong, Goryeong, and Gangseogun, their names reflect this naming convention. If scholars cannot reasonably postulate the excavation origins of a stolen artifact, then they simply name it after the owner or the place where it is exhibited.

Though the crowns of the Gaya Dynasty are much smaller and simpler compared to those of Shilla, they still have their own unique characteristics. For instance, the gold crown of Jeon-Changnyeong has a spade-shaped ornament attached to the crown frame at the center and two leaf-shaped branch ornaments on each side. The ornaments themselves are hung with tiny disc-shaped decorations. The crown in the Samsung Museum of Art has a bigger frame with four spade-shaped ornaments attached. While each ornament here has disc-shaped decorations as with the Jeon-Goryeong crown, this crown's frame boasts curved jades hung in around its circumference.

Figure 1-9 Reproduction of the Jeon-Changnyeong Gold crown of Gaya (Ogura Gold Crown) in the National Museum of Korea/ Unlike the Shilla Gold Crown, this crown is expressed with an onion-like shape in the center. It seems to express that the grass leaves are standing next to onion shaped center.

Naming the Seobongchong Gold Crown

- As mentioned earlier, when scholars cannot identify the original owner of a crown, they usually name it after its excavation site. But where there are rules, there are also exceptions—like the crown of Seobongchong. The name of this crown comes from the nickname of a historical figure who was involved in its excavation.

- Seobongchong is an ancient tomb of great historical significance located in Gyeongju, but its name has a rather absurd backstory. It was excavated in 1926 during the Japanese colonial period. Sweden's Crown Prince Gustaf visited Japan and its annexed Korean territories at the time, frequently visiting the excavation site and even participating in the excavation himself. Consequently, the character Seo (瑞) that is used to describe the name of Sweden (瑞典, pronounced Seojeon), and Bong (鳳), the first character of the two-character word Bonghwang (鳳凰, meaning phoenix or crown prince), were combined to name the tomb. This story may sound like a quirky historical fact, but to continue to refer to this ancient tomb in this manner is to disregard the long and storied history of this cultural heritage. Even if the owner and occupant of the tomb cannot be identified, the names of Seobongchong and the Seobongchong gold crown must be changed.

03

Shilla's gold crowns take the form of the Shin-dan-su tree

When I first saw Shilla's gold crowns, I was impressed by the distinctive Shilla style and sought to understand its hidden symbolism. Some say the prongs of the crowns look like the hanja character 山 for mountain. Others say they look like the antlers of a deer. But none of this made any sense to me. Why did Shilla artisans make these crowns in this unique style in the first place?

Andong University professor Lim Jaehae wrote in his book *Revealing the Origins of Shilla's Gold Crowns* (2008) that the crowns imitate and symbolize trees. His persuasive explanation relies on not just the shape of the crowns, but also the mythology and culture of the people of Shilla.

Professor Lim begins his book by talking about the roots of Shilla. Shilla started when Jinhan migrants of Samhan* settled in

---

* Samhan: Literal translation Three Han. Jinhan people of the three Han States

six villages. Lim points out that a mysterious forest called Gyerim features prominently in the mythology surrounding Kim Alji, the founder of the powerful Kim clan of Shilla.

Lim explains that Gyerim means "forest where the sacred rooster cries" and that legend says that Kim Alji was born from an egg in the forest of Gyerim. For a while, the nation of Shilla even called itself Gyerim, and its royal crowns were designed to imitate the trees of that legendary forest. After the end of Gojoseon (also known as Ancient Joseon (2333 BCE ~ 239 BCE)), the Three Hans of Mahan, Jinhan, and Byeonhan*, were established along with other states such as Buyeo**, Okjeo (3c.~ 2c. BCE ~ 56 CE), and Dongyeh (1c. BCE~ 6c. CE). The people of Shilla in particular held the legends of Ancient Joseon as sacred, and they passed down the story of Hwanung establishing the city of Shinsi and starting the nation of Baedal under the auspices of the shindansu tree.*** To the people of Shilla, the sacred forest of Gyerim was an important symbol, and it was only natural for such an important symbol to be expressed through Shilla's royal crowns. The very designs of Shilla's crowns essentially declared this firm belief: "Shilla is the descendant of Dangun.**** The legacy of Ancient Joseon has been handed down to us."

---

of Ancient Joseon migrated to the southern part of the Korean peninsula around time of the fall of Ancient Joseon.
* The Three Hans - Also known as Samhan. The migrants and refugees of Beon Joseon and Jin Joseon moved to the southern region of Mak Joseon to establish the three states. Three Hans were succeeded by Baekjae dynasty(Mahan, 18 BCE), Shllla dynasty(Jinhan, 57 BCE), and Gaya dynasty(Byeonhan, 1c. BCE).
** Buyeo - There are 8 different nation states that used the name Buyeo. There was Ancient Buyeo, Great Buyeo(Ancient Joseon changed its name. Succeeded by Northern Buyeo), Northern Buyeo(succeeded by Goguryeo, Jolbon Buyeo, Eastern Buyeo, Galsa Buyeo, Western Buyeo, Southern Bueyo(Baekjae)
*** Read. Ch. 7. Taegeukgi: the Universe Spread on Cloth Sect. 6 The geon, gon, garm, and ri trigrams.
**** Dangun is the title of the emperor of Ancient Joseon. There were 47 Danguns throughout its 2,096 years' lineage.

If you examine the vertical ornaments of the Geumryeongchong gold crown, you will find that they stand firmly erect toward the heavens, like trees that have grown straight and tall. Rounded leaves shaped like spades sprout from the branches and stems of these trees ornaments.

Who made the gold crowns of Shilla?

- In the early stages of Shilla, the Park, Seok, and Kim clans took turns in ruling the land. The crown of Silla found in Gyeongju was created when the Kim lineage was in power.

What is the shindansu?

The shindansu is a divine tree, a motif which can be found in legends all around the world, such as the tree of life or the cosmic world tree. The Korean people once had a tradition of choosing a sacred place called sodo to hold heavenly rituals and plant trees; the biggest tree was then selected as the shindansu. The shindansu was a medium that connected the heavens and the people. Next to the sodo, a special kind of school called Gyeongdang would teach unmarried youths reading, archery, and horse riding. Sodo culture was passed down to later generations of Koreans to become Sotdae culture. Even

Maypole, erected every year on May 1st.

now, if you visit a Korean village, you might see long wooden poles erected with the figure of a crane sitting at the very top of each. These symbolize the sacred tree, the shindansu.

Sotdae spread to Japan, becoming the dori-i, or the traditional gates that stand in front of Shinto temples. There are parallels to shindansu culture in other countries as well, appearing throughout both the Northern and Southern Hemispheres. In Islamic cultural tradition, Muslims planted trees and established schools for teaching the Quran, called Madreseh, in the innermost sanctums of their mosques. This is where they teach a variety of studies to empower future generations. The culture of the Evenki tribe of Russia's Saka Republic also shares similarities with Sotdae. Globally, there are a number of traditions surrounding the maypole held on the first of May, a celebration that is similar to Korea's Jeongwol Daeboreum festival. According to many of these traditions, which are still followed in parts of Europe and the Americas, the maypole is erected for the month of May at the peak of spring when life is vibrant with energy.

On the first of each May, all the youth of the village come to dance the maypole dance under the pole, where the young men and women take the ends of the ribbons attached to the top of the pole and spin in different directions. The ribbons form a knot, and when the knot is finished, the young men and women pair with the partner closest to them.

Traditionally, this was a very important spring courtship ritual, helping villagers pair off into couples who would marry and bear children. In places in England and the United States, they chose May queens and crowned them. Germans in Bayern and Austrians in particular have their own twist on this celebration. After the May dance, a couple of men wearing duck masks appear, making quacking noises and hopping and dancing their way around the village in a big circle. This ritual is a prayer that not only asks the god of thunder to send enough rain for ducks to play in ponds, but also for growing grass, grain, and beans for the year.

Some Western scholars claim that the pole used on the first of May symbolizes a male god's phallus descending from heaven to become one with the female goddess of the earth. In Eastern culture, this symbol represents the process of fulfillment through the unification of the heavenly and earthly realms. In some Western traditions, maypoles were decorated with spiraling white and red ribbons, with the red representing menstruation and the white representing sperm. This parallels the Sotdae tradition in Korea where a duck or a crane was placed on top of a Sotdae pole as a symbol of reproduction. Koreans would offer a ritual for the prosperity and well-being of the village under the Sotdae every first full moon of the year. This celebration of the Jeongwol Daeboreum festival was considered a holiday as important as the Lunar New Year, with more events that day than any other time of year.

While the Sotdae poles have counterparts like the maypole in Western traditions, the shindansu can be compared to the lindenbaum (linden tree), which was regarded as a divine tree in parts of Europe. The linden tree bears small fruits when its leaves sprout in the spring, and this ripened fruit has often been fashioned into prayer beads. Like the shindansu tree, the linden tree has left a remarkably long-lasting cultural impact. Austrian composer Franz Schubert even wrote a song titled "Lindenbaum" about this tree, which is currently the national tree in the Czech Republic, Slovakia, Slovenia, and Lusatia (a region between Poland and Germany). There are many locales and cultural products named after it or a version of its name; various Slavic language-speaking societies call the lindenbaum "lipa", but it has other names including lime and linden.

The names of the linden tree are scattered throughout a variety of European societies. For example, Croatia's currency, kuna, has a lower unit called the lipa. Croatians call the month of June "Lindenbaum" while people in Poland and Ukraine use this name for July. The German city Leipzig takes its name from Lipsk, a Slav word meaning "where the Lindenbaum stands". In the Slavic Eastern Orthodox Church, people prefer icons, or pictures of saints, that are illustrated on a lindenbaum board. The name of the famous village of Lipica in southern Slovenia means "little lindenbaum". Lipica is the home and namesake of the Lipizzaner, a horse breed of international renown. Many people seek out Lipica just to see its prized horses.

The Linden tree of a rural village of Austria that serves as the Shindansu tree in Europe.

Much as the linden tree has a range of names, it is also associated with a range of beliefs. People in the Baltic region held that Laima, the goddess of fate believed to intervene with matters of birth, marriage, and death, lived in the lindenbaum. According to this belief, whenever people prayed for wishes to come true, the goddess would appear from the tree in the form of a cuckoo bird and answer them. For this reason, Lithuanian women revered this tree as a place to make offerings of their personal belongings and pray for blessings. This is very similar to the Korean tradition of Grandmother Samshin, who was believed to live in the Seo-nang-dang tree; Grandmother Samshin bestowed blessings and helped couples get pregnant.

Prior to the advent of Christianity, the lindenbaum was considered a holy tree in Germany. Just like the

Slavs, they would dance under the tree and hold festivals, and they would also gather under its branches to handle the various issues that arose in the region around the tree. They believed that the presence of the lindenbaum revealed the truth, so even after Christianity was introduced, the lindenbaum served as a court of law where the important decisions were made. They used to call the lindenbaum "the tree of the law" and would plant it in an open gathering space in town. This tradition continued until the Enlightenment movement of the eighteenth century. Trees planted in the town center were called the Dance Linden, and people held festivals beneath them. The famous street Unter Den Linden, literally meaning "under the linden tree", is a street of lindenbaums where such festivals were once held. In German folklore, the lindenbaum was also called the tree of lovers, and the tree appears in the German novel *Der Ring des Nibelungen (Nibelungen's Ring)* as well. In it, the character Siegfried (also known as Sigurd) bathes in the blood of a dragon, making himself invincible to steel weapons. But he misses a spot due to a lindenbaum leaf stuck to his back, and that is exactly where an arrow later pierces him with a mortal wound.

If we go back further to the times of the Greek poet Homer and his Roman counterparts, we find that even they mentioned the virtues of the lindenbaum. Scythian oracles used to carry the leaves of the lindenbaum with them, and there are characters in Greek mythology who turned into linden trees. The most well-known among them was the mother of Kyron (Kyron was one of the

Centaurus), who turned into a tree immediately after she gave birth to the centaur. As demonstrated by these many tales and traditions, the European lindenbaum, like the Korean shindansu, has been talked about and considered a sacred tree for quite a long time.

Obelisk in the Karnak Temple in Luxor, Egypt

04

Outfits and ornaments as class and status symbols

There was a strong caste system in place during the Four Kingdoms Period (1c. BCE - 562 CE) *of the Goguryeo, Baekjae, Shilla, and Gaya dynasties. Clothing differentiated classes from the prehistoric era through the Joseon Dynasty (~1897), class-based attire ranging from everyday clothes to official hats. The existence of these official hats, which were commonly worn by government officials, is a perfect example of how different headgear was worn based on a person's class and status. In Shilla and Gaya in particular, kings and queens wore crowns of pure gold, feudal lords and regional representatives wore gold and bronze headgear, and lower officials wore silver; a similar tradition was true in Goguryeo and Baekjae as well.

---

* Four Kingdoms Period is referring to the period when Goguryeo, Bakjae, Shilla, and Gaya Federation had existed in Northeast Asia for more than 500 years. The Four Kingdoms Period comes to an end with the fall of Gaya Federation. Since there is no official set time period for the Four Kingdoms Period we used the date for Gaya's establishment and dissolving.

Figure 1-10 A replica of Baekje's gilt-bronze crown cap displayed at the Hansung Baekje Museum / A dragon and phoenix is carved in a hexagonal grid pattern

In her book *The Political History of Goguryeo's Gold Crown*, professor Park Seonhee of Sangmyeong University explores the period when the gold crown of Goguryeo was worn by the Great King Sosu-rim. During the same period, Baekjae was at the height of its golden age under the rule of King Geun-go-cho. Park reasons that if Goguryeo was producing gold crowns, its neighboring rival Baekjae would have responded in kind with its own production and implementation of gold crowns. Furthermore, Baekjae's gold crowns would

Figure 1-11 Silver ornaments of a crown from Baekje / Its is rare that such a large number of spangles are attached to it, making it look like a Sindansu tree with thickly grown leaves and branches. (Baekje Special Exhibition, National Museum of Korea)

differ from Goguryeo and Shilla's crowns given Baekjae's somewhat unique traditions. We can only hope that one day these gold crowns of Baekjae will be excavated to astonish the world with their own distinct beauty and history.

05

The splendid golden ages of the Four Kingdoms Period

As mentioned in the previous section, there is currently one known gold crown that has been traced back to Goguryeo. For a long time, scholars thought that Goguryeo lacked such a crown of its own, but this was disproved recently with the emergence of a previously unknown ancient gold crown. In 2008, an individual who had been privately preserving this crown revealed it to Professor Park Seonhee, an expert on the history of fashion, and a few other scholars. This is now known as the Jeon-Gangseogun gold crown of Goguryeo.

Park published her book called *The Political History of Goguryeo's Gold Crown* in 2013, bringing together the amazing stories of this particular Goguryeo Dynasty gold crown as well as the history of Goguryeo's politics. The crown is still being studied by experts, but hopefully it will be unveiled to the public soon. Due to the lack of detailed information about this Goguryeo crown, it was long assumed that there were only nine Korean gold crowns, but this number will officially increase to a total of 10 when the Goguryeo crown is revealed.

It is believed that the gold crown was found in Gangseo-gun County (Ganseong-li Village, Borim-myeon Township, Pyeongannam-do Province) during the Japanese colonial period*. The crown itself looks magnificent, with hundreds of shiny decorations made of pure gold from a main gold ornament shaped like a flame. The flame-shaped ornament alludes to the sun-worshipping customs of the people of Goguryeo.

Before the crown was revealed to the world through Professor Park's book, the popular belief about Goguryeo and Baekjae was that they did not have gold crowns of their own. Officially, the only extant relic of this type from Goguryeo was a bronze cap gilded with gold. But looking at history solely through the lens of material evidence like this leads to the biased assumption that Shilla was the only country with gold crowns. However, factoring in the existence of gold decorations for crowns from Baekjae and Goguryeo on display at the National Central Museum, it can be assumed that these two countries also had their own gold crowns like Shilla. According to Professor Park, Baekjae, Goguryeo, and Shilla all benefited from cultural heritage passed down from Ancient Joseon, so it is safe to assume that Baekjae had gold crowns during this era as well.

Shilla's luxurious gold crowns were made in the fifth and sixth centuries when Shilla's national power was rapidly growing, but Goguryeo and Baekjae had already developed long before Shilla began to flourish, making it unrealistic to claim that they were unable to create their own gold crowns. Then, why don't we have many gold crowns from Goguryeo and Baekjae in museums today? There are two key reasons. Firstly, the two countries' styles of tombs were structured in

---

* Japanese Colonial period - 1910~1945

Figure 1-12 A replica of the mirrored flame-shape pattern crown displayed at the Goguryeo Exhibition of the National Museum of Korea / This gilt-bronze crown was excavated from Toseong of Cheongam-ri in Daeseong Region of Pyongyang, and is estimated to have been produced between the 4th and 5th centuries. It shows that the Goguryeo crown was extremely elegant and splendid.

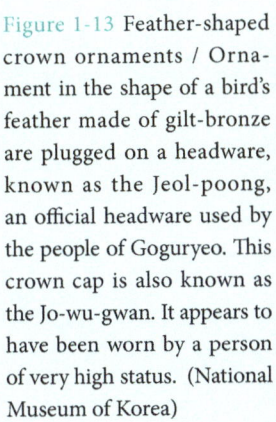

Figure 1-13 Feather-shaped crown ornaments / Ornament in the shape of a bird's feather made of gilt-bronze are plugged on a headware, known as the Jeol-poong, an official headware used by the people of Goguryeo. This crown cap is also known as the Jo-wu-gwan. It appears to have been worn by a person of very high status. (National Museum of Korea)

Figure 1-14 A gilt-bronze ornament in a mirror shape pattern excavated from the tomb of the Goguryeo Jinpari in Pyongyang / It has the three-legged crow (sam-jok-oh) inside the circle in the center. A phoenix is expressed on the top and two dragons on the bottom. (National Museum of Korea)

Figure 1-15 (Left) Gold crown ornaments excavated from the Royal Tomb of King Muryeong / The crown belonged to the king, and the ornaments have a number of spangles(glowing metal decorations attached to gold crowns) attached on them. Queen's crown has no spangles.(National Museum of Korea)

Figure 1-16 (Right) King Muryeong's gold earring found along with the golden crown ornaments / A curved jade ornament hangs down as it's sophisticated appearance is even comparable to the decorations of the Shilla dynasty (National Gongju Museum)

a way that was easier for graverobbers to raid than the burial mounds of Shilla. Secondly, majority of Goguryeo's tombs are in Manchuria which is an official Chinese territory now. Fortunately, the Jeon-Gangseogun crown's emergence has opened the door for the world to see a side of Goguryeo that was previously unknown.

While Baekjae's gold crowns are yet to be found, gold ornaments which were likely used to decorate those missing crowns have been discovered. The decorations for a king or queen's crown found in King Muryeong's tomb have shapes reminiscent of flames, which resembles the design used for Goguryeo's gold crown. We can also make an educated guess about the shapes of Baekjae's pure gold crowns based on the country's Jeol-poong-hyeong gold-bronze crown.

06

Curved jade, the great mystery of the gold crowns

There are relatively simpler forms of Shilla's gold crowns like the one from Jeon-Gyodong, and then there are splendid crowns found in Cheonma-chong and Geumryeong-chong, that are strung with numerous leaf-shaped and rounded ornaments made of gold and curved jade. Shilla and Gaya's curved jade pieces in particular take a very unique shape that is symbolic due to both material and design.

Firstly, it is important to know that jade itself was a prized and precious jewel in ancient East Asia for both its aesthetics and its functions. While it has a distinctive and beautiful color and texture, it was also believed to contain sacred powers. Jade was perfect for rulers who wanted to flaunt a strong sovereign authority and flourishing economy.

Secondly, curved jade pieces were crafted to imitate the shape of a dragon, symbolizing fruitfulness, seed, and life. According to Korean

Figure 1-17 Numerous curved jade ornaments (National Museum of Korea) on the gold crown of the Hwangnamdaechong Tomb

Figure 1-18 Curved jade artifacts excavated along with Shilla gold crowns / (Upper left) Geumryeongchong Tomb (National Museum of Korea), Cheonmachong Tomb (Upper right), and the Northern tomb of Hwangnamdaechong Tombs (Below) (National Gyeongju Museum)

tradition, dragons represented water and were sacred creatures that controlled water. The yin-yang and the five elements philosophy held that water was the life energy that all living things possess. Using jade to evoke a dragon was part of the long tradition of jade culture that had been passed down from the Hongshan culture (BCE 4,700 to BCE 2900.).*

Thirdly, the curved jade resembles a character that represented a dragon in an ancient script used by oracles and written on shells and bones. This use of curved jade in representing dragons has been traced as far back as the prehistoric era. Below are some examples of these "shells-and-bones characters".

Fourthly, people saw curved jade as a way to express their wish for the flourishing of their nation—a wish for their nation to be like the fruit-bearing sacred tree. A dragon was a symbol that vaunted the fact that the king or emperor was a ruler by divine right. In other words, the wearer of a crown with numerous curved jade carvings was a ruler chosen by the heavens, a ruler who would bring about a nation that prospered and grew. Along these lines, there are also scholars who claim that curved jade symbolizes a fetus. In the traditional sense, we can imagine that a fetus also symbolizes the birth and growth of a nation.

---

* Hongshan culture - also known as Hongsan Culture in Korean. Neolithic culture in the Liao River basin. Hongshan sites have been found in an area stretching from Inner Mongolia to Liaoning, and dated from about BCE 4,700 to BCE 2900. Read Page 50 of this book: 'What is Hongshan Culture?"

Curved jade pieces have been found among Baekjae artifacts as well; a gold earring strung with curved jade was found in the Tomb of King Muryeong of Baekjae. Artifacts crafted from iron, glass beads, and curved jade were also excavated from Gaya Dynasty ruins located in the Bonghwang-dong area of the city of Kimhae in South Korea.

There is an intriguing cloth painting on display at the Pazyryk Exhibition in the Hermitage Museum located in Saint Petersburg, Russia. It was found in a tomb of a king of the Hun civilization located in the Pazyryk Valley of the Altai Region. There is a person on horseback in the picture, which depicts curved jade on the person's chest and on the nose of the horse. From this picture and other pieces of nomad history, we can infer that curved jade was a common symbol shared across the cultures of nomadic peoples.

What is Hongshan culture?

The oldest Neolithic civilization in the world was located in the northeastern region of China next to its namesake, the Gulf of Balhae. The Balhae Gulf civilization (also called the Yoha(Liao He) civilization) is estimated to reach as far back as 9,000 years ago, and it encompasses different cultures in each subsequent time period. The highlights of the Hongshan period of the Balhae Gulf civilization are the stone tombs, goddess temple, and heavenly altars left behind in the Niuheliang ruins, but we have also found significant quantities of processed jade among the copper molds and copper artifacts of this period. The sizable excavation of jade from this period is noteworthy because jade jewelry is known to be difficult to produce.

Due to this mix of mediums, the Hongshan period is known as the period of mixed usage of copper- and stoneware. Scholars also refer to this period as the Hongshan civilization because the culture and society of this era was in the beginning stages of an early state. The Balhae Gulf civilization is older than the four major civilizations of Egypt (3150 BCE), Mesopotamia (3500 BCE), Indus Valley (3300 BCE), and Yellow River (2100 BCE). The Hongshan civilization is at least a thousand years older than the Yellow River civilization, which originated in a river basin widely regarded as the birthplace of Chinese civilization. The Balhae Gulf civilization was founded by the Dongyi people, the ancestors of Korean civilization. There are many opinions as to which civilization can legitimately claim the Dongyi people as a predecessor, but it seems valid to call them the ancestors of Korea due to the countless similarities between the cultures of the Dongyi people and Korean people. In fact, Dongyi was the name the Chinese people used to label the people who lived to their east—the ancestors of Korea.

China belittled these people, the Dongyi, as barbarians until recently. But after discovering the Niuheliang ruins of the Hongshan culture, China began incorporating the Balhae Gulf civilization into Chinese history, claiming that the Dongyi people were the originators of Chinese civilization. To that end, China has been working on four projects to rewrite this ancient history: the Xia-Shang-Zhou Chronology Project, the Northeast project, the Chinese Civilization Exploration Project, and the National History Revision Project. The intent is to link all preexistent history within the current borders of the People's Republic of China in one united history, but this ignores its historical and cultural neighbors and threatens to peg Korean civilization as merely a descendant of Chinese civilization.

Despite this, Korea's mainstream scholars have not paid much attention to the connections between the

Hongshan culture and Korea's ancestors. In the meantime, China has steadily progressed with its project to lay sole claim to this ancient history. Before it is too late, scholars of Korean history must take interest and study the Balhae Gulf civilization and the Hongshan civilization to protect the integrity of world history.

Figure 1-19 Picture of a king riding a horse excavated from the Pazirik Ancient Tombs in Altai, Russia/ Curved jade decoration is placed on the chest and on the nose of a horse. (Museum of Hermitage, St. Petersburg, Russia)

07

The origins of the ancient gold crowns

Beside the 10 gold crowns that grace the museums and research labs of Korea, there are two other surviving ancient gold crowns. One is the Tillya Tepe gold crown of Afghanistan, and the other is Sarmatian gold crown preserved in the Hermitage Museum in Saint Petersburg, Russia.

Some scholars choose to increase this number by including the Issyk gold crown exhibited in the Almati Central Museum in Kazakhstan and the gold crown from the Liao Dynasty's (CE 916~ CE 1125) Princess Jingook exhibited in the Guimet Museum in France. The Issyk gold crown has a conical hat shape, and Princess Jingook's gold crown covers the top and the back of the head like a helmet, making it difficult for scholars to determine whether these two headgear meet the right criteria to be called crowns. This means that the officially-recognized gold crowns of the world are the 10 crowns of Korea, the

Tillya Tepe crown, and the Sarmatian crown. Of the last two, it seems the Sarmatian crown was produced at an earlier time period.

Both the Tillya Tepe gold crown and the Sarmatian gold crown's estimated production periods date further back than Shilla's gold crowns. Some scholars claim that these early crowns could have affected Shilla's methods for crafting its own. This claim came under greater scrutiny in the summer of 2016 when the National Central Museum of Korea hosted a special exhibition of gold artifacts from Afghanistan, and the Tillya Tepe crown was revealed to locals and international tourists alike. Tillya Tepe is located in Northern Afghani-

Figure 1-20 Tilia Tepe Golden Crown of the Ancient Bactrian Kingdom

Figure 1-21 A replica of a 'golden man' dressed in golden armor and golden ornaments found in an ancient tomb in the Ishik region of Kazakhstan / The hat worn by the golden man, was not in the form of a crown, but in the form of a cone hat, using gold to decorate it with a mountain goat, tiger, mountain, sot-dae, arrow, and a hand holding an arrow. The mountain goats live in the Cheonsan Mountain Range(Himalayas), a mountain range extremely difficult for humans to access. So the mountain goats were revered as sacred animals that is close to the gods. The four bows mean that they dominated the four direction. Sotdae has the same meaning as a the Shindansu.(Kazakhstan Almaty National Museum)

stan and means "the hills of gold" in the Uzbek language; the hills were named after the crown was discovered. At a glance, it seems as though there are many similarities to Shilla's gold crowns. But the curved jade typical of Shilla's gold crowns is missing, and there are many floral ornaments and gems on this Afghan crown that aren't found on any of Shilla's crowns. Also, Shilla's crowns were worn by royalty, but the Tillya Tepe crown is assumed to have been worn by a priestess rather than a person with royal authority because it was recovered from the grave of a young woman.

The Sarmatian gold crown boasts many large jewels on its outer frame, which also bears the image of a woman. Smaller jewels line both sides of the crown while the top of the crown is embellished with trees and deer decorations. This design is significantly different from the gold crowns of Korea.

The Sarmatian gold crown and the Tillya Tepe gold crown from the Bactrian region were both crafted when nomadic tribes dominated those territories. According to professors Lim Jaehae and Park Seonhee, the underlying thread linking Shilla's gold crowns and the Tillya Tepe gold crown is that both feature a tree motif, but the crowns have nothing else in common in either their methods of expression or the methods of production. Furthermore, the plant expressed in the design of the Tillya Tepe gold crown is not a regular tree, but rather a type of vine.

The motif found on the Sarmatian gold crown looks like a small fruit tree. By comparison, the trees of Shilla's crowns bear thick trunks that stretch magnificently skyward as if their branches could brush the stars. If the Tillya Tepe gold crown calls to mind a lush, sprawling vine, Shilla's gold crowns weave together a balanced and elegant beauty. They also incorporate the legendary elements of the shindansu tree and the Gyerim forest (Gyerim is also another name for Shilla). While the two gold crowns of Sarmatia and Bactria were created earlier than Shilla's gold crowns and have common elements by virtue of being the artisanry of nomadic peoples, it is difficult to find clear evidence that the Tillya Tepe and the Sarmatian crowns had a direct impact on the crowns of ancient Korea.

08

How did Shilla become the nation of gold crowns?

It is more likely that Shilla's gold crowns were influenced by traditions passed down from Ancient Joseon than Afghanistan or the Sarmatians of Central Asia. A critical piece of evidence in favor of Shilla's Ancient Joseon heritage is the inner crown called the jeolpung, a conical headpiece which was worn over the Sangtu top knot* and was unique to Korean dress culture. Royalty of Buyeo, Goguryeo, Shilla, Baekjae, and Gaya all wore outer crowns over this inner crown, with the Goguryeo custom even adding two feathers of precious metal to the jeolpung and decorating it with a gold or silver hoop. This inner crown is a perfect example of the ubiquity of fashion as a status sym-

---

* Sangtu top knot - An ancient Korean tradition. Married men tie their hair in a knot on top of their head. A pin-needle called donggot was used to hold the top knot and a headband was worn over the head to stabilize the topknot. The term Sangtu originates from Sangdu which was originally a word that refers to the Big Dipper of the Northern Seven Stars. Ancient Koreans believed that by having the Sangtu on one's head, one becomes directly connected to the Seven Stars where Samsin Sangjenim (official title of God in the Ancient East Asian tradition) resides.

bol and a vehicle for a common culture for the Korean people.

There is a gold jeolpung with feather-shaped ornaments and a hoop made of gold on display at a musuem in Ji'an, a city in China's Jilin province. This was excavated from the tomb of the Great King Gwanggaeto (374-413 CE) of the Goguryeo Dynasty. But if we set aside this magnificent gold jeolpung from Goguryeo, the size and splendor of Shilla's gold crowns far outshines the designs of Goguryeo and Gaya. This begs the question: Why did the makers of Shilla's gold crowns craft them into such stunning shapes? To shed some light on this mystery, we must examine the history of the power dynamics between the four nations of Baekje, Gaya, Goguryeo, and Shilla.

Given the contents of the Great King Gwanggaeto's tomb and the varying regional footprints of these four nations, Shilla spent its early days in Goguryeo's shadow as a small neighbor dwarfed by Goguryeo's regional power. At this time, Baekjae also had a tendency to look down on Shilla since it was focused on competing with Goguryeo for regional influence. Even an examination of how this influence reached the Japanese Archipelago reveals that Shilla's reach was far less than that of Baekjae or Gaya. Shilla's diplomatic power also fell short in comparison to Goguryeo and Baekjae. This may have led the Kim clan, Shilla's governing elite at the time, to conclude that they should no longer share the throne with the Park or Seok clans; it was time to create a kingdom ruled solely by the Kims. They no longer wanted to stand in Goguryeo's shadow or be perceived as a weaker country than Baekjae, so they strove to portray the image of a new and stronger Shilla. This may have provoked the rulers of Shilla to create a gold crown that outshone the crowns of Goguryeo and Baekjae.

Though a culture that was ripe for the development of these beautiful gold crowns was shared among all four nations, Shilla's gold crowns distinguish themselves as particularly sophisticated and aesthetically pleasing. Imbued in the material elegance of these works of art, however, are the political ideals and prayers of the people of Shilla.

Korea can take great pride in the fact that the greatest number of ancient gold crowns in the world was found in Gyeongju. Curiously, the city of Gyeongju has chosen the Cheonmado flying horse picture as its symbol instead of these gold crowns.* But it is time that the rest of the world learned about the magnificent world heritage that was discovered in Gyeongju, and time for Gyeongju to shine on the world stage. While the Cheonmado flying horse is remarkable in its own right, Gyeongju's crowning achievement is none other than its array of pure gold crowns.

---

* Cheonmado (heavenly horse drawing) - Read Ch 2. Conquering the Continent: The Stirrup and the Gaemamusa Sect 7. The heavenly horse as a sovergin symbol

A Trip to the Museums in Korea

Conquering the Continent: The Stirrup and the Gaemamusa

01 The nomadic people who conquered Eurasia on horseback
02 The Parthian shot and the art of mounted archery
03 The rise of the stirrup
04 The development of horse riding skills and stirrups
05 The military might of the Gaemamusa
06 The horse-revering nomadic people
07 The heavenly horse as a sovereign symbol
08 The bronze pot: a must-have for nomadic life
09 The introduction and impact of stirrups in the West

01

The nomadic people who conquered Eurasia on horseback

Horse riding nomads left an indelible mark on the history of humankind that has lasted for more than 2,500 years(up until the 18th century). Nomadic peoples on horseback—Cimmerians, Scythians, Sarmatians, Huns, Avars, Khazars, Xiongnu, Göktürks, Uigurs, Mongols, Xianbei, and Khitans—dominated the Eurasian continent, placing Europeans under immense pressure. In response, Europeans developed weaponry to repel the influence of these nomadic peoples and consequently pushed warfare from the era of cavalry and arrows into the era of guns and artillery.

The horse riding nomadic peoples of Central Asia who became known in the West for invading and conquering European nations did not develop the useful habit of record-keeping. As nomadic peoples, they naturally relocated on a regular basis without settling down; therefore, they had no sense of land ownership and felt no need to leave records. In contrast, Europeans had a greater sense of land ownership, prompting them to create records and develop a sense of superiority that regarded the nomadic horse riders of Central Asia as barbarians.

In recent years, new light has been shed around the world on the significance of these horse riding nomadic peoples and their immense impact on the development of human civilization. When they swept across the Eurasian continent, they formed a bridge between the East and West that fostered the exchange of wealth and knowledge, causing a ripple effect that even brought an end to ancient and Middle Age Europe. The Huns in particular brought down the West-

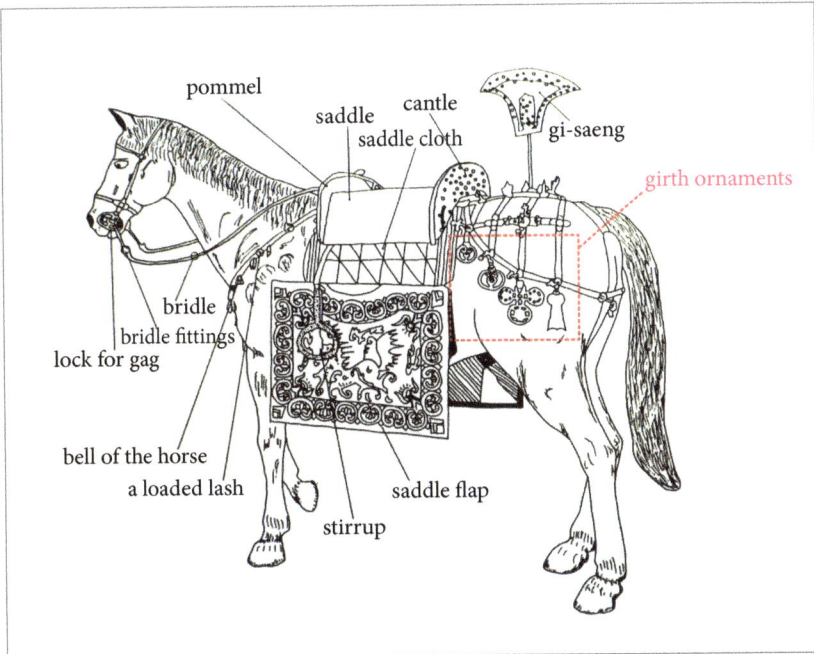

Figure 2-1 Drawing of a horse with full gear displayed at the Hansung Baekje Museum

ern Roman Empire and heralded the end of ancient Europe, while Mongol influence and the Turks (of Göktürk origin) destroyed the Eastern Roman Empire (Byzantine Empire), expediting the end of Europe's Middle Ages. Throughout these eras, the nomadic peoples continuously transferred advanced technology from the East to the West, providing stepping stones for advancements in Europe.

The mode of transportation chosen by these nomadic peoples, the horse, was at the epicenter of the tremors sent rippling through world history. The nomads may not have known how their horse riding would change the world forever, but for them, a horse was a member of the family, a personal necessity, and the greatest method of transportation before the advent of motor vehicles.

Over a span of 36 years, from the beginning of its dynasty until the tenth year of the Great King Sejong's reign, Joseon (1392-1897)

Figure 2-2 A silver stirrup from Koryo dynasty with a carving of a phoenix pattern (National Museum of Korea)

sent a total of 59,000 horses as tribute to the Ming Empire (1368-1644). With this effort to meet the weighty demands of Ming, Joseon saddled itself with a severe shortage of horses for its own use. Even during Goryeo's later period, Yuan Dynasty Mongolians (1279-1368) demanded that Goryeo (918-1392) provide them with horses. Since tribute items usually consisted of highly prized and valuable gifts, it is clear that the horse was a significant method of transportation in both China and Korea at the time.

Horse culture was passed down from the very early ancestors of Korea, staying strong in the proud descendants of these early nomadic tribes which started with Baedal (3897-2333 BCE) -> Ancient Joseon (2333-238 BCE) Northern Buyeo (239 BCE-58 CE) -> the Four Kingdoms period* (1c. BCE ~ 562 CE))-> the North-South States period (Later Shilla and Balhae) (668-926 CE) -> Goryeo(918-1393 CE) -> Joseon (1392-1897 CE). This love for horses, paired with prodigious horse riding skills, helped these Korean nations create and develop increasingly sophisticated and convenient tools to tame horses and even adorn them with ornaments. Among the many tools used to equip horses and their riders was a simple yet instrumental piece used for a rider's feet: the stirrup. This simple technology altered the course of human history.

A stirrup holds a rider's foot and is an important tool that helps the rider mount a horse's back, stay balanced, and adjust the direction of the horse. Scholars are not sure exactly who invented the stirrup or when, but by looking at extant artifacts from the past, we find that many of them come from Korea and China. A version of the stirrup from the fourth century (302 CE) was discovered in China and became known as the world's oldest stirrup, but this was a type known as the short stirrup. The short stirrup provided a foothold on only

---

* Four Kingdoms here refers to Four Korean dynasties of Goguryeo, Baekjae, Shilla, and Gaya. More popular term is Three Kingdoms, referring to Goguryeo, Baejae, and Shilla which lasted longer than the Gaya Federation.

one side of the horse, making it difficult to determine if this type of stirrup was used solely for mounting the horse or if it also had any use while riding. Then, paired metal stirrups dating from 415 CE were discovered in a Xianbei tomb, and it was revealed that this type of paired stirrup made its way to the West later in the eighth century, though the actual artifacts of that technological transfer date only to the tenth century. But why were these stirrups such a technological advancement? Riding a horse without any stirrups makes it extremely difficult for a rier to move their upper body, so they have to have excellent coordination and strength to use a bow at the same time. The rider also has to grip the reins with one hand, making it impossible to fire an arrow. As a result, early mounted warriors had to tie themselves at the waist to the neck of the horse to free up their hands to use a bow and arrow.

Figure 2-3 The Kimmerians, who were active in the Northern and Eastern Black Sea in the 6th century BCE, turning their upper bodies to the back to shoot their arrows on horseback / A replica of the Greek murals from the time when they didn't have a stirrup. The mounter warrior rider tied their bodies to the neck of the horses. (National Museum of History, Ukraine)

02

The Parthian shot and the art of mounted archery

The invention of paired stirrups didn't just help riders balance on horseback—it determined the course of world history. Though the concept seems simple, stirrups are essential for a mounted warrior. Without stirrups, a rider cannot maintain balance while fighting on horseback and will eventually fall off in the attempt. With the rise of the paired stirrups, nomads were able to balance themselves on galloping horses and freely alter their riding positions to attack an enemy. Even the finest infantry was no match for these mounted warriors with stirrups.

The exact date when people began riding horses is unknown, but an assortment of artifacts have helped estimate the earliest horse riding activities as far back as the twelfth century BCE (3,200 years ago). Before that, fully-equipped soldiers rode on chariots pulled by horses when they entered battle. Even after the introduction of cavalry units,

Figure 2-4 Parthian Shot is a method of archery where the mounted archer turns his body towards the back to shoot his arrow by leaning his body weight on the stirrup (Museum of Kazan Kremlin, Russia)

riders had to tie their thighs and knees to the horse and keep one hand on the bridle or reins.

The best method of attack for these mounted archers was to twist at the waist to shoot. They called this the baesabeob method, a phrase which describes the method of shooting arrows at enemies behind you. This became known as the Parthian shot in the West, and it is considered an advanced skill in archery.

Take a moment to imagine what it would look like if you saw a mounted warrior shoot an arrow at an enemy. On this imaginary battlefield, the archer approaches on a swiftly-moving horse; while

Figure 2-5 The mounted soldier shooting a Parthian shot (the Hermitage Museum in St. Petersburg, Russia)

moving, the archer shoots at the enemy with an arrow. If the first shot fails to critically damage the target, the archer then fires a second arrow immediately. This is done regardless of the direction in which the horse is galloping. Even if the horse and its mounted archer pass the target, if the archer is fast enough, the archer can rely on the stability of those paired stirrups to twist around and shoot a third arrow at the target that is now behind them. This ability to balance on a moving horse while shooting arrows instantly increased the range of attack of mounted archers.

The advanced combat method of the Parthian shot is easy enough to explain, but it is certainly not an easy set of skills to acquire. It fascinated the Romans who witnessed it firsthand. Rome, upon losing its war with Parthia due to this new set of archery skills that Roman soldiers had never seen before, began to call this the "archery of the Parthians", which is where the Western term "Parthian shot" originated. This fascinating history can be traced back all the way to the First Triumvirate of the Roman Empire (60-53 BC).

Parthia (247 BCE - 224 CE) was a kingdom established by the nomadic people who once lived along the Amu Darya River of the Middle East. It was founded after the fall of Persia, and it controlled the Silk Road, monopolizing trade between Asia and Rome. Parthia also prevented communication between China's Han Dynasty (202 BCE-220 CE) and Rome, making it impossible for Rome to learn the highly-coveted secrets of silk production.

Rome was ruled by three men during the First Triumvirate: Caesar, Pompey, and Crassus. Unlike Caesar or Pompey, Crassus built his wealth through real estate to become the richest man in Rome—but he lacked war experience. He therefore felt the need to bring home a great victory like Caesar and Pompey, which provoked him to proceed with the Parthian Expedition despite the elders who opposed his decision. But there was another reason for his warmongering: Crassus wanted influence over the Silk Road. In 53 BCE, the Parthian Empire and the Roman Empire fought the Battle of Carrhae (modern Harran, southern Turkey). There were 10,000 Parthian cavalry against 43,000 Roman foot soldiers on the battlefield, but Rome suffered a devastating defeat in the end. Crassus's own son died along with 20,000 Romans, and the Roman soldiers that were captured were later sold as slaves.

Although the Roman foot soldiers tried to fight close combat with their swords and spears, the Parthian cavalry shot endless volleys of arrows from afar. When the Romans used their shields to block arrows and reorganize their position, a highly skilled unit of spear-wielding cavalry as a Parthian cataphract would charge them to throw the Roman military back into disarray. The Parthian cataphract was then followed by mounted archers who would rain arrows on the Romans. The mounted archers used camels to carry arrow supplies to

Figure 2-6 **Parthian shot of the Goguryeo archers**/ Image from the Muyongchong Tomb of Jiban-hyeon in modern day Jilin, China

Figure 2-7 The mural paintings in Deokheung-ri, Pyeongannam-do / Figures 2-6, 2-7 are all replicas displayed in the special exhibition of the Goguryeo tombs at the Hansung Baekje Museum.

a nearby spot on the battlefield. When archers ran out of arrows, they could swiftly resupply themselves from the camels and then resume shooting at the enemy. Unable to rely on their famous close combat techniques, nearly half of the Roman foot soldiers died under this assault. The Romans who survived were witness to a daunting new tactic for close combat archery that they dubbed the Parthian shot. They had never seen anything like it. The Parthians would fake a retreat, drawing the Romans into a chase, only for the Parthian archers to twist around and fire arrows at the Romans behind them. This Parthian shot later became synonymous with cowardice in the West.

The Parthian shot that decimated the Roman legions was not used solely by the Parthians. Depictions of this technique can be found in the wall painting of the Goguryeo Dynasty known as the Su-ryeob-do (painting of hunting), the drawings of the ancient burial mounds of Goguryeo, and the gilt-bronze incense burner of Baekjae.

While the question of whether the Parthian Empire used leather or wood for its early stirrups—or whether it used any stirrups at all at that time—has not been answered, Parthia's stellar horseback riding skills certainly played a key role in using this archery technique. But what happened after the introduction of stirrups? The destructive force of the nomadic people only grew. After the introduction of stirrups, the missing elements for perfecting horse riding had finally come together. Even if a horse picked up speed or jostled in formation with neighboring horses, riders were able to maintain their positions and even change riding positions at will to attack the enemy. Stirrups were an indispensable tool for the nomadic people.

The nomads lived a life of animal husbandry, so they had to move with their livestock and, at times, defend their livestock from predators. They also had to hunt. Archery was perfect for killing or deterring wild animals at a distance. In particular, it was good for hunting animals like deer, which constantly change direction when fleeing a hunt—the archers simply needed to twist on horseback to shoot the deer down. They didn't have to adjust the direction of their mounts. Overall, stirrups made hunting significantly easier. Riders could shoot to the side or behind, avoiding shooting directly forward where the horse's head blocked the view.

03

The rise of the stirrup

When did the stirrup first appear in Korea?

According to the historical record *Samguk Sagi* (also known as *History of the Three Kingdoms*), Goguryeo mobilized 6,000 armored and mounted soldiers during the war against former Wei Dynasty China (220-226 CE) in 246 CE. Goguryeo Dynasty stirrups made from gold and bronze were found in the Chilseongsan Mountain burial mounds near the Guknaeseong fortress and estimated as originating in the early fourth century. Shilla Dynasty's Ho-woo-chong, a fifth-century tomb, also became known as an excavation site for other Goguryeo-style stirrups. Stirrups are depicted in such detail in fourth- and fifth-century Goguryeo wall paintings that it appears this riding tool was already in use between the third and fourth centuries.

During the third and fourth centuries, Goguryeo fought wars both great and small with the Wei Dynasty of China and the Murong Xianbei. A tribal branch of the Xianbei, the Murong Xianbei were a nomadic horse people who acquired parts of the Liaodong region and established the Yan Dynasty (337-370 CE).* During the reign of King Gogukwon of Goguryeo, the Murong Xianbei captured the capital city of Goguryeo and took the dead body of King Micheon (King Gogukwon's father). They took hostage the queen dowager (King Gogukwon's mother) and many other people of Goguryeo.

This kind of armed conflict with the northern nomadic horse people lasted for over a century, driving Goguryeo to develop a variety of new weapons and war tactics. This sparked the inventions of metal stirrups and the Gaemamusa, the fully-equipped mounted warriors of the Goguryeo Dynasty. Gaema refers to equipping a horse with its own armor, and musa means warrior, so the cavalry of armored horses ridden by the warriors of Goguryeo were called the Gaemamusa. This may seem like a tale from a time and place far from the Korean peninsula that we know today, but the mounted warriors of Goguryeo used to gallop across the Gaema Plateau—a highland that takes its name from the Gaemamusa and still exists in modern North Korea.

---

* Liaodong region is located in Northeast of China, west of North Korea, and Northwest of South Korea. It lies on the Northern shore of the Yellow sea. It was formerly under the rule of Ancient Joseon, Gogureyo, and Daejin-guk(Balhae).

04

The development of horse riding skills and stirrups

The earliest stirrups were made of leather or cloth. Compared to the metal versions that were developed later, these leather stirrups performed poorly when riders needed to step on the stirrup or apply more pressure. More importantly, they broke easily in the thick of battle. These unwieldy leather stirrups were soon followed by wooden stirrups that used a combination of wood and leather or wood and cloth. Then, in the late third century, metal stirrups were introduced that combined bronze plates with wooden pieces. These were more durable than their wood and leather predecessors and performed well in battle, but they came at an exorbitant production cost and took too much time to make.

The deungja, a fully-developed version of the metal stirrup, came into use after the middle of the fourth century. The "deung" (鐙) part of the word deungja (鐙子, meaning stirrup) includes the character for metal (金). See how 金 is squeezed into the left side of the 鐙 char-

Figure 2-8 Goguryeo stirrup excavated from Acha-san Mountain (National Museum of Korea)

Figure 2-9 Metal stirrup excavated from the Altai region / On the right is a tempered iron stirrup made by striking the iron. This was a style that was also popular within Goguryeo (the Hermitage Museum in St. Petersburg, Russia)

acter? Based on the component meanings of this name, the wooden stirrups and the leather stirrups that preceded the deungja metal stirrups may not have been considered true stirrups.

With the introduction of these metal stirrups, training for horse riding was shortened significantly from several years to a matter of days.

We know how the stirrup evolved, but who was the first to make metal stirrups? Given the artifacts discovered thus far, it seems the Xianbei lead the charge by a close margin. But considering that the fully-equipped mounted warriors of the Gaemamusa entered history as early as the middle of the third century, it is reasonable to assume that metal stirrups were in use back then even though such an artifact is yet to be found. Why? This is due to the fascinating implications of other artifacts found in the Gangwondo province.

In 1994, the foundations of three Goguryeo buildings from third century were discovered in the Chullyeong region of Gangwondo Province, accompanied by a variety of miniature models of Gaemamusa. There were 54 iron and four bronze horse figurines as well as dragon, turtle, snake, and other animal figurines made of iron. The horse figurines fashioned from iron featured metal scale (char-gap) armor and even riding equipment, including the highly detailed shapes of stirrups. Based on the existence of these figurines, it can be assumed that Goguryeo used bronze or metal stirrups before Xianbei. In other words, it is possible that the world's first set of stirrups came from Goguryeo and that Goguryeo-style stirrups may have been introduced to China through the northern nomadic tribes.

In a comparison of stirrups dating from after the middle of the fourth century, Goguryeo's metal stirrups are superior to the Xianbei stirrups down to the method of production. The Xianbei cast-iron stirrup was made through a process of pouring molten iron into a mold, yet while this process was easier and made harder stirrups, they were also heavy and brittle. In contrast, Goguryeo's wrought-iron stirrups were made by forging iron. Forging is a method of

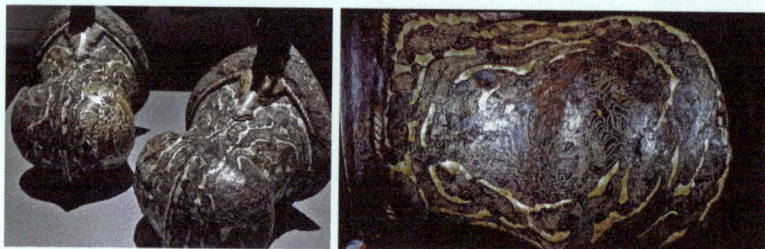

Figure 2-10, A glamorous iron stirrup with gold and silver engraving of a heavenly horse and a backgournd scenery, Unified Shilla dynasty (National Museum of Korea

Figure 2-11 Russian emperor's golden stirrup / It is said to be a gift from the Ottoman Turks as a means to maintain peace between the nations (Russian Kremlin Palace Armory)

The Development of the Stirrup

Development Stages	Description	Production Time and Other Details
1) Leather stirrup	Stirrups made from leather	Nomadic people implemented this before the Common Era (CE)
2) Wood-and-leather stirrup	Wood shaped into stirrup and then covered with leather	Found near the Dongjin ruins from mid-fourth-century Wei and Jin's Northern and Southern period
3) Wood-and-bronze stirrup	Bronze plate nailed to wooden stirrup as reinforcement (theory based on burial goods found in graves)	Discovered in late third-century Xianbei mound, early fourth-century Ji'ansi (Goguryeo) artifact
4) Metal stirrup (cast iron)	Stirrups made using iron-working methods (casting)	Found in Tomb No. 1 from late fourth-century (Xianbei) period, located in Jeon Chang, Chaoyang County, Liaoning Province, China
5) Metal stirrup (wrought iron)	Stirrups made with iron-working methods (forging)	From Goguryeo's Ohnyeosan-seong fortress, late fourth century

pounding and shaping heated iron to forge it into a desired shape. Forging techniques are more complicated, but they actually strengthen the iron, making a final product that lasts significantly longer.

05

The military might of the Gaemamusa

The stirrups of Goguryeo feature heavily in the history of horse riding not only due to their design, but due to how their inventors engaged with neighboring tribes and nations. Although Xianbei developed stirrups during ongoing conflict with Goguryeo, its development of stirrup technology was discontinued when Early Yan (or Former Yan 337 CE - 370CE) fell. In contrast, Goguryeo continued to cultivate relations with other nomadic tribes. By doing so, it enabled the spread of its stirrups across Central Asia and eventually to the West.

The proliferation of the stirrup formed the foundation of numerous military tactics. Goguryeo was no exception to this; new strategies came about through the usage of these stirrups as shown by the strategic operations of the Gaemamusa.

Visit the Goguryeo exhibit in the National Central Museum in

Seoul, and you can see firsthand the footgear worn by these mounted warriors. These shoe-like pieces of equipment are spiked with nails and seem more like accessories that would have been attached to a rider's shoe than like shoes themselves.

Indeed, these "nail shoes" were part of the extensive equipment of the proud and mighty mounted warriors of Goguryeo, and they were attached to the sole of the foot as a weapon for kicking one's enemy. But who exactly were these nail shoe-wearing, fear-inspiring Gaemamusa?

The Gaemamusa were known as the Gaema mounted warriors, a cavalry force equipped with char-gap, a type of lamellar or "metal scale" armor. The char-gap armor was fashioned from overlapping bits of metal that looked like fish scales. Pieces of metal were placed close together, overlapping each other in a somewhat flexible sheet. The resulting armor was then wrapped around the warrior's body. When the lightweight char-gap armor was removed after use, it could be flattened into a portable bundle. The Gaemamusa wore this metal scale armor from the back of their head down their necks to their legs, and completed their battlegear with helmets, leather gloves, and nail shoes.

Even the Gaemamusa horses were armored, with char-gap armor protecting their bodies and iron armor tailored to their heads. A depiction of Gaemamusa warriors and their horses thus equipped has been found in Goguryeo burial mound No. 3 in Anak, North Korea. While it might seem that wearing so much armor would inhibit movement, the versatility and movement allowed by the char-gap armor ensured that the Gaemamusa had no problem piercing enemy ranks, wielding swords, and shooting arrows with ease.

Another advantage of char-gap armor was that it was easily fixed. If damaged by an arrow or sword, only the damaged portion of the metal sheet needed to be removed, making for easy partial replace-

Figure 2-12　A warrior and his horse is armed with a the char-gap armor while holding a long spear, the main weapon of the Gaemamusa Warriors.(Yongsan War Memorial)

Figure 2-13 A nail shoe of a mounted Gaemamusa of Goguryeo dyansty/ A supporting equipment which is worn over the shoes, primarily used to kick the enemy in close combat. (National Museum of Korea)

ments that enabled the armor to last longer. Moreover, the overlapping elements of these metal sheets were effective in absorbing the impact of enemy arrows and spears. The downside of this equipment lay in its initial creation: a high production cost due to the use of many leather and metal pieces, and the demand for iron-working skills and a sufficient supply of iron.

The metal armor worn by the Gaemamusa were not mere iron, but steel. Goguryeo had the advanced technology to produce solid, lightweight, high-quality steel that allowed them to equip the Gaemamusa as a powerful army with steel gear. Goguryeo's smiths could even work this steel into the thin, overlapping semblance of fish scales.

But even with impressively lightweight char-gap armor, the sum of a warrior's gear would have amounted to at least several dozen pounds. A warrior had to be in peak physical condition to wear armor and wield a weapon at the same time. They also had to twist and evade enemy spears—feats that would have been impossible without metal stirrups. Like the stirrups found in the Ohnyeosan-seong fortress of China's Jilin province, stirrups had to be forged from iron for a warrior of the Gaemamusa to stay balanced.

The fact that the fully-fledged cavalry of the Gaemamusa existed in the middle of the fourth century indicates that these metal stirrups were probably in use during the early fourth century, if not earlier. However, fully-equipped mounted warriors did exist before the invention of stirrups. An example of this can be seen in depictions of the Sarmatian soldiers who lived in the region that is now southern Russia and Ukraine. These soldiers bore a resemblance to the Goguryeo mounted warriors who wore char-gap armor. Their swords were also shaped similarly, taking the form of the hwandudaedo, which was a type of sword with a ring pommel. But they did not have metal stirrups, so these mounted warriors were unable to have as strong of an impact on the battlefield. The proliferation of metal stirrups never reached Sarmatia.

Figure 2-14 Char-gap armor of Goguryeo's Gaemamusa warrior (Yongsan War Memorial of Korea)

Figure 2-15 A replica of the mural paintings of the gaemamusa warriors' race displayed at the National Museum of Korea.

The cost of char-gap armor alone was high, but the cost to fully equip a single Gaemamusa warrior and warhorse was even higher. Converted to modern standards, it would cost about the same as a mid-range car now. The Gaemamusa were supported by their nation's economic strength and could be compared to modern mechanized infantry or armored corps. The five-yard spears called sak that were used to penetrate the enemy line and the short spears, arrows, and daggers that were launched in battle were all part of the Gaemamusa equipment as well, making for a cavalry force without equal.

Take a moment to imagine a vivid battle scene featuring this mighty military in action. When the order to attack is given, the Gaemamusa form into strategic lines and begin to trot their horses towards the enemy. The sight of this well-equipped cavalry thundering across the land makes the enemy shake with fear. Though their ears are deafened, the soldiers facing the Gaemamusa still feel the vibration under their feet, and their vision is filled with Gaemamusa warriors drawing near. Archers on foot rush to halt the approaching waves of mounted warriors by shooting so many arrows that their volleys darken the sky.

But the armor worn by the Gaemamusa is not so easily penetrated, and their horses pick up speed. The sight of the Gaemamusa barely affected by a downpour of arrows eats away at the morale of every enemy soldier. Now the first ranks of the Gaemamusa are mere seconds away, and they have five-yards long spears wedged under their arms. The enemy soldiers fling their spears in another preemptive attack at the nearing Gaemamusa warriors. But it is too little, too late. The Gaemamusa come clashing into the enemy's spears with their own, far outreaching what the enemy holds. The horses are at full gallop and carrying significant weight; it seems like nothing will stop them. And nothing does. The victory goes to the Gaemamusa with their thunderous attack, their warriors seeming all but invincible in their heedless charge into the enemy's arrows and spears. To their

Figure 2-16 The image of a Sarmatian soldier wearing an armor as he holds his sword with round pommels/ The formation of the bow reminds us of Goguryeo's Gaemmamusa warriors. (National Museum of Kazan, Russia)

Figure 2-17 A replica of the Sarmatian mounted warrior holding the long spear/ There have been no stirrups that were found in Sarmat and the replica does not have a stirrup either. (Kremlin Musuem of Kazan, Russia)

contemporaries, they are like the modern tank or armored vehicle.

This same outcome played out in each and every battle. The Gaemamusa were invincible.

Ancient Joseon, the Originator of the Armors of East Asia

- The armor of Ancient Joseon was far more advanced than those of its contemporaries in China, and it served as the predecessor to the char-gap or metal scale armor of Goguryeo. The earliest armor made by the Chinese people was a primitive type of leather armor from the reign of Qin Shi Huang, the founder of the Qin Dynasty (221-206 BCE).

06

The horse-revering nomadic people

To the nomadic tribes who traversed the Eurasian continent, horses were a vital part of life. Their great love for their horses could be compared to a modern person obsessed with the best luxury cars of today. In this section, we will explore how the nomads and their descendents expressed that immense appreciation for horses.

If you visit Heejeong-dang Hall in Changdeokgung Palace in Seoul, be sure to look for the beautiful chimney there. On its north side is a drawing of an elephant; its south, a deer; west, a crane; and east, a heavenly horse. Although the painting of the heavenly horse is simple, it still portrays the distinct characteristics of heavenly horses. A heavenly horse was believed to leap across a flowing body of water with a single flap of its wings and fly through the clouds to the open air above. The power and vivacity emanating from this drawing's hair and tail flowing in the wind and its fierce glance with quivering nostrils call to mind the heavenly horse drawings found in the ancient Cheonma-chong tombs of the Shilla Dynasty.

The symbol of the heavenly horse can also be found on Goryeo Dynasty artifacts like the bronze mirror (known as the po-do-su-mun-dong-gyeong) in the Goryeo exhibition in the National Central Museum. A toad sits in the middle of this mirror, surrounded by six other animals: three heavenly horses and three wild beasts that resemble lions. The wild beasts are on the hunt for deer, startling birds that sit in a vineyard into flight. The three heavenly horses soar above the hunt with wings outspread. Heavenly horses like these were a popular motif loved by the people of Goguryeo as well, as shown in the images of heavenly horses that adorn Goguryeo wall paintings. The use of this motif was an expression of the affection for horses held in common by Korea's ancestors. Unsurprisingly, drawings of heavenly horses are found throughout the Eurasian continent as well.

Figure 2-18 A rubbed copy of Cheonmado(heavenly horse drawing) on the chimney of Heejeondang in Changdeokgung Palace (National Palace Museum of Korea, Gyeongbokgung Palace)

Figure 2-19 Po-do-su-mun-do-gyeong, a bronze mirror in the Goryeo Dynasty (National Museum of Korea)

07

The heavenly horse as a sovereign symbol

Mention of the heavenly horse, or the cheon-ma, inspires most Koreans to think of the cheona-ma-do, a painting of the heavenly horse found in the ancient Cheonma-chong tomb in Gyeongju. The tomb itself is named after the cheonmado painting on a saddle flap found in the burial chamber. With one attached on each side of the saddle, saddle flaps were used to protect the horse rider's clothes from dirt and other filth. These flaps were called jang-ni. Saddle flaps were usually made from leather, cloth, or wood.

Evidence of this reverence for horses is also found in the name of a ruling-class clan that preceded Goguryeo and Baekjae. These two nations developed from Northern Buyeo, which succeeded Ancient Joseon. The Maga (Horse Clan), Wuga (Cow Clan), Jeoga (Boar Clan), and Guga (Dog Clan) were known as the ruling elite under the king of Buyeo, each overseeing one of the four divisions of their nation.

Figure 2-20 Cheonmado drawn upon a dahrae excavated from the Cheonmachong tombs (National Gyeongju Museum)

Figure 2-21 Horse decorations carved with a heavenly horse / Made during the 13th century in the Mongolian Empire with bronze. Excavated from the city of Astracan, a grassland town adjacent to the Caspian Sea.(The Hermitage Museum, St. Petersburg, Russia)

As far back as Ancient Joseon, horses had secured a place in society as the best form of transportation, pulling chariots and carriages and enabling riders to see farther than people on foot. A rider on horseback could feel a rush of exhilaration from galloping across the great plains of Central Asia, a feeling that has been described as flying through the sky. While this desire and need for swiftness, paired with a strong fondness for horses, might be sufficient to explain why the nomads would draw the cheonma (heavenly horse) on a saddle flap or name an elite clan after the horse, it does not fully explain their reverence for the cheonma.

To better understand this reverence, we have to lift our eyes to the stars. The cheonma (heavenly horse) was closely related to a constellation that the people of these horse-loving societies saw every night. More details can be found in the explanation of the Cheon-sang-yeol-cha-bun-ya-ji-do (Chapter 5), but in Eastern tradition, constellations were categorized into three central points and 28 constellations. The three points of origin are the Jamiwon, Taemiwon, and Cheonsiwon. The Jamiwon is a constellation that includes Polaris (the North Star) and the seven stars of the Big Dipper believed to sit at the center of the cosmos. The 28 constellations that surround and guard the Jamiwon in a circle are called the 28 su. Among these 28 constellations is a star called Sung, and the creature used to represent that star is the horse. Essentially, the heavenly horse was seen as a gift from the Heavenly Emperor to the king who ruled the land in his stead. It was both a gift from the heavens and a symbol of power.

By embellishing tools and equipment with paintings of the heavenly horse, these people were declaring their nation to be a sovereign one, an empire recognized by the heavenly realm. This is also why various nomadic peoples upheld the tradition of burying the symbolic heavenly horse with their ruler so that he could ride his heavenly horse in the afterlife. An example of a typical heavenly horse outside of Korea is displayed in the Scythian tomb at the Central State Museum in Almaty, Kazakhstan. When a Scythian king died, his horse was buried with him, along with other horses decorated with ram horns. Rams lived in the high mountain ranges surrounding the Scythian people's heavenly mountain (Tian Shan) so they were believed to be holy beings, close to the heavenly god. As such, the front of the headgear worn by the "Golden Man" found in Almaty's Central State Museum is decorated with a ram—or possibly a heavenly horse bearing the horns of a ram.

Figure 2-22 A recreation of the king's tomb at the Almaty National Museum in Kazakhstan / A horse decorated with the horns of a mountain sheep is the heavenly horse. There was a traditional belief that the kings and queens will ride them to the heaven in the afterlife. Also, a cloth covering the back of a horse has the heavenly horse on them.

Figure 2-23 A replica of the Golden Man, a king of Scythia, unearthed in Ishik, Kazakhstan, / A mountain goat or winged heavenly horse is adorned in the front part of the hat.(Kazakhstan Almaty National Museum)

08

The bronze pot: a must-have for nomadic life

Besides stirrups, another item essential to life as a nomad was the bronze pot. You can see a statue of a nomadic man holding one such pot in the Shilla exhibition in the National Central Museum of Seoul; there is also a replica of this nomad statue in the Gyeongbokgung Palace station on Line 3 of Seoul's subway.

Figure 2-24 A clay doll of the Shilla dynasty mounted figure carrying a bronze pot on the horse's buttocks (National Museum of Korea),

The bronze pot was an absolute necessity for any of the nomads who controlled the Eurasian plains. Each person had one, and the pot was buried with its owner as part of funerary rites. These pots were used to make stew for eating or for ritual offerings. The nomadic people were constantly on the move looking for fresh pasture for their livestock to graze. While on the move, for meals, they dismounted from their horses to build a fire over which they hung the bronze pot to cook their food. After the meal, they would carry the bronze pot with them as they mounted their horses and began moving again. Along with the majority of the nomadic people, the Huns who stormed through Europe also used bronze pots, but with a slightly different shape.

Bronze pots have been discovered in nomad graves in Central Asia, Russia, Ukraine, Bulgaria, Serbia, and Hungary as well. Evidence of a societal norm of carrying around a bronze pot has also been found in the ruins of Gaya and Shilla. This refutes the common misperception in modern Korean society that Korea's ancestors formed an agricultural society and solely lived in settlements. Even a quick look around Korea's museums reveals numerous artifacts from nomads that were passed down to their successors. For a people who spent daily life eating and even sleeping on the backs of their horses, it was only logical that they crafted tools of convenience for regular use in such a lifestyle.

Figure 2-25 Bronze pot on display at the National Museum of History in Moscow, Russia

09

The introduction and impact of stirrups in the West

Motivated by its many wars with neighboring countries, Goguryeo developed methods of forging iron, horse riding skills, and strategies for its char-gap-armored cavalry. These developments significantly impacted the northern nomadic people's battle tactics. The nomadic people of Rouran took the effective fighting strategies they learned from Goguryeo and, under the name Avar, went to reign terror over Europe.

The Rouran was a branch of the people of Xianbei. The last surviving nation of Gojoseon (Ancient Joseon) was Beon Joseon (this was also known as Dongho in *The Book of Later Han*, a Chinese text), which was brought down by the Xiongnu Empire (BCE 3rd c.~ 1st c. CE). Beon Joseon split into two groups, one becoming Wuhuan, and the other, Xianbei. The people of Xianbei were united under a leader named Tanshihuai to create a vast empire that stretched all the

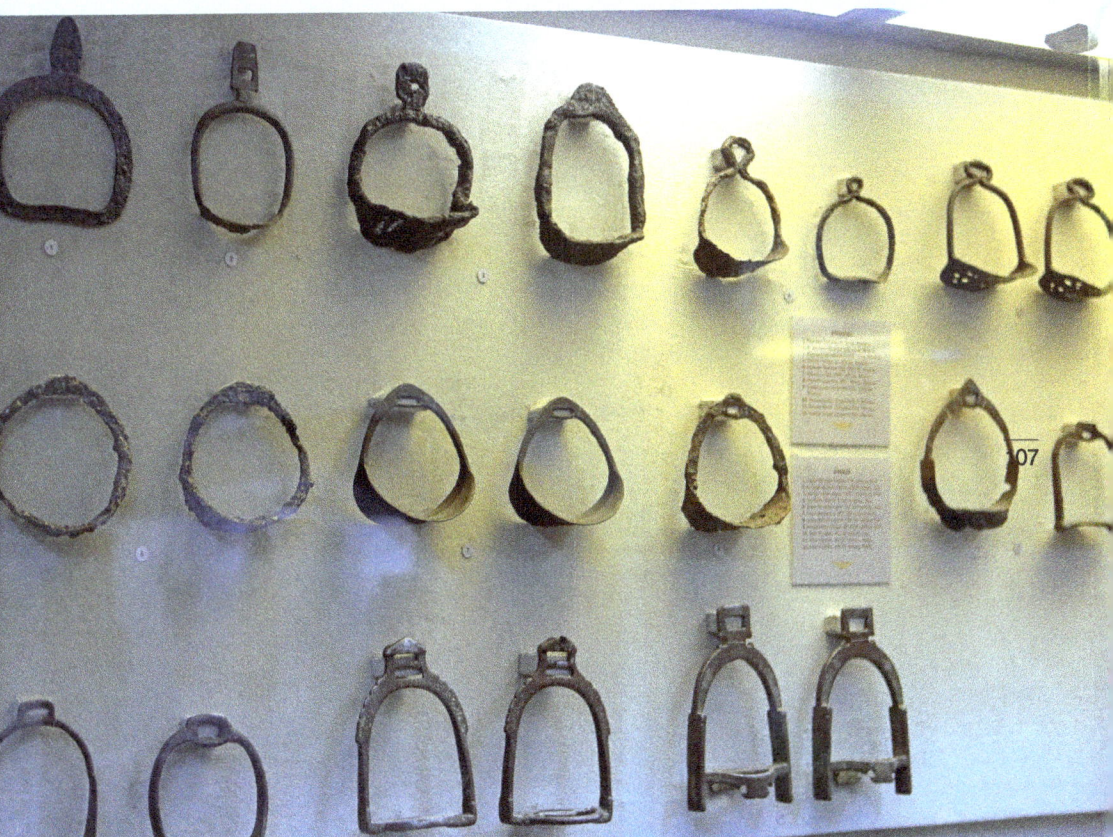

Figure 2-26 Stirrups arranged by era excavated from the Altai Mountains and East Siberian region / First stirrup from the upper left is the Goguryeo stirrups found in 5-6th century Siberia (National Museum of Novosibirsk, Russia)

way to the northern Siberian region of Lake Baikal and to Tian Shan. After Tanshihuai's death, many Xianbei tribes moved into the inner regions of China, igniting the Five Hu and Sixteen Kingdoms period (304-439 CE). This is when Rouran migrated to a central region of China and established a nation in 402 CE.*

The Rouran were a nomadic tribe that controlled the northern plains between the fourth and sixth centuries CE. Through interactions with Goguryeo, they embraced skills related to stirrup usage and the Gaemamusa. But in the middle of the sixth century, the Rouran disappeared, seemingly overnight, fleeing westward to escape the Göktürks. The Göktürks were a people who had once forged iron under Rouran rule, and with these skillfully-forged weapons, they rebelled and were able to establish the Göktürk Empire.

The ousted Rouran made their way to Europe equipped with Goguryeo stirrups and Goguryeo-style cavalry. They were called the Avar, and they swept across the Balkan Peninsula, Hungary, and the Pannonian Plain. The Avars who conquered vast regions of sixth-century Central Asia and Europe were as infamous as the Huns (or Xiongnu), making their mark as they made their way west.

The State Museum of Local History and Nature in Novosibirsk, a city located in central Russia, features Goguryeo-style stirrups from the Altai region, fifth and sixth centuries CE, in its exhibits. The Avar burial mounds, stirrups, belts, and saddles are markedly similar to the ones found in Altai. Goguryeo-style stirrups and Siberian longswords were found in ruins near the Volga River region as well. In contrast, the predecessors of the Avar, the Scythians and the Sarmatians, left no sign that they used metal stirrups. Turks, Magyars, and Mongolians, three combative nomadic peoples with highly developed

---

* 5 hu 16 state period - Chaotic period in Chinese history from 304-439 CE. 5 non-chinese people, Xiongnu, Xianbei, Di, Jie, and Qiang joined forces in overthrowing the Western Jin dynasty and established their own dynastic states.

battle techniques, followed the Avars to the west. After the fall of the great empire of the Göktürks, they established the Seljuk Turks and the Ottoman Turks, bringing down Constantinople, the capital city of the Byzantine Empire (Eastern Roman Empire), and dominating the Mediterranean to flourish for a long time as a mighty empire.

In the ninth century, when the Magyars arrived on the Hungarian Pannonia Plain, they were like the second coming of the Huns who had humbled Rome. The Magyars went as far as modern Spain, making western Europe tremble in fear. There is still a road in Aquileia, an ancient city in northeastern Italy, that the Huns and the Magyars once used. Along the road, there are the ruins of a monastery that bear a depiction of the Parthian shot and an inscription of a prayer that reads, "O God, please save us from the arrows of the Magyars."

Thirteenth-century Mongols had a more developed organizational system and weapons that allowed them to conquer Europe in the blink of an eye. They used swords and a variety of other weapons including bows crafted from the horns of water buffalo. Such powerful bows had never been seen in many of the lands they conquered. The front and rear of a Mongol's saddle, also known as the pommel and cantle, were made with wood that kept riders firmly astride and enabled them to sleep on horseback. It was the invention of stirrups, however, that was the foothold for the rise of the combat-ready nomadic people and their bid to conquer history.

The invention of these metal stirrups brought about radical changes across the continent. Nomadic peoples who already boasted superb horse riding skills grew capable of even greater destruction, and they swept across the continent. According to the history told by artifacts that have been excavated thus far, Goguryeo was at the center of this change. With advanced forgery techniques, the people of Goguryeo were able to craft and use metal tools and technologies that were far superior to those of their neighbors, including stirrups, the lamellar armor called char-gap, swords, and spears. The spirit of the nomadic peoples lives on in the small but significant metal stirrups that are now museum artifacts. When you see one of these stirrups in a museum, keep in mind that it holds the soul and story of these formidable forebears.

Figure 2-27 Turkish cavalry with striking similarity to Gaemamusa Warrior of Goguryeo(The Hermitage Museum, St. Petersburg, Russia)

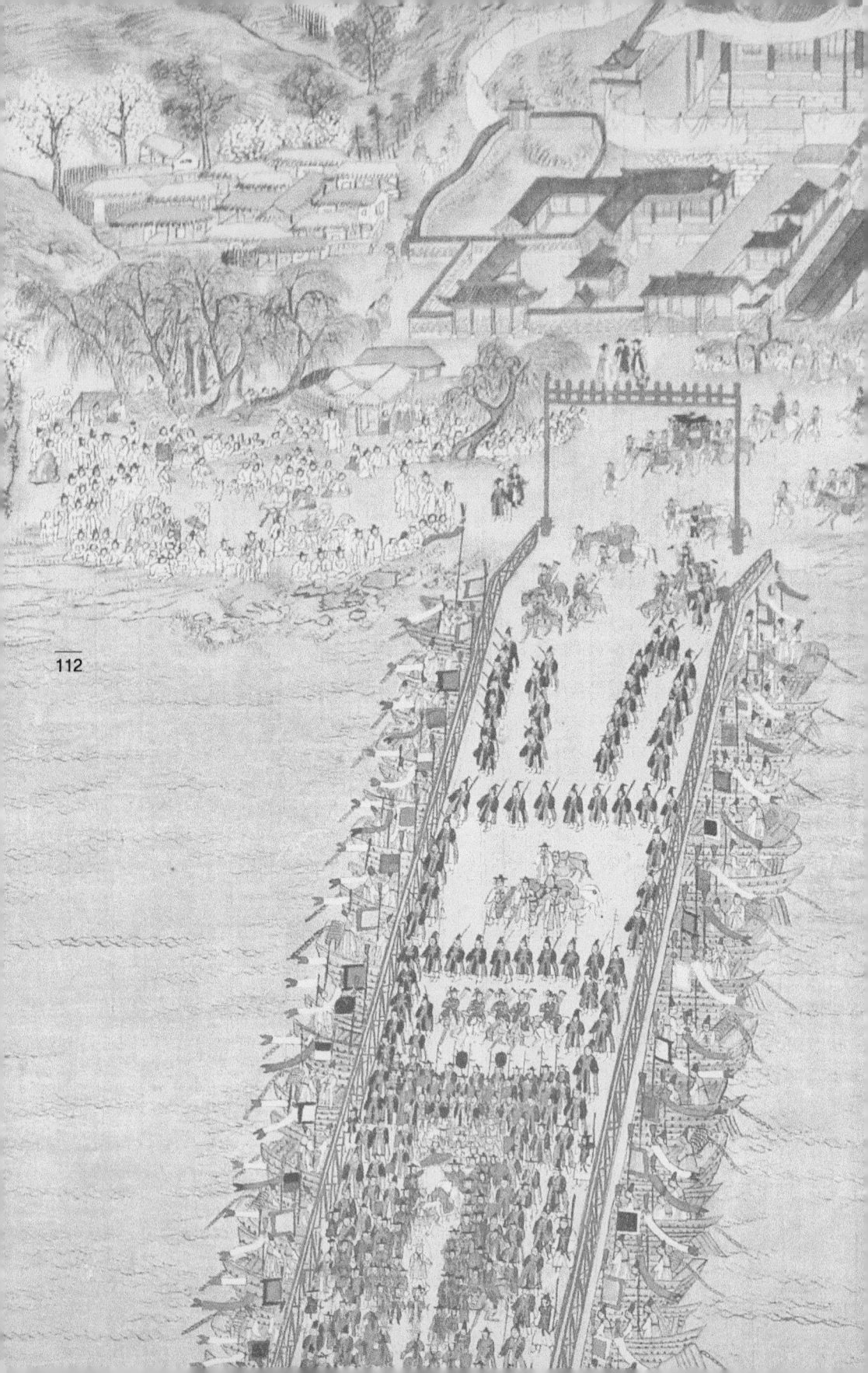

PART 03

A Trip to the Museums in Korea

The first metal printing of humanity that flipped the world upside down

01 The paradox of the Gutenberg Bible in film
02 Eastern paper and printing technologies in Europe's cultural awakening
03 Goryeo, the land of advanced wood and metal printing technologies
04 Did Gutenberg copy Goryeo's movable metal type printing press?
05 Meeting Iran's Gutenberg
06 Jeungdoga, predecessor of Jikji by 138 years
07 Korea's metal-refining and manufacturing technology gives birth to movable metal type

01

The paradox of the Gutenberg Bible in film

In 2004, Hollywood premiered a disaster movie called *The Day After Tomorrow* in which the Northern Hemisphere suddenly is locked in glaciers due to global warming. In one scene, a group of people take refuge in the New York Public Library and burn books to stay warm in the cold weather. The setting seems like a snapshot of the end of human civilization until a character named Jeremy clutches the famous Gutenberg Bible against his chest and refuses to let it be burned. Another character asks derisively, "You think God's gonna save you?" Jeremy responds that while he does not believe in God, the Gutenberg Bible is the first book ever printed, and so he will protect it even if Western civilization must come to an end. According to Jeremy, the Gutenberg Bible represents the dawn of the Age of Reason and thus Gutenberg's printing press is the greatest achievement that humanity has ever made.

I was lost for words when I first saw this movie at its release. These

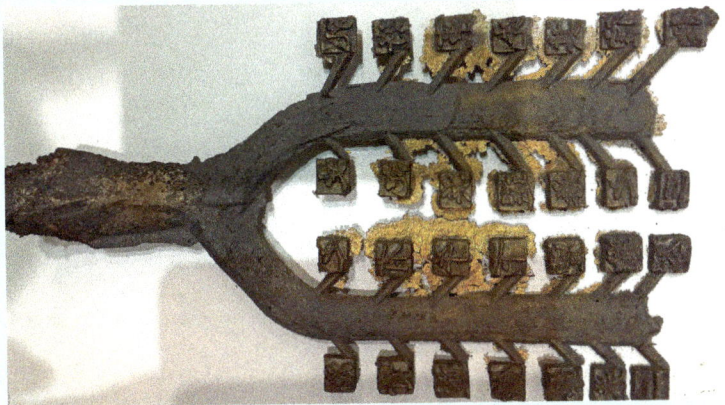

Figure 3-1 Metal branch with printing types / When the melting metal is poured into the mold and the metal cools down, the printing types are removed off from the metal branch for use. (Cheongju Early Printing Museum.)

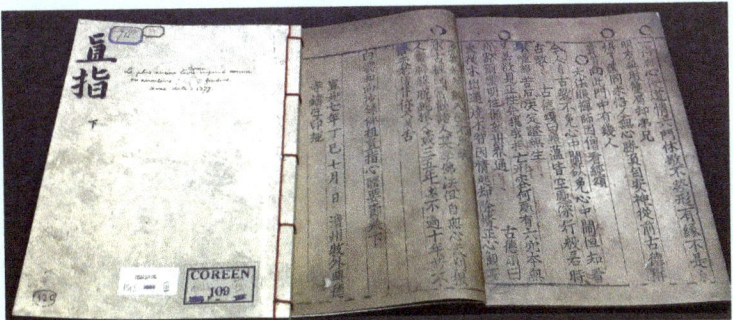

Figure 3-2 The Young-in Version of Baek-un-hwa-sang-cho-rok-bul-jo Jik-ji-shim-chae-yo-jeol displayed at the Cheongju Ancient Printing Press Museum. Commonly referred to as Jik-ji-sim-che-yo-jeol. "Jikji Simcheyojeol," is a book compiled by the Buddhist monk Baekun, the national sage at the end of the Koryo Dynasty. This book is a collection of the teachings of Buddha and the ancient monks. Only the second volume of the two books remains.

Figure 3-3 A monument commemorating the Jik-ji erected in front of the Cheongju Early Printing Museum

days, it is more widely known that *Jikji* is the oldest movable metal type-printed book in the world, but the Gutenberg Bible was thought to be the record-holder until recently. The oldest woodblock-printed book, which is called the *Mu-gu-jeong-gwang-dae-da-ra-ni-gyeong* (produced around 700-751 CE) and the oldest movable metal type-printed book, *Jikji*, are both from Korea. Korea is the motherland of printing technology when it comes to both woodblock and movable metal type printing.

There are two main types of printing technology: woodblock printing and movable metal type printing. In woodblock printing, letters are carved directly onto a wooden plate or block, while in movable metal type printing, a combination of metal letters are arranged to make a single plate and then pressed onto paper. Woodblock printing has numerous issues, such as requiring hundreds of large blocks of wood just to print multiple editions of one book, being easily damaged or destroyed due to fire or accident, and simply being difficult to make. If the woodcarver makes a mistake with the letters, the process has to start again. In contrast, a movable metal type printing press does not have these complications. With the right combination of letters, a bookmaker can start printing hundreds of pages. Movable metal type printing was a revolutionary technology.

Prior to the start of the new millennium, *Life* magazine published an article about the 100 most influential events in the last millennium. Sitting proudly at No. 1 on the list was the "Printing of the Bible through the invention of Gutenberg's press." Around the same time, *Time* magazine chose the most influential person in the last millennium as Gutenberg, who was lauded as the inventor of the printing press. When I read these articles, I felt as if the West had stolen this celebration from its rightful participants.

02

Eastern paper and printing technologies in Europe's cultural awakening

What makes Western societies laud Gutenberg to such a degree? To understand this phenomenon, we must first understand how the technologies of paper and the printing press made their way to Europe. We begin with examining Silk Road cities in what is now Uzbekistan.

Uzbekistan is a fertile land between the Syr Darya and the Amu Darya rivers of Central Asia. In Arabic, it is called the Maverannakhr, which means "place across the river." It is the only area in Central Asia where nomads settled and pursued an agricultural life.

During the Tang Dynasty (618-683 CE, 795-904 CE), major Silk Road cities such as Tashkent (which is the modern capital of Uzbekistan) and Samarkand occupied the region. The people of Tashkent asked for aid from their Arab neighbors to drive out the Tang

Empire, sparking war between the Abbasid Caliphate (750-1258 CE) and Tang. An Eastern method of making paper spread to the West through this war, and at the center of this historical scene was military general Go Seonji, the son of a Goguryeo immigrant. Go Seonji was born in the Tang Empire after the collapse of Goguryeo and became a great general during the reign of Emperor Xuanzong of the Tang Dynasty. In the year 751 CE, Go Seonji led the Tang army in a battle against the army of the Abbasid Caliphate, which had conquered the Mediterranean. The battle took place in the Talas Valley (modern Kyrgyzstan). But after an internal revolt rocked the Tang army, even the astute general Go Seonji could not win the war. Around 20,000 people were taken to the Abbasid region as war slaves, paper-making technicians among them.

With a stroke of luck, the Abbasid Caliphate obtained the most advanced paper production technology of its time, which was rapidly followed by a revolutionary change in the governance of this huge empire. Previously, the Arabs had used lambskin and papyrus for their records, but this was considerably inconvenient. The production of a single Qu'ran was a bloody and costly process, requiring the slaughter of 300 lambs, and if the lambskin came in contact with water, any writing on it was easily damaged or even erased. As for papyrus, this plant-based paper ripped easily and came at an exorbitant price. Books made from either product were difficult to make and therefore treated as an expensive luxury.

Figure 3-4 The Quran made of 9th-century parchment on display at the Chehel Sotun Palace in the central Iranian city of Espahan.

Figure 3-5 Choral score recorded on a parchment paper (Museum of Duomo Di Siena, Italy)

But once this empire learned how to produce a paper that was lightweight, easy to make, and capable of retaining writing with limited warp or fade, it brought substantial changes to the recording, sending, and saving of documents. Arabs set up numerous paper factories and translated many books in Arabic using what they called Samarkand paper.

During this same period, Europe, too, had only books written on lambskin. When the Arabs made this leap with the technology learned from their war slaves, Europeans were still living in the past. Europe had to import expensive paper from Arabian cities such as Damascus (capital of modern Syria). Once this paper production technology spread through Arabia, Northern Africa, and the Mediterranean, it finally came within the grasp of the Europeans, and they

Figure 3-6 Copy of the Wooden carving of Tripitaka Koreana (Incheon Ganghwa History Museum)

strove to acquire it. The Europeans finally acquired the technology in the twelfth century CE.

Spain was under Arab rule for about eight centuries (from the eighth century to the fifteenth century CE). Naturally, they also came to possess this paper making technology and made many books of their own.

Then, when Toledo, a region near Madrid, fell to a Christian nation, a vast collection of these books and the paper production technology itself passed to France. France built its first paper factory in the twelfth century, and this technology then spread throughout Germany, Italy, England and the rest of Europe. The first Italian paper production company was set up in the thirteenth century, and with this supply of paper, Italy started importing Arabic books and translating them into Latin. Consequently, the Renaissance began.

Figure 3-7 Toledo near Madrid, Spain / Once a glamours Islamic city, it played the role of bringing paper-making technology into the West in the 12th century

There is a tendency to think of Michaelangelo, Leonardo Davinci, and other geniuses of architecture and painting when talking about the Renaissance, but the word Renaissance itself means "a revival of academy and art," and it was a cultural and spiritual movement throughout all types and forms of art—including paper, printing, and book-making.

We have established how paper production methods traveled from the East to the West, but what about the spread of woodblock printing press technology? Researchers have yet to identify when exactly the woodblock printing press made its way to Europe, but it seems likely that the seafaring merchants who traveled between the East and West would have been the agents of this. In his book *Hong Seongwook's Science Essay*, Seoul University professor Hong Seong-wook explains that wooden blocks were used in the production of gaming cards and religious paintings in the West at the beginning of the fifteenth century. It is possible that they used the method of copying text by hand even after the introduction of woodblock printing press technology into Western societies.

Although the paper production technology made its way to Europe, it remained such a luxury that only monasteries, royalty, and aristocrats owned books. With a high rate of illiteracy in Europe then, information and knowledge stayed as an exclusive privilege for the very few while commoners were trapped in the Dark Ages. To make matters worse, the bubonic plague broke out and national systems collapsed to the point that Christianity lost its foothold. Europe plunged into chaos as peasant revolutions challenged religious authority. In Prague, Hussites led the first religious revolution in Europe.

In the midst of this fifteenth-century turmoil, Johannes Gutenberg of Germany printed his first pages from a movable metal type printing press. Books made with Gutenberg's press gave commoners the

Figure 3-8 An English version of the 42-line Bible printed by Gutenberg in 1455. (Cheongju Early Printing Museum)

chance to share information and knowledge. These books of the Renaissance period began to spread far and wide, and European commoners were able to seize their place in an era of enlightenment.

Once available only in Latin, the Christian Bible was translated into German so that people could learn more about the Church. This led to religious reformation as information spread to the general public and the power structure of the very few people who had monopolized information started to collapse. From a Christian-centric world sprouted an age of reason and enlightenment. This prompted Europeans to venture out of the Mediterranean Sea and into the Atlantic Ocean, launching the Age of Exploration in which they conquered and brought in vast amounts of wealth in gold and silver from the Americas. European countries that had long suffered under enormous debts to China finally repaid them in full and began to cement themselves as powerful nations on the pages of world history.

Then Habsburg Spain came into power, followed by the rise of the mighty British Empire. The accumulation and distribution of knowledge sparked the First Industrial Revolution. In France, there was also a civil revolution. The introduction of printing press technology was a watershed moment for Europe, opening a door to a world of possibilities. In other words, the printing press took the West from the troubled shadows of the Dark Ages to the height of enlightenment on the world stage. The Renaissance that has won great praise and scholarly consideration in the West could not have taken place without the paper production and printing press technologies that came from the East. This is why Gutenberg, who neglected to mention the true origin of his so-called invention, has been so revered.

When European civilizations still could not even manage to make paper, an early Korean civilization had made the world's first movable metal type printing press. The printing technology that had begun in the Goguryeo Dynasty eventually led to the invention of movable metal type in the Goryeo Dynasty. The world's oldest woodblock-printed book, *Mu-gu-jeong-gwang-dae-da-ra-ni-gyeong*, was later found in Bulguksa Temple's Seokgatap pagoda in Gyeongju of Shilla dynasty, and the world's oldest movable metal type-printed book, *Jikji*, was chanced upon in the National Library of France by Dr. Park Byeongseon of Korea. *Jikji* was produced at least 75 years prior to Gutenberg's first press on the lambskin paper of his famous 42-line Bible. Through Dr. Park's discovery, Korea was finally recognized as the founder of printing press technology.

03

Goryeo, the land of advanced wood and metal printing technologies

The transition from handwriting to printing press technology was a revolutionary process that began with the woodblock printing press. Scholars have yet to determine who first used woodblock printing press technology. In Korea, it was first used during the Three Kingdom Period (58 BCE~668 CE),* and this woodblock printing technology then blossomed during the Goryeo Dynasty.

The foremost example of this is the *Tripitaka Koreana* found in Hae-in City (Hapcheon, Gyeongsangnam-do Province), a staggering feat of printing prowess that was meant to repel Mongolian invasions with the blessing of Buddha. The *Tripitaka Koreana* was 16 years in the making, and the wooden blocks used for the project number 81,258. Such an extensive collection of woodblocks for printing can-

---

* This is counting from Goguryeo's succession of Northern Buyeo in 58 BCE to the fall of Goguryeo in 668. Shilla unites the three kingdom and continues for more than 250 years.

not be found anywhere else in the world. It is also the most extensive collection of Buddhist writings in the world. The *Tripitaka Koreana* was added to the UNESCO Memory of the World Register out of recognition for its significant cultural value.

The woodblock printing press was indeed a world-changing technology in its own right compared to handwriting, but its inconvenient features led to another invention: a method to make a combination of movable metal letters for printing. The world's oldest movable metal type book, *Jikji*, was originally written by the monk Baek-woon of the Goryeo Dynasty, and it discussed the teachings of Buddha and venerable monks after Buddha who had passed down the teachings of Zen Buddhism. The book was divided into two volumes, but only the second has survived the ravages of time.

Jikji was originally kept in Korea, but a French diplomat to Korea, Collin de Plancy, purchased it with his own money to add it to his personal collection, which he took to France. It was then purchased by a prominent European jeweler named Henri Véver. According to Véver's will, Jikji was donated to the National Library of France in 1950.

It is truly regrettable that Korea's proud cultural heritage is currently kept in France. However, it is likely that *Jikji* only survived the chaotic latter era of the Joseon Dynasty and the Japanese colonial period that followed because it was safe in France. Over 200,000 valuable historical books were burned by the Japanese colonial government in order to fabricate a false version of Korean history that justified Japanese occupation of Korea. Given this gross treatment of Korean texts, *Jikji's* preservation in France was likely a blessing in disguise.

The person that brought attention to *Jikji* was Dr. Park Byeongseon, a Korean librarian at the National Library of France who took a break in the storage area. She was preparing for a book exhibition to commemorate the Year of World Literature when she found a book titled *Jikji*. Due to the minute powders of metal on its pages and the year it was published, she swiftly realized that the book was made by a movable metal type printing press. Through her research, *Jikji* became internationally recognized as the oldest movable metal type-printed book in the world, and in 2001 it was listed on the UNESCO Memory of the World Register. To highlight the significance of this cultural item, UNESCO presents a biennial award recognizing people and organizations who have contributed to the safeguarding of world heritage and records. This award is called the UNESCO/*Jikji* Memory of the World Prize.

Unfortunately, when Dr. Park informed the South Korean government that she had also discovered royal records looted from the library of Oegyujanggak by French soldiers in 1866, she was immediately dismissed from the National Library of France. King Jungjo of the Joseon Dynasty had ordered the *Uigae* (books that recorded royal ceremonies and rites) be kept in the Oegyujanggak, a library in Ganghwado Island. This is where the name "Oegyujanggak books" originated.

Thanks to Dr. Park's sacrifice, South Korea was able to demand the return of the Oegyujanggak books. After about 20 years of negotiations between the two countries, the royal records made their way back to Korea in the form of a loan that is renewed every five years. Dr. Park passed away in 2011, but I would like to express my respect for her efforts; her sacrifice helped Korea's great cultural heritage see the light of day again.

04

Did Gutenberg copy Goryeo's movable metal type printing press?

Although Koreans developed the world's oldest movable metal type printing press, Gutenberg still wins copious praise in the West. However, using *Jikji* as evidence, British professor John Hopson asserted that Gutenberg's movable metal type press was an imitation of the Goryeo printing press. While Korea had laid the foundation for the invention of movable metal type printing technology through the innovative development of woodblock printing, it was not until the twelfth century that Europeans had even acquired the updated paper technology. The right environment to swiftly invent a movable metal type printing technology simply did not yet exist in Europe.

Paper production and printing technologies had long been developed in the East, with Korea at the center of innovation. The East and West had maintained a cultural exchange for thousands of years prior to these inventions, and naturally, many innovations in one society would spread to another and be taken into new stages of development through that exchange. The printing press was no exception to this process. The issue, however, is the timing.

Claiming that Europe, which had just begun to take its first steps with the use of what it had learned from other civilizations, suddenly invented movable metal type printing technology is simply illogical. Gutenberg himself was not even a printing professional, making it hard to believe that he originated his press completely on his own.

In 2005, former U.S. Vice President Al Gore made a visit to South Korea for the Seoul Digital Forum. In his speech, he took the audience by surprise by telling them that Gutenberg received his printing press technology from Korea. According to Gore, the truth was that a papal emissary from the West had visited Goryeo and brought back a diagram of the movable metal type printing press. The drawing made its way to Gutenberg, who failed to attribute the idea to Korea. Gore told the crowd that he learned this from Switzerland's printing press museum. Soon after, the

Swiss Museum for Paper, Writing and Printing (also known as the Basel Paper Mill) also announced their own research paper that supports Gore's claims. While his words were unexpected, they have continued to gain credibility.

Then, the production crew for the documentary called Dancing *with Jikji* found a copy of a letter in the Vatican that had been sent by the Pope to King Choongsook of Goryeo in 1333. This is much earlier than the official publication year of *Jikji* (1377). The fact that Goryeo and the Vatican had a direct exchange was proven. Moreover, Gutenberg was revealed to be a personal acquaintance of Cardinal Niclaus, who was part of the delegation that visited Korea.

The list of evidence goes on. Daegu MBC, a branch of a major broadcasting network in South Korea, produced a documentary called *Gutenberg Steals* from Goryeo. It features French printing press specialist Dr. Olivier Deloignon, who studied the pages of the 42-line Bible and came to the conclusion that Gutenberg made his letters using methods identical to those used by Goryeo. The book had traces of sand on the surface of the printed portions that were typical of metal letters made with the foundry sand casting method. This confirms that Goryeo's technology for making movable letter type did reach Europe, and that Gore's claim of the Vatican acquiring this movable metal type printing technology from Goryeo and giving it to Gutenberg was true all along.

05

Meeting Iran's Gutenberg

I have traveled all around the globe, and every Iranian I have met along the way has told me that there is a city in Iran that I must visit: Isfahan. Isfahan is located in central Iran, and its beautifully adorned cityscape does indeed live up to its name, which literally means "half of the world."

In this ancient Iranian city, there is a district called New Julfa that holds the city's largest concentration of Christians. This district is where Armenians, who were known as "the gods of commerce," were designated to settle. Abbas the First of the Safavid Dynasty (1501-1736) wanted to use the Armenians' entrepreneurial skills to increase the country's growth in the early seventeenth century, a sign of their exceptional abilities in business.

In New Julfa, there is a church that was repurposed from a Muslim

Figure 3-9 Khachatour Vardapet, also known as 'Iranian Gutenberg,' / His statue is standing in front of a printing press he had developed and is looking at a printing type (In front of the VANK Cathedral located in the Julfa district of Isfahan, Iran).

Figure 3-10 The Julfa Printing Press made in 1841 / Khachatur's Printing Press underwent several changes and this image is his third version (Armenian Museum, Isfahan.)

Figure 3-11 Books printed with the third version of the Julfa Printing Press are displayed along with the printing types per each period. (Armenian Museum)

temple, and its inner walls have been decorated with depictions of stories from the Christian Bible. The Museum of Khachatur Kesaratsi, an Armenian museum, is part of this church's compound. It contains the movable metal type printing press made by the Khachatur Kersarati(1590~1646), also known as the Iranian Gutenberg.

The machine is decorated with a sitting eagle, under which are two animals that look like snakes or dragons. The existence of this printing press led professor Jeong Su-il, a top expert on the Silk Road, to team up with German scholars for an academic symposium called "Finding a new movable metal type printing press," which revealed more of the story of how the printing press traveled from Korea to the West.

The team's research concluded that there were two routes by which the movable metal type printing press transferred to Germany. The route by oases began in Korea and moved respectively through China, Central Asia, Iran, greater Europe, and then finally into Germany, whereas the route through the plains began in Korea and then moved respectively through Mongolia, southern Siberia, greater Europe, and finally into Germany. Whatever the exact roads in between may have been, the fact remains that Iranian movable metal type printing technology was also based on Korean technology.

06

Jeungdoga, predecessor of Jikji by 138 years

Jikji is the oldest extant publication by movable metal type printing, but there are records of movable metal type-printed materials that existed even before Jikji. Unfortunately, copies of these no longer exist. Until recently, the oldest publication referenced in historical texts was *Sang-jeong-go-geum-ye-mun*.* Copies of this book on law and virtue were produced by royal decree during the reign of Goryeo's King Injong. While the copies of the book itself have not survived, it is mentioned in *Dong-guk-ee-sang-guk-jib*,** authored by Lee Gyubo (a Goryeo Dynasty scholar), that Sang-jeong-go-geum-ye-mun was printed with movable metal type and distributed to each government office.

---

* Literal translation of *Sangj-jeong-gog-geum-ye-mun* is 'Book of rites and proprieties of the past and present in detail.'
** Literal translation of Dong-guk-ee-sang-guk-jib is 'A compilation of poems of Eastern Land (referring to Goryeo).'

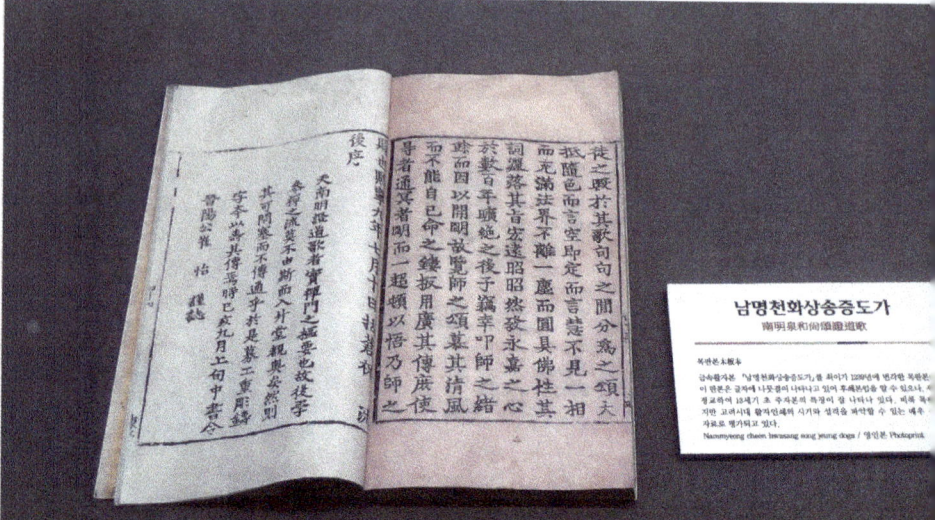

Figure 3-12 Yeong-in Version of Nammyeong-cheonhwa-sangsong-jeungdoga (Cheongju Early Printing Museum)

Even more recently, it became known that a book predating even King Injong's publication on law and virtue once existed, entitled *Nam-myeong-cheon-hwa-sang-song-Jeungdoga*. This was a book of commentary by the venerable Nammyong "Beobchon" of the Song Dynasty (960-1279 CE) on the *Jeungdoga* text written by monk Hyun-gak of Tang Dynasty China. Hyun-gak's book was a Zen Buddhist guide for monks to relieve the agony of humankind through chants and songs. It is known as the book that led monk Sungcheol to decide he wanted to become a monk after reading it during his youth.*

The publication year of the commentary on *Jeungdoga* is recorded

---

* The printed commentary known as *Nam-myeong-cheon-hwa-sang-song-Jeungdoga* is commonly referred to as Jeungdoga by scholars, after the text it comments on. Likewise, this book refers to *Nam-myeong-cheon-hwa-sang-song-Jeungdoga* as simply Jeungdoga.

as 1239, during the reign of Goryeo's King Gojong. At first it was widely believed to come from a woodblock print, but later this view shifted to movable metal type technology based on the shape of the letters and traces left on the book. Printed copies of this are preserved in the Samsung Publication Museum, the Gongin Museum (Yangsang, Gyeongsangnam-do Province), and Il-san-mun-go in the Daegu National Central Museum. Although scholars continue to debate the exact form of production for the *Jeungdoga* commentary, the fact remains that if it is recognized as a product of Goryeo's movable metal type printing technology, the *Jeungdoga* commentary will officially be the oldest work printed by movable metal type in the world.

07

Korea's metal-refining and manufacturing technology gives birth to movable metal type

Movable metal type printing presses were not easy technology to implement. First, this kind of printing required the mass production of paper. Second, the right ink for use with movable metal type had to be developed. Third, the technology for metal forgery had to be highly refined. Long before the invention of printing with movable metal type, Korean civilization boasted an advanced technology of carving letters and images on metal.

The Sacred Bell of the Great King Seongdeok (also known as the Emile Bell) is an excellent example of this. Made during the reign of Shilla's King Gyeongdeok in 771 to honor his late father, this huge bronze bell weighs 18.9 metric tons and is covered with around 1,000 letters, 36 lotus flowers, and an image of flying fairy in exquisite detail. It was made with such skill that when crafters in the modern era tried to hang the bell by

Figure 3-13 (left) A divine bell of King Seongdeok with more than a 1,000 characters engraved on it (National Gyeongju Museum), (right) Rubbed copy of King Seongdeok's divine bell (National Museum of Korea)

replicating a steel cable to attach to the tail of the dragon figurine at its top, they failed, giving rise to a popular anecdote in South Korean history classes. It is astounding to think that the Shilla Dynasty had the technology to create such an elaborate bell—technology that we have yet to fully understand, let alone replicate.

Another example of impressive craftsmanship is found at Yongdusa Temple, which is estimated to have been built during the reign of Gwangjong, the fourth king of the Goryeo Dynasty. Most of the temple was destroyed by Khitan and Mongolian invasions, so all that remains is the Iron Flagpole left in Cheongju, Chungcheongbuk-do Province. Standing 12.7 meters high, the Iron Flagpole of Yongdusa Temple is finely carved with 393 letters that pay homage to the fascinating skills involved in forming this beautiful writing on steel.

A similar type of exquisite carved lettering is also found on a bronze plate from Goguryeo. Goguryeo's King Jangsu had 10 bronze plates made in memory of his father, the Great King Gwanggaeto.

Only one has survived to the modern era, but it bears highly sophisticated writing that is still legible.

This range of artifacts tells us that Korea's technology for forging metal was significantly advanced and handed down through numerous generations.

Figure 3-14 Bronze bowl with the words "Great King Gwanggaeto" engraved, unearthed from Gyeongju's Howu-chong tomb / Bronze Bowl made by Emperor Jangsu for commemorating his father, the Great Emperor Gwanggaeto (National Museum of Korea)

The fact that the Goryeo Dynasty printed its own books with movable metal type is significant because it shows that Goryeo had a thriving culture with advanced technologies that even conquerors could not truly take from them. For example, during the reign of the twenty-fifth king of Goryeo, King Choongryeol, this Korean nation was defeated by the Won Dynasty (1201-1368), and the rulers of Goryeo started calling themselves kings instead of emperors. Despite this new power dynamic, Goryeo's advanced culture and technology remained essentially undamaged.

Figure 3-15 Restored printed edition of Jik-ji-sim-che-yo-jeol (Cheongju Early Printing Museum)

However, the introduction of movable metal type did not mean that woodblock printing fell into disuse. Woodworkers were able to sustain such a high speed of carving letters to create a woodblock that this technology remained in use until the late Joseon Dynasty.

The variable sizes of the letters of the first movable metal type of the Goryeo Dynasty made for rather untidy printing. But when it came to the Joseon Dynasty, the movable metal type technology began reaching impressive new milestones in its development. Notably, the

movable type letters made during the reign of King Sejong were known as "kap-in" in Korean and included around 200,000 letters that came in small and large sizes. The kap-in letters were also more balanced and had fixed spacing between letters. It is no stretch to say that these letters were the peak of Korean movable metal type technology. They were made by scientists who also built astronomical observation devices, so it makes sense that such advanced technicians would produce high-quality printing presses. Throughout the reigns of many kings who followed King Sejong, new generations of scien-

Figure 3-16 Hwansong-Songyouk-Eugye. A book detailing the process of building the Hwaseong Fortress in Suwon with details from the regulations to rituals along explained using images. (National Palace Museum of Gyeongbokgung Palace)

tists built upon this foundation to make a variety of calligraphic fonts that increased the practicality of movable metal type.

Through this rapid advancement of printing technology, Joseon was able to amass a great number of records for posterity, such as the *Veritable Records of Joseon Dynasty* and the *Seungjeongwon Ilgi*. The *Veritable Records of Joseon Dynasty* has a total of 64 million characters and is a collection of more records of history than any found in China or Japan. It contains the daily records of every king from the first to the twenty-fifth king of Joseon. The records' objectivity remains highly praised because even a reigning king was proscribed from reading his own records. But the *Veritable Records of Joseon Dynasty* are not the only notable records. There is another collection of records called the Uigwe, also of the Joseon Dynasty.

The *Uigwe* is a collection of books that recorded major events across the nation and within the royal court during the Joseon Dynasty, using painstaking detail and even illustrations to capture the

Figure 3-17 Part of ceremonial procession of King Jeongjo's travel to Hwaseong Royal Tomb/ The sequence of the ceremonial procession is meticulously recorded accordingly. (National Palace Museum at the Gyeongbokgung Palace)

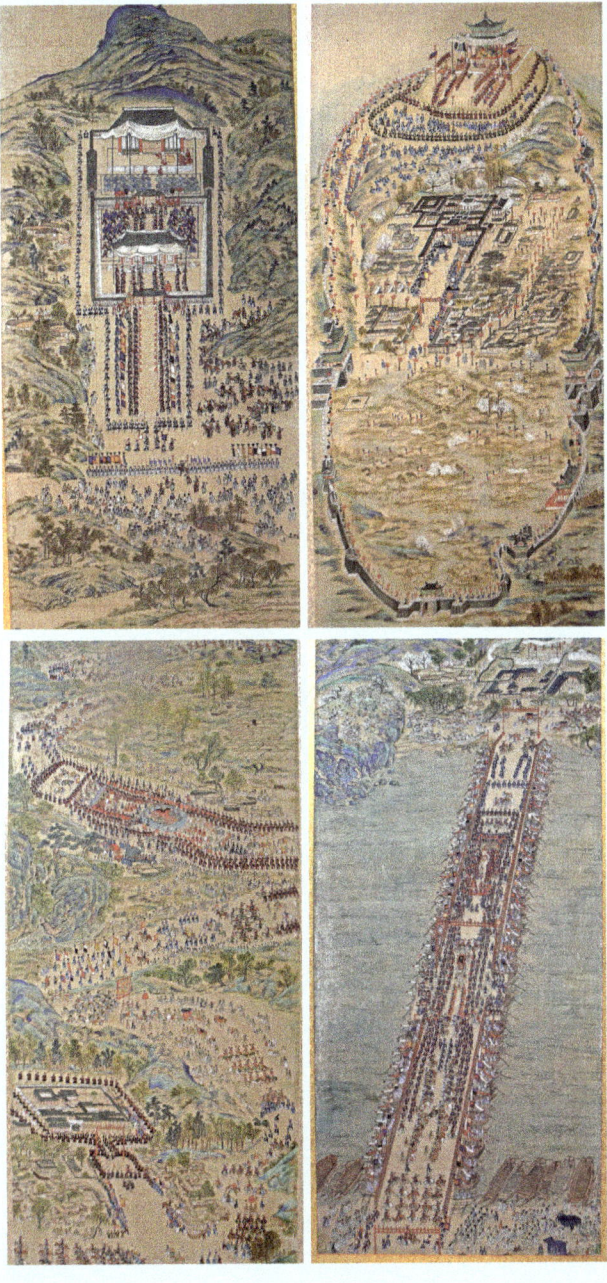

Figure 3-18 Part of the eight-panel folding screen with an image of the King Jeongjo's Travel to Hwanseong Royal Tomb/ (From the left) Paying respect to the Myeongnyundang Shrine, night training, procession to Hanyang, and above the bridge of the Han River on his return to the palace (National Palace Museum of Gyeongbokgung Palace)

scenes, tools used, process, participants, and cost. Essentially, it is a compilation of official event reports augmented with pictures. Talented artists participated in its creation, lending the feel and high artistic value of a book of photographs.

Among East Asian nations, Korea is the only country with a book collection of this type and magnitude; it is a unique and rare piece of the world's cultural heritage. Currently, a total of 3,895 books are distributed between Seoul University's Gyujanggak Library, the Academy of Korean Studies' Jangseogak Library, and the National Central Museum of Korea. The sheer number of texts in this collection is astounding. While an additional part of the collection is currently preserved in France and Japan, everything that remains within South Korea has been formally included in the UNESCO Memory of the World Register. Among these is a set of classics from the *Uigwe*, *the Wonheng-eulmyo-jeongli Uigwe*, which is the record of when the Great King Jeongjo held an eight-day festival in 1795. This was the longest festival of the Joseon Dynasty, and its records alone take up eight volumes.

Along with *Uigwe*, there is the *Hwa-seong-neung-heng Banchado* of the Great King Jeongjo, which records his visit to Hwaseong Fortress with both text-based commentary and visual depictions. King Jeongjo went to pay honor to his late father by visiting his father's royal burial mound, the Hyeong-ryoong-won, with his mother Lady Hon of the Hyegyeonggung Palace. The *Banchado* depictions are drawn like a woodprint panorama, precisely detailing the king's parade and even the order of the participants. A staggering 1,700 people, 800 horses, and even colored flags are portrayed in fine relief. Yet while the *Banchado* is impressive, the Hwa-seong-neung-haeng-do-byeong folding screen, which depicts major events of its era, is even more well-known. Together, these artifacts demonstrate how much Korea's ancestors valued documenting history.

There are 16 written records from Korea listed on the UNESCO Memory of the World Register, putting the country second in number globally behind Germany, and first in Asia.

1. The Hunmin Chongum Manuscript,
2. Royal Seal and Investiture Book Collection of the Joseon Dynasty,
3. Nanjung Ilgi: War Diary of Admiral Yi Sun-sin,
4. Human Rights Documentary Heritage 1980 Archives for the May 18th Democratic Uprising against Military Regime, in Gwangju, Republic of Korea,
5. Archives of the National Debt Redemption Movement,
6. The Archives of the KBS Special Live Broadcast "Finding Dispersed Families,"
7. Documents on Joseon Tongsinsa / Chosen Tsushinshi: The History of Peace Building and Cultural Exchanges between Korea and Japan from the 17th to 19th Century,
8. Baegun hwasang chorok buljo jikji simche yojeol (vol.II), the second volume of "Anthology of Great Buddhist Priests' Zen Teachings,"
9. Confucian Printing Woodblocks,
10. Archives of Saemaul Undong (New Community Movement),
11. Donguibogam: Principles and Practice of Eastern Medicine,
12. The Annals of the Joseon Dynasty,
13. Ilseongnok: Records of Daily Reflections,
14. Uigwe: The Royal Protocols of the Joseon Dynasty,
15. Printing woodblocks of the Tripitaka Koreana and miscellaneous Buddhist scriptures,
16. Seungjeongwon Ilgi: the Diaries of the Royal Secretariat.

Despite the fact that Korea is a global leader in terms of written records, there are only 16 of these texts listed on the UNESCO Memory of the World Register. Sadly, this is the result of a variety of internal and external issues including political turmoil, rebellions, and seven different wars.

While there are many historic examples of how Korea's vast catalogue of written records was winnowed down to what exists today, this book will mention only a few. During the reign of Goguryeo's King Dongcheong, the Wei Dynasty invaded the capital city Hwandoseong and burned all records. Shilla and Tang allied forces took over Baekjae's capital and burned its book storage buildings to the ground along with all the books inside. Books were also burned during the Mongolian invasion during the reign of Goryeo's Gojong, and burned or lost during the Japanese invasion of Imjin-waeran and the Chinese invasion of Byeongjahoran. Japan's burning and confiscation of over 200,000 Korean books occurred after Japan forcibly annexed Korea with the Japan-Korea Annexation Treaty of 1910. But one of the most shocking series of destructions took place during the reigns of King Sejo (the second son of Great King Sejong), King Yejong, and King Sungjong. These three kings ordered the collection and destruction of history books during their reigns. Anyone who hid history books at home was executed. Consequently, untold numbers of books printed by a nation that prided itself as having the most advanced technology for written records vanished, leaving behind a country that cannot remember the full extent of its own history.

If those burned books had survived to be passed down to today, imagine the depth and breadth of the amazing cultural heritage that could have been shared with the world.

Today, Korea ranks near the bottom of the OECD nations for the number of books read per person. It seems hard to believe, considering that Korea once was the world leader in printing press technology and that Korean people used to be so well-read. But it has become exceedingly rare to see a Korean person reading a book on the subway in Seoul.

No matter how much progress has been made through digital culture and the technological revolution, the most successful people in the world still read. They have not abandoned the "analog" way of life, nor have they put down paperbacks and hardcover books for good. The modern person is inundated with information from the internet, but so much of it is of low quality, not usable or useful. More advanced and important information is often printed on paper.

When I see subways full of Koreans without a book inside, it makes me think of how society was long ago, when the printing press had not yet been developed and knowledge and information still belonged to only a handful of powerful people. There was a higher purpose for why Korea developed the printing press technology that has shared information and knowledge throughout the generations since: the purpose of building a world where everyone lives in abundance. The people of the most developed nations in the world, such as the U.S., Germany, Japan, Sweden, and Finland, do one thing really well, and that is reading. It is easy to simply marvel at the progress of these countries, but it is more important to consider how they have attained such abundance and wealth.

Korea's ancestors understood the importance of record-keeping and documentation. Through the use of advanced printing press technology, they wanted to raise the overall quality of life of their people and enjoy a more refined culture. This applies to the modern day as well. There used to be a saying in Korea: "Our national power is equal to our physical fitness." These days, physical fitness has become more of a given, and how much a nation's citizens read is now what truly equates to its national power. It is my hope that the seeds planted and cultivated by the active minds of Korea's ancestors will come to full fruition during this generation and all those to come.

> Where paper and printing press are, there too is a revolution - Thomas Carlyle

大東千古開矇矓

用字例

初聲ㄱ。如 감爲柿 굴爲蘆 ㅋ。如 우
ㄷ。如 두 為茅 담
ㄴ。如 노로為獐 에為流澌
ㅁ。如
為獺 시為
為未春稻
ㅎ爲大豆 ㅇ。如 리
ㅔ為
為

A Trip to the Museums in Korea

The dream of all languages, Hangul

01 The beautiful design of the Korean alphabet
02 An alphabet to rival all others
03 King of communication and debate:
    Great King Sejong and his secret project
04 Great King Sejong's dream lives on in UNESCO award
05 Traditional lifestyle philosophy within Hangul's
    consonants and vowels
06 Hangul was not made in a day
07 The future of the Korean language

01

The beautiful design of the Korean alphabet

Many years ago, I visited the red dunes that surround the Sossusvlei desert region in Namibia. When I arrived at my oasis-like destination, a porter in his early twenties came to take the luggage from the car into the lodgings. When I spoke with him about my luggage, he asked me if I was from Korea. Intrigued, I smiled and asked him how he knew, and he told me that he recognized the Korean writing on my luggage tag. I had never expected to meet a Namibian person who was interested in Korean, especially in the middle of the desert with no other town nearby, and I was so delighted that I expressed that I wanted to offer him a gift of some kind. The young worker asked me to write his name in Korean on his arm because he loved the beauty of the letters; he wanted to get it tattooed. The Hangul that Koreans use every day and take for granted is seen in the eyes of foreigners as a beautiful design.

But it was not until I saw the Hangul-inspired floor and stone chairs of Gwanghwamun's Sejong Center for the Performing Arts in Seoul that I personally experienced that same admiration for Hangul's aesthetic. This was only after I had been impressed by seeing firsthand the way Islamic culture has relied on language and writing as an element in its architectural designs.

Islamic nations have a long history of using language and writing in their designs and decorations. Examples of this include Iran using Persian, also called Farsi, as its official language, and Turkey, Egypt, Morocco, and Tunisia using Arabic. Another example can be found at Alhambra Palace in southern Spain. The very walls of this palace bear distinct traces of this cultural influence. In Islamic culture, it is forbidden to create images of sentient beings; this is an avoidance of idolatry called aniconism. Islam therefore did not develop a culture of painting icons like that which is found in Christianity, but rather created sophisticated patterns far beyond what Christian Europeans could do. Of those many designs, the mosaic tiles are particularly complex, involving a breathtaking array of shapes and colors that are beautifully refined, neither gaudy nor plain. Yet while Islamic calligraphy and European paintings were developed through religion, Hangul came into existence without any religious influence. Hopefully, Hangul will become more widely known and be reimagined into many new forms and uses in the near future.

Figure 4-1 Next to the Sejong Center for the Performing Arts in Gwanghwamun /Stone chairs and floors decorated in Hangul, the Korean writing system

Figure 4-2 Decoration of God's name in the Persian alphabet on an entire wall (the Friday Mosque in Yazd, Iran)

Figure 4-3 The Arabic characters adorned the walls of a Koran School in the ancient Silk Road city of Buhara in Uzbekistan / Decorations of sun god and phoenix are quite unique.

02

An alphabet to rival all others

Among the 3,000 languages in the world today, the Korean alphabet of Hangul is the only script with both a name and a known date of invention. Unsurprisingly, the excellence of this written language is widely acknowledged outside of Korea, as can be seen by the numerous appraisals by world-class scholars from around the world on display at the National Hangeul Museum in Seoul.

Among the scholars who sing the praises of Hangul is Columbia University professor of Korean History emeritus Gari Ledyard, who has described Hangul as an "unparalleled grammatological luxury." British history documentary writer John Man opines in his book *Alpha Beta* that Hangul is the best alphabet, one that other languages can only dream about. Even the American magazine *Discovery's* June 1994 issue featured an article that claims Hangul is the most rational alphabet in the world. Across the pond, British linguist and University of Sussex professor Geoffrey Samson has remarked that Hangul is undoubtedly one of the greatest intellectual achievements in human history. The litany of praise from world-class scholars goes on, so their evaluations have been summarized below in three main points.

First, Hangul is extraordinarily easy to learn. It is a phonetic alphabet system composed of shapes that imitate the mouth forming the sounds that they represent—and there are only 24 letters to remember. Jeong Inji writes in *Hunminjeongeum Hye-rae-bon* that "a wise person can learn [Hangul] in the space of a single morning and even a fool can learn it in 10 days." The memorization of the shapes is straightforward, and Hangul is an ideal system for the modern era of information and internet technology. In the age of the smartphone,

Figure 4-4 Statue of King Sejong at the Gwanghwamun Square

Hangul requires just 10 buttons to create most syllables and has received recognition as a great fit for the information technology environment.

Second, Hangul is a scientific writing system of vowels and consonants that look like vocal organs. Each consonant takes the shape of the speech organ when pronouncing its sound, a system that far exceeds any of its contemporary (fifteenth century) language theories and demonstrates that the Korean alphabet was created using scientific methods. Dr. Werner Sasse, professor emeritus of Korean Studies at the University of Hamburg in Germany, remarked on the extent of Hangul's advanced development when he said, "King Sejong systematized the phonological theory five centuries earlier than the West, which completed its phonological theory in the twentieth century."

Third, the vowels of this system are founded on Eastern ideologies and philosophies. Dr. Sasse evaluated it as "the best alphabet in the world, which combines traditional philosophy and science theory." His reason for praising it as "the best alphabet" is that Hangul weaves together traditional philosophy and science without tangling them.

"The most complete alphabet among those in existence…"

From a report to the British Mission Headquarters (1883) by Missionary John Ross, 1842-1915

"King Sejong's invention of Hangeul is a brilliant achievement in the history of humanity…"

From *The Korean Alphabet* (1882) by Homer Hulbert, Ph.D. (1863-1949)

"Absolutely original and astonishing phonemic letters... The most scientific notation system available among all the scripts of the world..."

From *East Asia: The Great Tradition* (1960) by Harvard professor Edwin Reischauer (1910-1990)

"The Koreans invented the best alphabet in the world."

From *Korean Writing: Idu and Hangul* (1964) by Leiden University professor Frits Vos (1918-2000)

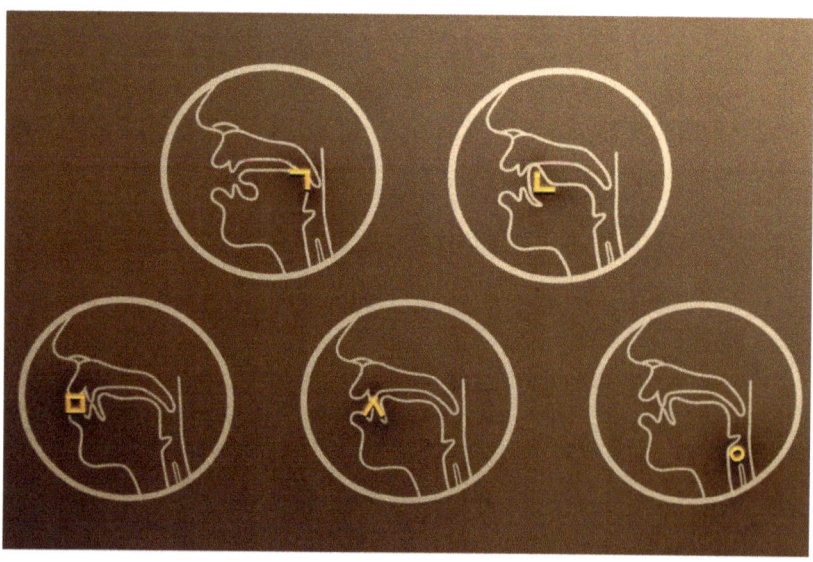

Figure 4-5 Images showing the shape of the vocal organs per each consonant on display at the Hangul Museum

03

King of communication and debate: Great King Sejong and his secret project

When King Sejong took the throne in 1418 during the Joseon Dynasty, his first words were, "All right, let the discussion commence." He was a king of communication, an expert scholar, and a genius. He is rightfully remembered today as a king among kings. With the aid of his court officials, he engaged in constant debate, research, and invention to improve the lives of his people, going to great lengths to be a good ruler. Yet of his many special projects, why did King Sejong choose to make the creation of Hangul a secret?

The popular explanation is that King Sejong was well aware that his court officials would fiercely oppose the project. This common justification is also the most believable one, and it is supported by the fact that a state minister named Choe Manli wrote an appeal to the king in which he strongly opposed the creation of Hangul. The chorus of appeals against the king's actions—like Choe's—gives us a deeper un-

Figure 4-6 King Sejong's image of researching for the creation of Hangul (Hangul Museum)

derstanding of the state of national affairs and international relations during King Sejong's reign, and even a glimpse into the king's intentions.

Today in South Korea, almost everyone can read. But not so long ago, many people were utterly illiterate. In fact, the rate of literacy would have been even worse during the Great King Sejong's reign, when illiterate individuals made up the majority of the population. Take the alphabet out of consideration, and many commoners did not even understand enough of the terms used in spoken language due to extreme differences in education. This made communication in a language of complex speech levels and honorifics exceedingly difficult. Many of these people suffered unjustly either because they experienced an unfair situation or committed illegal or criminal acts without any knowledge of what was legal and what was considered a crime. This is what drove King Sejong to write the *Samganghaengshildo**. Hangul was created to resolve the problems brought on by communication problems.

---

* *Samganghaengshildo* - A collection of real acccounts of loyal ministers, devoted sons, and faithful wives. It was published by King Sejong to teach his people to practice propriety in their daily relationships among 'Sovereign and his Subjects,' 'Parents and Children,' and 'Husband and Wife.'

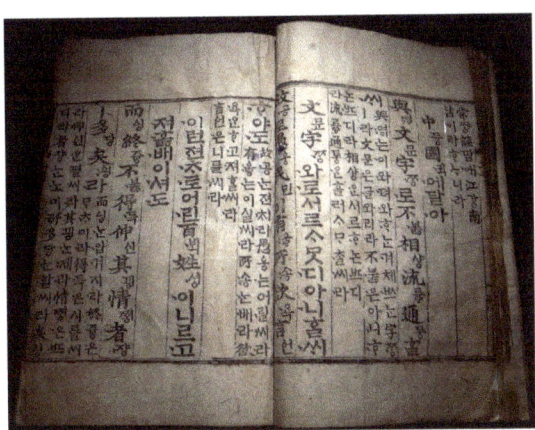

Figure 4-7 The "Wol-in-seok-bo" and "Hunmin-jeongeum Eonhae" displayed at the Hangul Museum. Here, King Sejong wrote the purpose of Hangul's creation.

The following describes the arguments outlined in the appeals that Choe Manli offered to the king. The real reason for his opposition to the creation of Hangul can be found in the fourth item of the list.

1. If we use implement a written language of our own (Hangul), we will be turning our backs on the Ming Empire and becoming their enemy*.

2. If we use Hangul, our people will not learn Neo-Confucian philosophy. Letters and knowledge must not be divided, but they will be divided with the creation of this script.

3. You must debate and discuss with the royal court first and then seek the permission of the Ming Emperor to make the new script.**

4. If the national exam is given in the new script, the Han-mun (the extant characters-based writing system) that the people of the noble class have learned until now will become useless.

---

* Prior to the invention of Hangul, literate Korean citizens (predominantly male scholars and nobles) relied on characters taken from the Chinese writing system. Choe Manli argues that opting for a Korean vernacular instead of Chinese symbols when reading and writing could be interpreted as a message that Joseon is no longer content to pay tribute to the Ming Empire.

** (royal court) - A government led by the Monarch and his ministers through discussions and debate to decide upon national policies for the purpose of governing.

5. Since the Crown Prince is involved with the creation of the alphabet, there will be problems when he becomes king if he only concentrates on the strange art of the alphabet and does not study Confucius and Mencius.

In reality, the fear of the threat to his own and other noble's vested interests is what led to such a strong opposition from Choe Manli. King Sejong rebutted Choe Manli's appeals with the following:

1. The alphabet is for the people. When Sulchong made the Ee-du writing system for the convenience of the people, he was highly praised, so then what do you mean by telling me I have done wrong?*

2. The *Hun-min-jeong-um* (*The Proper Sounds for the Instruction of the People*) is excellent from a linguistic perspective.

3. The Crown Prince has already taken charge of matters at a national level, so for him to participate in this is only natural.

This rebuttal seems simple, but there were fundamental reasons for the Great King Sejong's creation of Hangul.

The first was to cultivate a sense of community. Once the nation had an alphabet that was a clear and unified system, King Sejong's subjects would be able to properly communicate with words and better understand each other. Then, with the spoken language integrated, the people would gain a proper sense of community, and politics would also unify so that the nation could be led in the right direction.

---

* Ee-du alphabet writing system was found by a famed scholar Sulchong, of Shilla dynasty. However, it was still difficult to learn and use. It also became the basis of Japanese writing system.

Secondly, King Sejong wanted to prevent class division. He wanted to make a method of communication that enabled him to hear even the quietest of voices among his people so that no one would be trapped in an unfair situation. This was the only way that he could prevent the separation of the dominant ruling class and the subjugated working class. These intentions behind his creation of Hangul are clearly outlined in the *Hunminjeongeum* Eonhae as well.

---

* *Hunminjeongeum Eonhae* – A book that describes the principle, purpose, reason, and usage of Korean alphabet Hangul.

04

Great King Sejong's dream lives on in UNESCO award

The UNESCO King Sejong Literacy Prize is an award that was instituted in 1989 in honor of the mind behind the internationally-acclaimed Hangul alphabet. This special prize is the world's recognition of an alphabet that was designed to combat illiteracy and free commoners from a life of unfairness, and the king who made it happen. When International Literacy Day is commemorated annually on September 8, the award of the King Sejong silver medal, $20,000 USD in award money, and a certificate of merit are presented to individuals and organizations chosen for their efforts to fight illiteracy. The 2015 recipients were Mozambique NGO Associação Progresso and Sri Lanka's National Institute of Education.

Associação Progresso was recognized for promoting women's participation in poverty eradication and social development by providing a range of education opportunities for local residents, especially women and children, in their mother tongues rather than the country's official but less widely-used language of Portuguese. Similarly, through its Open School

Programme, Sri Lanka's National Institute of Education offers education to people who have not completed their primary education. It has also contributed to poverty eradication and income creation by providing vocational technology education for young people and adults outside of school. These two organizations were selected for the award as a result.

05

Traditional lifestyle philosophy within Hangul's consonants and vowels

Hangul was not invented by accident. It was intentionally established using Korea's traditional ideologies as its foundation. But in order for us to fully understand the traditional philosophy that is the basis of Hangul, we would have to translate each and every line of the original written characters used in the Hunminjeongeum *Haerye*—that information alone would fill an entire book on Eastern Philosophy. The following is a summary of a few notable elements.

The principles used in *Hunminjeongeum* (*The Proper Sounds for the Instruction of the People*) are based on yin-yang and the five elements, which ultimately represent the natural laws of the universe. The sounds made by humans, animals, and nature are all created from and according to these natural laws. *Hunminjeongeum* originally took these sounds and created a system of 28 letters that represent the sounds in writing.

Consider the labial consonant called "mieum" in Korean, which looks like a small box when written: ㅁ. There are two of these used in the Korean word "eomma," which means "mom" and is written in Hangul as 엄마. Can you see the two rectangular boxes in the word? The first box is at the bottom of the first syllable, eom (엄). When the mieum consonant is pronounced by closing your mouth and putting your lips together (like when you say "um"), it is written at the bottom of the syllable block. When the mieum consonant is pronounced by opening your mouth and pulling your lips apart, it is placed at the beginning of its respective syllable block, in this case, ma (마). Because this sound comes from the opening and closing of the lips, it is called a labial sound. The shape of your lips surrounding that sound resembles the earth that embraces all living things. Therefore, this is categorized as the central energy of the five elements: Earth. As for the four seasons, this falls under late summer, and of the five sounds, it is known as the gung (宮) sound.

Five Elements Categorization of Consonant Pronunciation

Hangul Consonant	Pronunciation	Five Elements	Seasons	Five Sounds
ㄱ, ㅋ	Velar sound	Wood	Spring	Gak
ㄴ, ㄹ, ㄷ, ㅌ	Ligual sound	Fire	Summer	Chi
ㅁ, ㅂ, ㅍ	Labial sound	Earth	Late Summer	Gung
ㅅ, ㅈ, ㅊ	Dental sound	Metal	Autumn	Sahng
ㅇ, ㅎ	Guttural sound	Water	Winter	Wu

The chart above includes the seasons because *Hunminjeongeum Haerye*'s explanation assigned a season to each of the five elements.

While the consonants are based on the ideology of yin-yang and the five elements, the vowels consist of the Samjae: heaven, earth, and humanity. The • dot, usually written as a short line in Hangul today, represents the round heaven. The — horizontal line represents flat and even ground: earth. Last but not least, the ㅣ vertical line represents a person standing upright. These three shapes based on the principle of Samjae—heaven, earth, and humanity — combine into all of the letter representations of vowels, which in turn combine with consonants. A single syllable can thus be formed from an initial consonant, a middle vowel, and a final consonant.

The simultaneous simplicity and complexity of a single syllable offers a glimpse of why scholars around the globe praise Hangul as one of the greatest achievements of humankind and as the greatest alphabet in human history, a system where traditional philosophy and scientific theory come together in harmony.

06

Hangul was not made in a day

Before the creation of Hangul, Korea's ancestors had their own unique letter system. The shell and bone characters that form the root of the Chinese characters are the work of those ancestors, the Dongyi people.* There are also 128 letters from the period of Daejinguk (698-1116 CE), also called Balhae, that survived on a fragment of a roof tile made during that era. The existence of a written language unique to Daejinguk is further corroborated by records of Lee Taebak, a poet renowned for his genius during the Tang Dynasty. Reportedly, he was the only person who could decipher diplomatic documents sent to Tang from Daejinguk.

Many of the historical texts and records that discuss the invention of Hangul write that its creators designed it to imitate an "old script"

---

* Dongyi refer's to the people of Korea. Dong means East and Yi means those who are skilled archers.

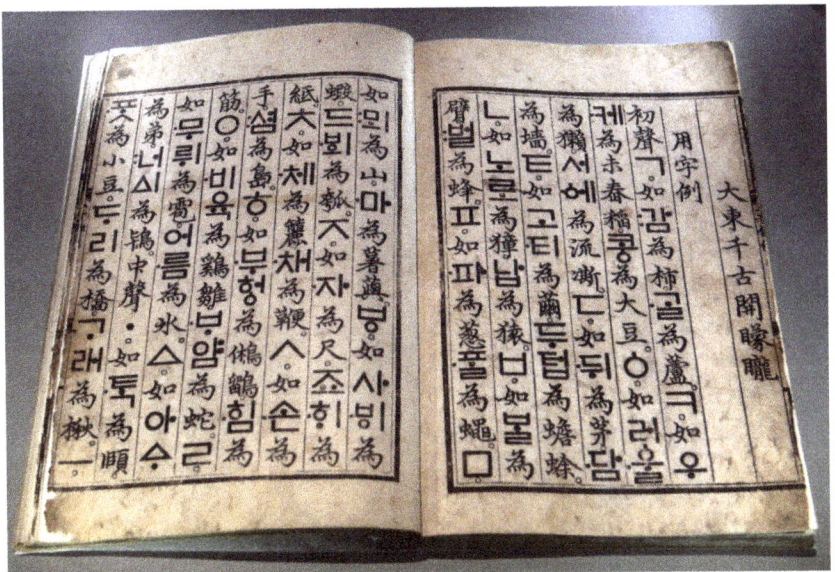

Figure 4-8 The Hae-rye-bon of Hunminjeongeum exhibited at the National Hangul Museum// The Haeryebon is an appendix to Hunminjeongeum, which is composed of examples and application related to Hangul which was composed by Jeong In-ji and Shin Sook-ju. Hunminjeongeum, which means the correct sound for teaching the people, can be categorized in to the Hanmunbon Version, consisting of Chinese characters, and the Eonhaebon Version, consisting of Hangul. The Haeryebon of Hunminjeongeum is commonly referred to as Hunminjeongeum.

once used by their ancestors.

While this old script has not been conclusively identified, the following records make it clear that King Sejong did create Hangul from an old written Korean language.

"This month, the King himself created 28 letters, and the letters were imitated from old writings…"

From *King Sejong's Daily Records,* in the second article from December 30, 1443, during his 25th year of reign

"Even though Your Majesty says that they are not new letters because the Korean alphabet is all based on the old script, and so it is an imitation…"

From the appeals of Choe Manli and others opposing the creation of the Korean alphabet, 1444

"His Majesty created the 28 letters, giving us succinct examples, and he made a name for the characters called the Hunminjeongeum, which is like a pictographic alphabet based on the old letters…"

From the preface of *Hunminjeongeum* Haerye, by Jeong Inji, 1446

"Our nation had a system of pictographic letters used in antiquity, but it was incomplete, and the shapes were not organized, making it insufficient for one to use it practically."

From *Hunminjeongeum* Unhae by Shin Gyeongjoon, 1750

07

The future of the Korean language

In the previous sections of this chapter, we explored the foundation and history of Hangul as a highly efficient and scientific system admired by scholars around the globe. But what about Korean as a spoken language? How does the Korean language rank overall in terms of usage worldwide?

There are over 7,000 known living languages today. Of those languages, Korean ranks twenty-first in terms of number of native and secondary users. The three most-used languages in the world today, in order, are English, Mandarin Chinese, and Hindi, according to Ethnologue, the top research center for language intelligence. More information on the Korean language's position among world languages can be found in the National Hangeul Museum next to the National Central Museum in Seoul—the first museum in the world to be dedicated to a language system. Recently, French media noted that Korea is a country to keep an eye on because it innovated its own unique and independent writing system.

The rise of the Korean Wave has spread Hangul and the Korean language in general far and wide. Non-Koreans are not only consuming Korean music, movies, and other cultural and creative content that has spiked in international popularity in recent years, but an increasing number of people are actively choosing to learn the language as a result. Hangul can express a vast range of sounds with great efficiency. It is my hope that the use of Hangul will continue to spread and find new and exciting uses around the world.

When I considered the best way to distribute the Korean language around the world, I came to a simple conclusion: people. Many people come to Korea because they are attracted by Hallyu (the Korean Wave) and end up learning the Korean language. A popular Korean TV show called *Abnormal Summit* has showcased a range of talented non-native Korean speakers from different countries for several years, elevating awareness both in South Korea and abroad. If Korea continues to produce high-quality cultural content and make it accessible to people, it seems likely that people around the world will take notice and take it upon themselves to learn the language.

There was, however, a South Korean media report that claimed Hallyu did not begin the way that most people believe. According to this media source, travelers began with layovers and visits to Incheon Airport through word-of-mouth recommendations. These travelers then ended up touring around nearby Seoul, where they discovered Itaewon, a cosmopolitan neighborhood that often is described as a heaven for tourists. These tourists then left the cityscape of Seoul's Itaewon to seek out South Korea's beautiful, mountain-covered countryside, where they fell in love with the rich variety of delicious regional delicacies. This is reportedly the real reason tourists became deeply interested in Korea and its people, enabling the rise of Hallyu. While this may have some merit as an explanation of earlier interest in Korea, the dynamic has shifted in recent years. More and more people are choosing to live in South Korea due to the excellence of Korean cultural content—and because the country is simply a great place to live. There is no doubt that this is the tangible impact of Hallyu. When visitors living in South Korea eventually return to their home countries after learning the Korean language, the language is naturally disseminated to new people across the globe.

Another way to encourage the use of the Korean language is to operate Korean language schools that provide Hangul and Korean language education to second- and third-generation Koreans abroad. This would require that they are willing to learn, of course. Many do not know all the ins and outs of the language because they rarely communicate in Korean in their everyday lives and they lack opportunities for formal language education as heritage speakers.

The very existence of the Korean language and alphabet was greatly threatened during the harsh laws of the Japanese colonial era, when the Korean language and even Korean names were forcibly replaced by Japanese versions. Even now, Hangul is technically incomplete because a handful of King Sejong's original letters have fallen into disuse. The work of restoring the complete set of 28 letters created for *Hunminjeongeum* is yet to be done. In order for a full range of linguistic sounds to be accurately written using Hangul, the four lost letters must be restored. Moreover, modern society in South Korea has to work to set and maintain a standard for written language in

the era of the internet and instant communication. The extensive shortening of words, the strange combinations of letters and special characters used online, and the instant messaging environment are slowly destroying the Korean language. Considering the value and importance of the Korean language, this is not an issue that can be taken lightly.

Figure 4-9 National Hangul Museum, the world's first museum on letters are located next to the National Museum of Korea.

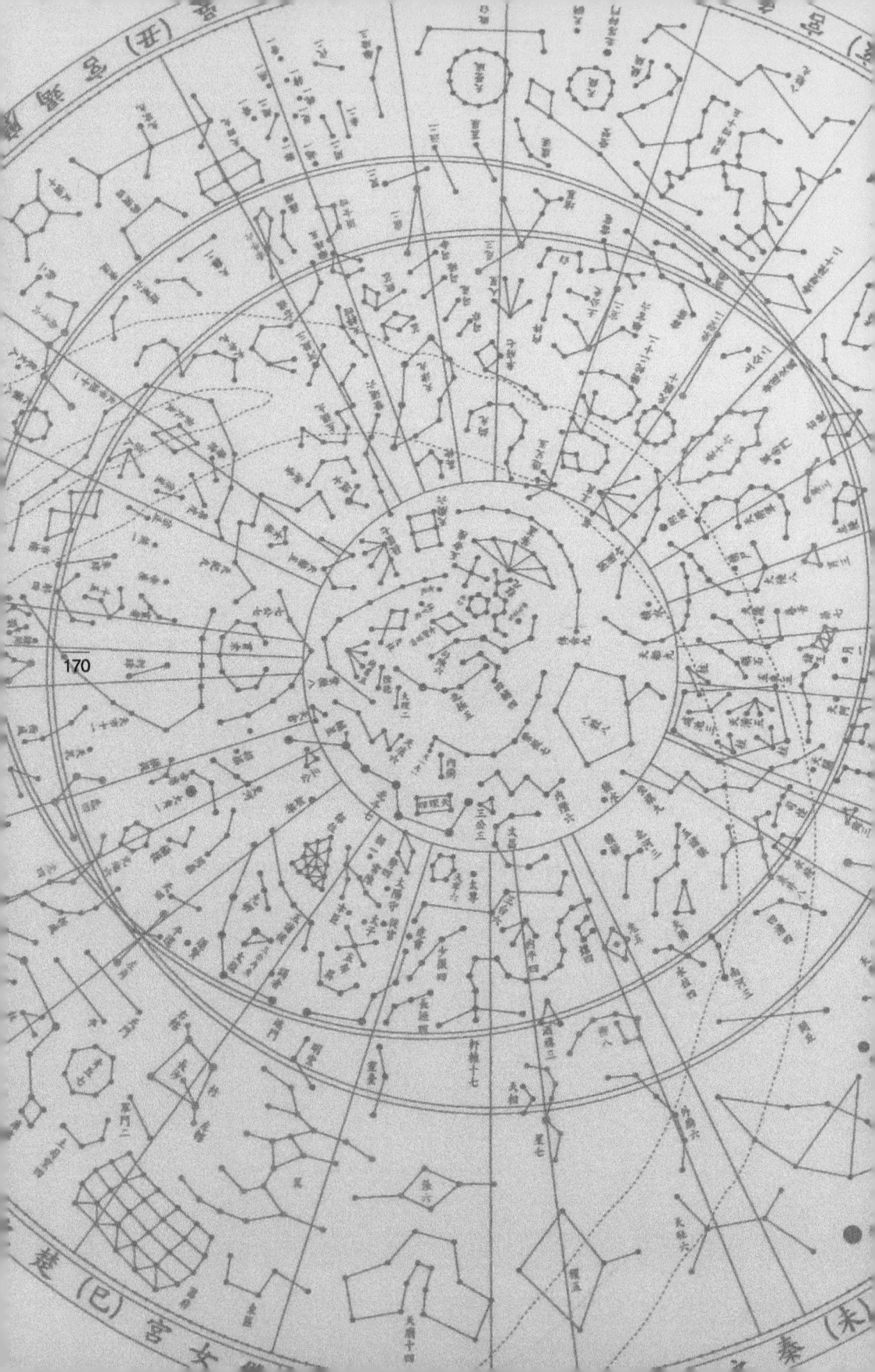

PART 05

A Trip to the Museums in Korea

My dear, if you see a shining star The cheonsangyeolchabunyajido

01 The universe within the 10,000 won bill
02 The troubled travels of the Cheon-sang-yeol-cha-bun-ya-ji-do
03 Depicting the vast majority of Northern Hemisphere constellations
04 Gyeongbokgung Palace, the auspicious site of Heaven on Earth
05 Guardians of the auspicious sites: Blue Dragon, White Tiger, Red Phoenix, and Black Tortoise
06 The heavenly guardians of Gyeongbokgung Palace
07 Governing the land in the image of the heavenly realm
08 Goguryeo astronomers draw the world's oldest constellation
09 Goguryeo's conception of the cosmos through astronomy
10 Astronomy in Shilla, Baekjae, and Goryeo
11 Astronomy inherited from Ancient Joseon

01

The universe within the 10,000 won bill

Next time you have the South Korean 10,000 won bill in your wallet, take it out and look for the cheon-mun-do, an ancient diagram of constellations and much more. The constellations can be found in the background of the bill's depiction of a celestial globe, which was a type of celestial observation device. Celestial globes were used since the Three Kingdoms period (58 BCE-668 CE), but the one that appears on the 10,000 won bill was made during the time of the Great King Sejong. The stars that shine in the background of this globe on the bill are the constellations of the Cheon-sang-yeol-cha-bun-ya-ji-do.

Even among Koreans, there are many people who do not know that these historically and culturally significant constellations exist on the 10,000 won bill. The Cheon-sang-yeol-cha-bun-ya-ji-do is notable because it is a storied drawing of all the constellations that were visible to the naked eyes of its makers, and it is the oldest astronomical chart of its kind in the world.

From ancient times, the Korean people were curious about the movements of celestial bodies in the skies above and spent copious amounts of time examining the heavens. The result of this long-lasting and close relationship with the stars is illustrated on the 10,000 won bill, making it as if Koreans carry the universe around in their wallets.

To put it simply, the Cheon-sang-yeol-cha-bun-ya-ji-do is an astronomical chart. But why does it have such a long and difficult name? The following section breaks down the name's meaning into the distinct elements of cheonsang, yeolcha, bunya, and jido.

The best place to start is actually at the end of the Cheon-sang-yeol-cha-bun-ya-ji-do's name. If you know a little Korean, you might think that jido simply means map, as in a map of Seoul or a map of South Korea. In this case, it actually means "drawing or depiction." Next we move to the beginning of the name: Cheonsang is an abbreviation of Cheonmunhyeonsang, meaning celestial phenomenon. Again, if you know some Korean, you may think that yeolcha is asso-

Figure 5-1 10,000 won bill with a map of the cheon-sang-yeol-cha-bun-ya-ji-do and hon-cheon-ui.

ciated with the word gicha, or train, but here it means that the celestial bodies have been divided into sections. Bunya means to associate or pair a certain region on Earth with a certain constellation. In sum, Cheon-sang-yeol-cha-bun-ya-ji-do means "drawing in which the divisions of the constellations of the heavens are reflected in areas on Earth."

As human beings, we naturally try to assign locations and directions to the world around us, but this is no easy task when it comes to the vastness of outer space and the twinkling stars that fill it. For this very reason, the cheon-mun-do was drawn based on directions and locations used on Earth, which enabled people in antiquity to better understand how stars were distributed in space. Additionally, they believed that the land itself and the constellations in the sky were connected and reactive to each other, so they divided the land into 12 different regions and paired them with 12 different constellations. This is what they called bunya.

The long name of the standard cheon-mun-do found on the 10,000 won bill is layered with meaning, offering us a glimpse of how the Korean people once lived and unveiling some of the secrets still hidden in history.

02

The troubled travels of the Cheon-sang-yeol-cha-bun-ya-ji-do

The Heaven and Science Exhibition of Gyeongbokgung's National Palace Museum includes the Cheon-sang-yeol-cha-bun-ya-ji-do and other tools and artifacts that were used to observe the cosmos, but you will also discover a unique type of Cheon-sang-yeol-cha-bun-ya-ji-do carved into stone. The black stone was made during Joseon Dynasty's King Taejo's reign (1335-1408 CE), and the gray stone was made during King Sukjong's reign (1661-1720 CE).

The real story of how the cheon-mun-do came to be carved into stone sounds like it came straight from a movie script. The black stone astronomical chart was a version made during the fourth year after the establishment of Joseon as a nation (found in 1392). It was copied from an as-yet unknown original from Pyeongyang, which was once the capital of Goguryeo. The original memorial stone that bore the astronomical chart is said to have been lost in a river in the

Figure 5-2 A cheonmundo(an astronomical map) carved on a stone - Taejo Stone Sculpture and Sukjong Stone Sculpture.(National Palace Museum at Gyeongbokgung Palace)

midst of warfare, but a commoner carrying a copy of the astronomical chart from Goguryeo offered it to King Taejo, the founder of Joseon. At last, the ability to make this special astronomical chart had come to Joseon.

But this was in the early years of Joseon's establishment, and there was no time to spend on producing astronomical charts because people were busy building the foundation for their new nation. It also was difficult to entice talented individuals who were still loyal to the Goryeo Dynasty. After Goryeo fell, its greatest astronomer, Yu Bangtaek, secluded himself in his hometown, but he was eventually coerced into completing the cheon-mun-do on a black obsidian stone brought from Mt. Baekdu in 1395. King Taejo offered Yu a position in his government and a feudal allowance on par with the top level officials who had helped establish Joseon, but Yu refused, saying that he could not serve two kings.

The Cheon-sang-yeol-cha-bun-ya-ji-do made during King Taejo's reign is called the Taejo-seokgakbon. In Our *History Carved in the Heavens*, astronomer and professor Park Changbeom writes that this is the world's oldest record of all visible constellations in a single chart; he calls it the complete version of the Eastern skies.

W.C. Rufus, an American who worked at Pyeongyang Soongshil School (a Presybyterian mission school) during the Japanese colonial period, wrote in his 1936 book *Korean Astronomy* that the Cheon-sang-yeol-cha-bun-ya-ji-do was a complete integration of Eastern astronomy resulting in an elaborate and accurate drawing of the heavens. But his book and its assertions attracted little attention when it was published, and it was not until much later that the long-ignored Cheon-sang-yeol-cha-bun-ya-ji-do revealed itself again. This carved stone copy of the Cheon-sang-yeol-cha-bun-ya-ji-do had been hidden in the rafters of the Myeongjeongjeon Hall of Changgyeonggung Palace where it was eventually found by science historian Jeong Jinwoon in the 1960s. Reportedly, palace tourists had been using the stone as a table when they ate their boxed lunches, their children playing games by piling sand on it. In the 1960s, national cultural treasures were not as carefully protected as they are today, so the carved cheon-mun-do was treated just like any other rock on a road.

After the recovery of the Cheon-sang-yeol-cha-bun-ya-ji-do, awareness of this important cultural treasure was raised, and in 1985, the astronomical chart was officially designated as a national treasure (both carved stones were chosen: King Taejo's Seokgakbon and King Sukjong's Seokgakbon). They were also recognized as the second-oldest astronomical charts carved in stone in the world. Given the historical turmoil and rough treatment this valuable heritage encountered, it is fortunate that the brilliance of the astronomical chart was carved into a stone that could withstand the ravages of time.

03

Depicting the vast majority of Northern Hemisphere constellations

In total, there are 1,467 stars and 295 constellations in the Cheon-sang-yeol-cha-bun-ya-ji-do. Given the sheer number of stars and the use of stone as the medium, it is quite difficult to distinguish one from another. Its maker tried to include as many stars on the rock as possible, and parts of the stone have worn away over the centuries. To overcome this challenge, the National Palace Museum of Korea displays an enlarged image on the exhibition wall to make the constellations more easily discernible. At first glance, the chart appears extremely complicated, with many concentric circles and numerous lines that stretch from the center to the very edges of the piece. But upon closer look, you will realize that the chart is far easier to understand than it first seems.

The first step to understanding the astronomical chart is to identify its four circles. Do you see them? The large outermost circle is called the waegyu, which is the horizon. Within this circle are two medium-

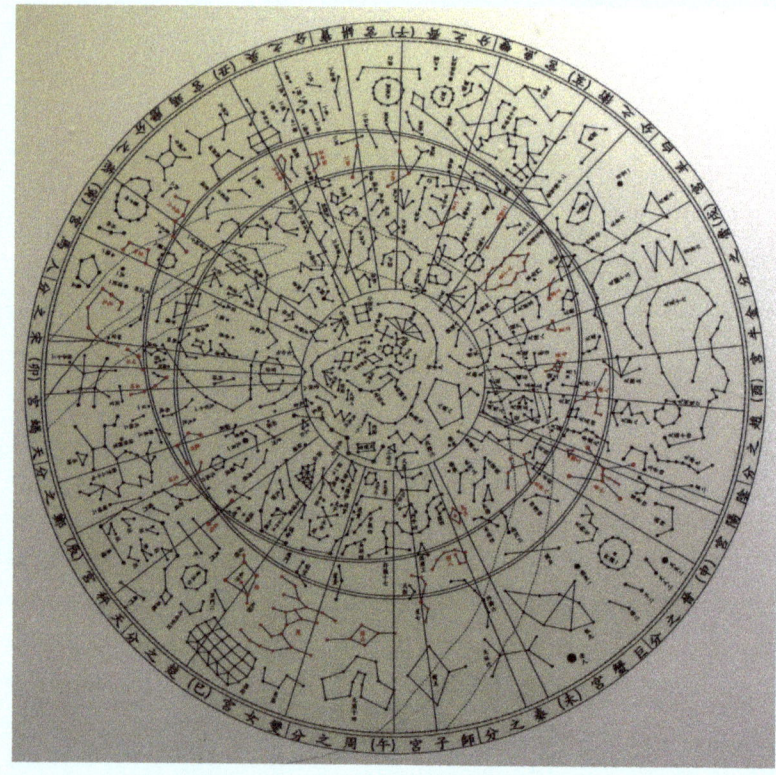

Figure 5-3 A partial replica of the astronomical map of cheon-sang-yeol-cha-bun-ya-ji-do displayed at the National Palace Museum of Gyeongbokgung Palace

sized overlapping circles. The circle that fits perfectly around the center is the celestial equator, and the circle that sits off-center is called the Emperor's Path, as it is the route that the sun takes during a one-year cycle.

The circle closest to the center is the naegyu, also called the Jamiwon. Once you have identified these four circles, your eyes might naturally shift to the lines radiating from the Jamiwon. These lines divide the 28 representative constellations into 28 sections. Their irregular spacing is not a mistake or issue of inconsistency, however; the 28 representative constellations are divided based on size, so the sections vary in size accordingly.

These 28 constellations are called the 28 su. For now, you do not need to know the names of each of the 28 su or what shape they take in order to understand the astronomical chart. As long as you keep in mind the fact that the radiating lines on the Cheon-sang-yeol-cha-bun-ya-ji-do are included to divide the 28 constellations into sections, you will be able to view it without it seeming so complex.

The Cheon-sang-yeol-cha-bun-ya-ji-do includes almost all constellations that can be seen from the Northern Hemisphere, and it displays these along with details about the Sun, the Moon, and the Milky Way. It even features information about the 24 divisions of the lunar calendar, too, demonstrating the height of astronomical knowledge at the time of its creation.

04

Gyeongbokgung Palace, the auspicious site of Heaven on Earth

Koreans are used to hearing a range of feng shui (geomancy) terms such as the auspicious sites of the Left Blue Dragon or Right White Tiger.* Historical Korean TV dramas in particular are filled with references such as these. But what exactly is an auspicious site? Simply put, it is a place that bestows good fortune. One version of this is called eumtaek, where good fortune is bestowed on the descendents of a deceased individual buried at an auspicious site. Alternatively, if a person lives on an auspicious site, they receive those blessings and good fortune directly. This is known as yangtaek.

The requirements for designating a place as an auspicious site, such as the Left Blue Dragon and Right White Tiger, come from the four gods: Black Tortoise of the North, Red Phoenix of the South, Blue Dragon of the East, and White Tiger of the West. These gods are

---

* Feng shui is the Chinese name for geomancy and the term that is widely known in the West. Korean geomancy is called pungsujiri.

represented by the mountains that protect an auspicious site, and an auspicious site cannot exist unless these four mountains are present.

It is a little-known fact that the auspicious sites of feng shui on the ground are based on constellations of stars in the sky. At its essence, Korean geomancy is about using an auspicious site in the heavens to identify its earthly counterpart. This begs the question: Where are those auspicious sites in the sky? It was once believed that the Heavenly Emperor ruled all of the universe (he was also known as the Jade Emperor). Naturally, this resulted in the belief that the Seven Stars of the Northern Dipper, which served as the Heavenly Emperor's chariot, shone in the most auspicious site in the heavens. This is why the center of the Cheon-sang-yeol-cha-bun-ya-ji-do is the Jamiwon, or the Jamigung Palace. It is the greatest and most auspicious site of them all.

Since ancient times, the early societies of Korean civilization made great efforts to manifest this auspicious site on Earth. Gyeongbokgung Palace is a perfect example of this effort to recreate the Jamiwon on Earth. The establishment of the Jamiwon on Earth holds great cultural and historical significance because it is a physical representation of the "descendant of Heaven" or "son of Heaven" ideology of earlier Korean societies. This ideology is also referenced on the Gwanggaeto Stele, a memorial stone erected at the tomb of the Great King Gwanggaeto, the nineteenth ruler of Goguryeo. The engravings on the stele refer to Goguryeo's founder, the Great King Gochumo, as the Heavenly Emperor's Son. This title comes from the Far East concept that the Heavenly Emperor resided in the Jamiwon and did not rule Earth directly; he ruled it through his son, who was born to rule the world in his stead.

This "descendant of Heaven" concept was passed down to Joseon, which built Gyeongbokgung Palace in 1395 to reflect the Jamigung Palace. The Forbidden Palace in Beijing was also based on this concept, although it was built several years later in 1407.

No empire or monarchy would be complete without the loyal vassals and subjects of its ruler, and the dominion of the Heavenly Emperor was no exception to this. While the emperor himself was believed to reside in the Jamiwon, the place where his celestial government carried out its work was called the Taemiwon, and the emperor's subjects lived in the Cheonshiwon. Together, the Jamiwon, Taemiwon, and Cheonsiwon are known as the Samwon, or the 3 Won, and they appear alongside the 28 su in East Asian astronomy. The Samwon and the 28 su are the foundation of the East Asian astronomical chart.

The Joseon Dynasty did not only build Gyeongbokgung Palace where the Jamiwon is on Earth; they sought to recreate the layout of three won as a whole. The earthly manifestation of the Taemiwon in the Joseon Dynasty was Yukjo Street, which is Gwanghwamun Square today. Yukjo Street passed between the buildings that housed the six central branches of government: yijo, hojo, yejo, byeongjo, hyeongjo, gongjo, and the ui-jeong-bu (as the executive branch, the ui-jeong-bu was the highest branch of government). There was also the hansungbu, which is equivalent to Seoul City Hall today, and the siheonbu, which functioned much like the Board of Audit and Inspection in modern South Korea. Beside the Taemiwon was the earthly version of the Cheonsiwon, an area filled with the hustle and bustle of people's everyday lives, much like a shopping mall or department store today. During the Joseon Dynasty, the area where the government-licensed stores of Hanyang (an old name for the city of Seoul) thronged with people exchanging products and goods was considered the Cheonsiwon.* Today, this place is called Jongno, but it is still part of a capital city meticulously designed to reflect the arrangements of the skies above.

---

* Seoul has had several names over its existence. Hanyang and Hansung were both used to refer to Seoul during the Joseon Dynasty.

5-1. Samwon's Earthly Sites in Joseon's Capital

Samwon in the heavens	Jamiwon	Taemiwon	Cheonsiwon
Hansung on Earth (capital city of Joseon Dynasty)	Gyeongbokgung Palace	Yukjo Street Government Offices (modern Gwanghwamun)	Sijeon market (modern Jongno)

Modern astronomy and the Buk-du-chil-seong (Seven Stars of the Northern Dipper)

- A recent study found that the Seven Stars of the Northern Dipper radiate cosmic rays of energy 10,000 times stronger than human technology can synthesize. The joint international research team that published this report in 2014 is known as the Telescope Array (TA) team and is composed of South Korean, American, Japanese, and Russian scientists. Their report analyzed five years of data gathered by installing 500 particle detectors and three large-scale telescopes in an area the size of Seoul.

- These cosmic rays from outer space are extremely high-energy microparticles. The TA team reported that 19 of the 72 extreme high-energy cosmic rays they measured came from the Seven Stars of the Northern Dipper region. This provides an interesting scientific basis for why the Seven Stars of the Northern Dipper might have been identified by people long ago as the most auspicious site in the universe.

Purple, the color of the Heavenly Son of the East and the West

- The "ja" in Jamiwon signifies jaju, which is a shade of the color purple.* As described earlier in this chapter, the Heavenly Em-

---

* The ja or jajusaek (紫朱色) type of purple in Korea is a reddish purple that is sometimes called plum, wine, or claret on the color spectrum. It may be classified under different names depending on culture and language.

peror was believed to reside in the Jamigung Palace in the sky, and his Heavenly Son was believed to live at the corresponding place for the Jamigung Palace on the land as his agent and servant. Jaju purple was used extensively in the palace of the Joseon kings who ruled Earth on behalf of the Heavenly Emperor. It features heavily in Gyeongbokgung Palace's design in particular, where it appears throughout the central building of the palace, called Geunjeongjeon Hall, and throughout all surrounding palace buildings as well. Jaju purple also adorns the walls of the Forbidden City in Beijing, China, where only the emperor could wear clothes of jaju purple.

- This color and its connotations of sovereignty can also be found outside of the Far East, in ancient Rome, where jaju purple was reserved for the emperor alone. During Emperor Nero's reign, it became a law that disallowed even the most powerful aristocrats from using jaju purple as they pleased. This meaning is also referenced in an inscription on the Constantine Obelisk, an ancient structure that was named after Constantine VII and that still stands in Constantinople, which used to be the capital city of the Byzantine Empire. The engraving on this obelisk bears the word "Porphyrogenitus," which can be directly translated as "born in the purple." In other words, the inscription states that Constantine VII was born to a father who had already risen to the throne as an emperor; Constantine VII was an emperor begotten of an emperor. The shade of purple referenced by this inscription is often referred to as royal, imperial, or Tyrian purple. While the the Roman Empire of Constantine VII's era does not appear to have had astronomy-based philosophies that might have identified a Roman Jamiwon, the imperial significance of jaju purple was commonplace in both the East and the West at the time.

Figure 5-4 **Obelisk of Constantine VII in Istanbul**

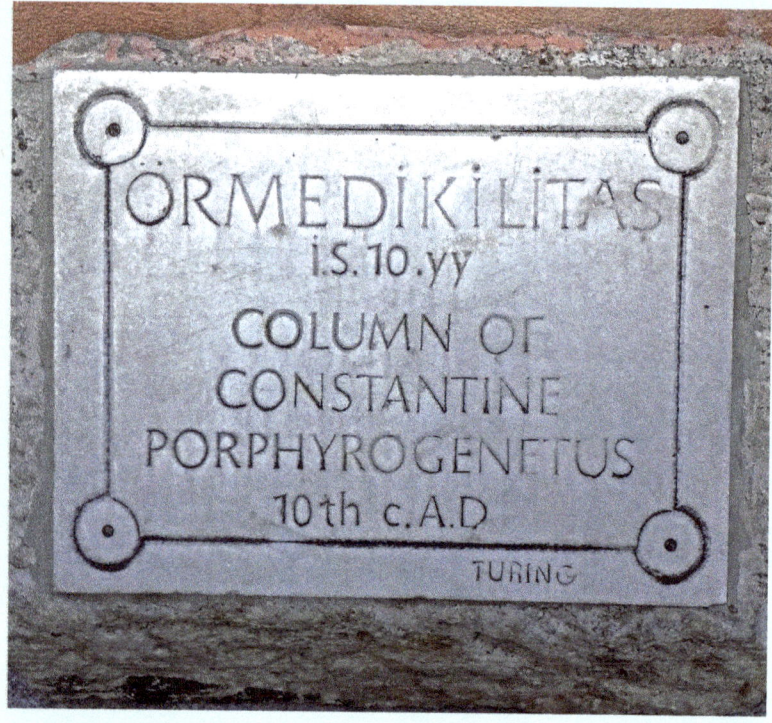

Figure 5-5 The stone plate in front of the obelisk of Constantine VII has a carving of the phrase "PORPHYROGENETUS," meaning "born of purple." The plate is erected in Hippodrome Square, where the Roman Chariot stadium used to stand.

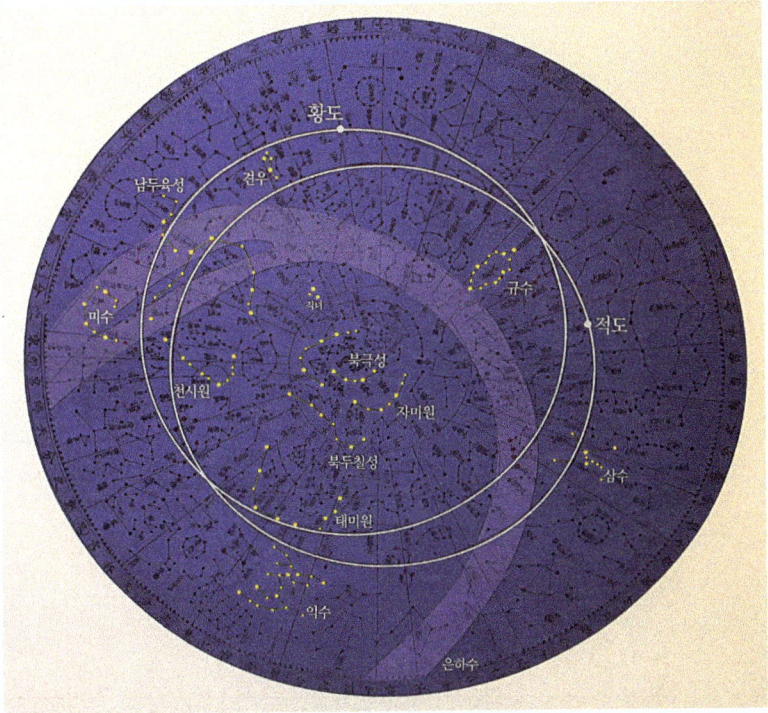

Figure 5-6 Conceptual map of the cheon-sang-yeol-cha-bun-ya-ji-do displayed at the National Palace Museum of Gyeongbokgung Palace

05

Guardians of the auspicious sites: Blue Dragon, White Tiger, Red Phoenix, and Black Tortoise

In the Eastern astronomical chart called the cheon-mun-do, the cosmos is divided into the 3 won and the 28 su (constellations). The Jamiwon stands at the center of the 3 won where it is surrounded and protected by the 28 constellations. This section will look at how the layout of these 28 constellations correspond to places on Earth.

The 28 constellations are manifestations of the four deities that together protect Gyeongbokgung Palace on all sides. The four deities are composed of four sets of seven constellations each, forming the Blue Dragon, White Tiger, Red Phoenix, and Black Tortoise. These divine animals are positioned in the four directions of the heavenly realm to become the Left Blue Dragon, Right White Tiger, Southern Red Phoenix, and Northern Black Tortoise.

While the cardinal directions that we use on Earth do not properly

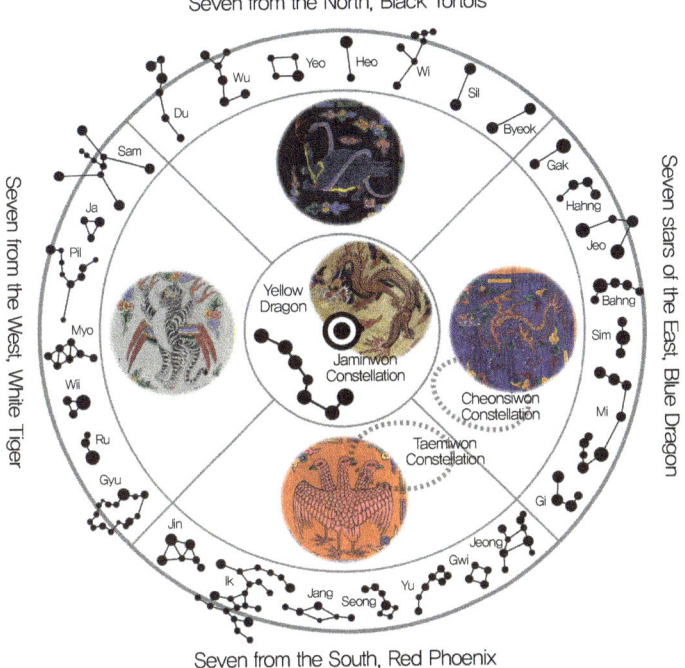

Figure 5-7 The 28 constellations surrounding the Jamiwon are divided by four directions, each with sevens constellations, as each of the four direction represents a divine animal.

translate to use in outer space, the cheon-mun-do marks the placement of constellations on a flat surface like a geographical map of land. The four directions of north, south, east, and west can then be applied. The next step is to express them through seasons and colors, where east is spring and blue, south is summer and red, west is autumn and white, and north is winter and black. This is what gives us the East Blue Dragon, West White Tiger, South Red Phoenix, and North Black Tortoise.

The four deities that protect Gyeongbokgung Palace are manifested through paintings of these sacred animals on the four gates that lead to the palace, but they are also manifested through the mountain

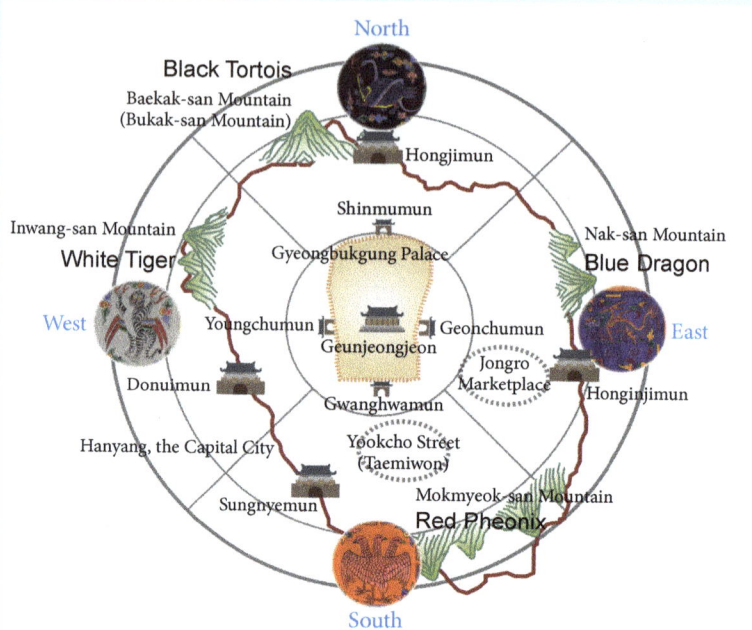

Figure 5-8 Conceptual diagram of the city walls of Hanyang (present day Seoul) which was created by bringing and comparing the image of the celestial body to the geography of Hanyang.

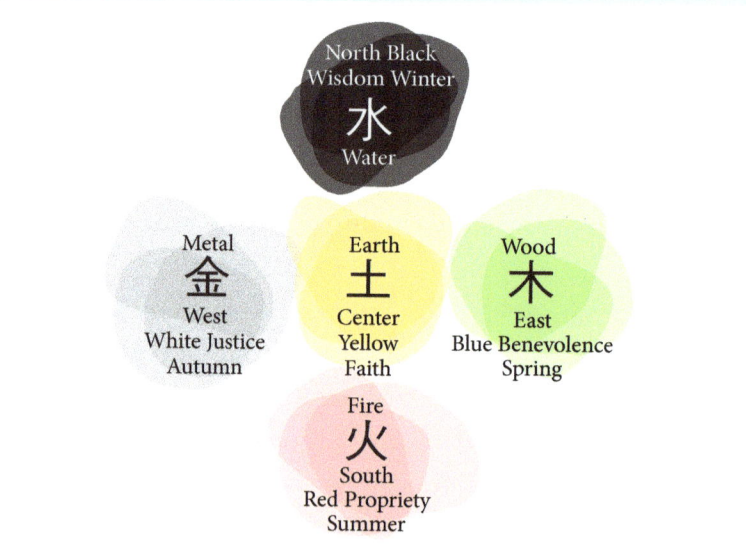

Figure 5-9 The diagram of the five elements depicting the Jamiwon as the center of the land and 28 constellations as the four directions in figures 5-7 and 5-8, / The five elements are wood, fire, earth, metal, and water. Each color, season and symbols are indicated accordingly

range that surrounds Gyeongbokgung Palace. Another manifestation is the four gates to the capital city, one located in each earthly direction of north, south, east, and west. Joseon's capital city of Hanyang was built so that the four deities could protect Gyeongbokgung Palace and its royal occupant, the Heavenly Son who ruled on behalf of the Heavenly Emperor. This ideology also contained the intentions of the founders of the Joseon Dynasty: safeguard Gyeongbokgung Palace.

1. Gyeongbokgung Palace's 4 cardinal direction gates and the 4 deities:
   Blue Dragon to the Geonchoonmun Gate of the East, representing spring,
   Red Phoenix to the Heungraemun Gate of the South, representing summer,
   White Tiger to the Youngchumun Gate of the West, representing autumn, and
   Black Tortoise to the Shinmumun Gate of the North, representing winter.

2. The four mountains that surround Gyeongbokgung Palace are Naksan Mountain (East Blue Dragon), Inwangsan Mountain (West White Tiger), Mokmyeoksan Mountain (commonly known as Namsan Mountain; South Red Phoenix), and Baekaksan Mountain (North Black Tortoise).

3. The four gates for entering the capital city of Hanyang from the four directions were named according to the principles of In (virtue), Ui (righteousness), Ryeh (decorum), Ji (wisdom), and Shin (trust and belief).
   The eastern gate is the Heung-in-ji-mun, the western gate is the Don-ui-mun, the southern gate is the Soong-ryeh-mun, and the northern gate is the Hong-ji-mun (it was later changed to Sook-cheong-mun). In the center of these is the Bo-shin-gak pavilion.*

---

* Bo-shin-gak pavilion - An annual tradition known as the New Year's Eve Bell, an event where the leaders of South Korea ring the bell in the Bo-shin-gak pavillion 33 times starting midnight between the New Year's Eve and New Year's Day. The purpose of ringing the bell 33 times Ringing the bell 33 times was for their prayer for the peace of the nation and the people to reach the 33rd heaven known as Do-ri-cheon Heaven where Je-seok-shin(the guardian god of Buddhism) resides.

The divine animals that represent each direction are emblazoned on their respective gates. You may recognize these gates by different names—the popular area of Dongdaemun, for example, meaning Great East Gate, is where the Heung-in-ji-mun still stands in modern day Seoul.

As described above, Gyeongbokgung Palace, the earthly counterpart of the heavenly Jamigung Palace, is protected by the mountains of the four directions, the city gates to the four directions, and the four gates to Gyeongbokgung Palace itself. On each of these gates appears its designated member of the four deities—Blue Dragon, White Tiger, Red Phoenix, or Black Tortoise.

The four deities can also be found around burial mounds for the purpose of protecting the king at his auspicious burial site. Examples of this include the Goguryeo Dynasty Gangseodaemyo tomb, the Goryeo Dynasty tomb in Gaepoong-gun County, Kaesong (North Korea), the Baekjae Dynasty tomb in Songsan-ri, South Chungcheongdo Province, and the royal tombs of Mokneung, from the Joseon Dynasty.

Figure 5-10 The Gyeongbokgung Palace and Baekaksan Mountain (Bukaksan) seen from the Gwanghwamun Square. Baekaksan Mountain corresponds to the Hyunmu of the North.

The table below shows how the 28 constellations are manifested on land. Note that the central Earth energy of the five elements was omitted because it is the symbol of the king

Forms of the 28 Su				
28 Su Names	Gak, hang, jaw, bahng, shim, mee, gi	Jeong, gwi, yu, sung, jang, ik, jin	gyu, ru, wi, myo, pil, ja, sam	Du, wu, yeo, huh, wi, shil, byeok
Four Deities	7 Su of the Blue Dragon	7 Su of the Red Phoenix	7 Su of the White Tiger	7 Su of the Black Tortoise
Direction	East	South	서(西)	North
Season	Spring	Summer	Autumn	Winter
Five Elements	Wood	Fire	Metal	Water
Five Virtues	Virtue (in)	Decorum (ryeh)	Righteousness (ui)	Wisdom (ji)
Four Great Gates	Heunginjimun	Sungryehmun	Donuimun	Hongjimun

06

The heavenly guardians of Gyeongbokgung Palace

In order to recreate the heavenly auspicious site of the Jamiwon on Earth, the Joseon Dynasty builders of Gyeongbokgung Palace incorporated images of and references to many mythical beasts throughout the palace. These legendary animals were believed to be the guardians sent from the heavenly realm.

One notable example of this is the pair of dogs seated on the second level of the Gwanghwamun gate. The type of dog in this depiction comes from the 28 su, specifically the Ru of the western constellations (which are the gyu, ru, wi, myo, pil, ja, and sam) that guard the west side of the Jamiwon. Another famous example is the pair of guardian animals that sits calmly in front of Gwanghwamun: the haetae. The haetae comes from the Du of the northern constellations (du, wu, yeo, huh, wi, shil, and byuk) that keep watch over the north of the Jamiwon.

Figure 5-11 Haetae statue erected on the right side of the Gwanghwamun Gate

Figure 5-12 One of the four sacred beasts that guards the Geumchon Stream of Gyeongbokgung Palace. It is said that they descended from the heavens to guard the waters. It's fun to see that it is staring at the water with it's tongue sticking out.

Figure 5-13 Geunjeongjeon Hall of Gyeongbokgung Palace / Geunjeongjeon Hall, which is equivalent to the center of Jamigung Palace, has the four gods that represents the 28 constellations in the four cardinal directions, and the 12 zodiac gods who brought the five elements of the heaven to earth is placed around the boundaries of the Geunjeongjeon Hall..

Guardian animals also appear on the ceilings of the three gates of Gwanghwamun. These are the North Black Tortoise and the paired Bong (male phoenix) and Hwang (female phoenix) of the South Red Phoenixes. The paired giraffes known as Gi (male) and Rin (female), which are said to only appear when a truly auspicious event occurs, are also depicted here.

If you pass Gwanghwamun and enter by way of the Heungryemun gate, you will see an artificial stream called the Geumcheon. This stream was made to reflect the Milky Way as it bisects the Jamiwon of the cosmos. Four guardian animals watch over the stream, and amusingly, one even has its tongue stuck out in a playful manner.

Unsurprisingly, this animal was believed to have been sent from the 28 constellations to block negative energy. It looks somewhat like a girin (giraffe) and somewhat like a haetae, but there is not an established official explanation for this animal. It might be the boar, the guardian of the water. The boar comes from the Shil of the northern constellations (du, wu, yeo, huh, wi, shil, and byeok) and controls water. Also, the Shil is the heavenly overseer of construction, so it could be interpreted as relating to the building of the artificial Geumcheon stream. If the boar is protecting the Geumcheon stream, this could explain why the dog and the boar are missing from the 12 zodiac gods that are placed around Gyeongbukgung Palace's Geunjeongjeon Hall. The dog is busy keeping watch over external affairs from the upper level of the Gwanghwamun gate, and the boar is overseeing the care of the Geumcheon, so neither is needed near Geunjeongjeon Hall.

28 Guardians, 28 Directions

7 yo	Jupiter	Venus	Saturn	Sun	Moon	Mars	Mercury
Eastern Blue Dragon	Gak - Monstrous Serpent	Hang - Dragon	Jeo - Marten	Bang - Rabbit	Shim - Fox	Mi - Tiger	Gi - Leopard
Northern Black Tortoise	Du - Haetae	Wu - Cow	Yeo - Bat	Heo - Rat	Wi - Swallow	Shil - Boar	Byeok - Alyu*
Western White Tiger	Gyu - Wolf	Ru - Dog	Wi - Pheasant	Myo - Chicken	Pil - Crow	Ja - Monkey	Sam - Ape
Southern Red Phoenix	Jeong - Wild Dog	Gwi - Sheep	Yu - Roe Deer	Sung - Horse	Jang - Deer	Ik - Snake	Jin - Earthworm

Gwanghwamun is the main gate located on the southern side of Gyeongbokgung Palace, but the palace itself is located in the northern region of Seoul, giving Gyeongbokgung Palace another name: the Northern Palace.** For this reason, the wild dog that protects the south and the haetae that guards the north work together to safeguard the palace.

Haetae, discerner of good and evil

- The haetae is a mythical creature that looks similar to a lion but has a horn on its head. It is known by many other names, such as Gaeoh, Haechi, Haecheon, and Shinyang. The pair of haetae guard-

---

* Alyu (known as yayu in Chinese mythology) - Some accounts say it looks like a cow with the hoofs of a horse. Some say it's a serpent that has a human face. Some say it looks like a dragon or a tiger and it cries like the cry of a baby. This mystic beast feeds on humans.
** The other 4 Grand Palaces in Seoul are Changdeokgung Palace, Deoksugung Palace, Changgyeonggung Palace, and Gyeonghuigung Palace.

ing the front of Gyeongbokgung Palace stand where people had to dismount their horses and palanquins before entering the sacred ground inside the palace.

It was said that the haetae had the tremendous ability to differentiate between good and evil, and if it found a sinner or an unrighteous person, it would ram them with its horn. Its huge eyes were believed to put the court officials in check, set traditions right, and resolve unfair cases during the Joseon Dynasty, so the judicial branch (Saheonbu) used the haetae as its symbol. A haetae statue stood in front of the Saheonbu building, and Saheonbu officials placed a horn on the top of the official hats they wore as part of their uniform. The daesaheon (the South Korean equivalent today would be the Prosecutor General) had a haetae embroidered on the front of his official uniform.

Legends tell of the haetae defeating fires and disasters, so the Heungseon Daewongun* (1820 CE ~1898 CE) had two haetae statues installed in front of Gwanghwamun. There is even a story that tells of how Heungseon Daewongun specifically chose the statues to control the fire energy of Gwanaksan Mountain, which was known for having the geomantic shape of a blazing flame. These haetae were removed during the Japanese colonial period but now stand in front of Gwanghwamun once again. Haetae statues also stand guard in front of South Korea's National Assembly Building, the Supreme Prosecutor's Office, and the Ministry of National Defense.

---

* Heungseon Daewongun - The Great Archduke was a regent of Joseon during the King Gojong in the 1860s. He was a central political figure of late Joseon dyansty Korea until his death.

07

Governing the land in the image of the heavenly realm

If you pass through the Geunjeongmun gate, you will find Geunjeongjeon Hall (Gyeongbokgung Palace's main throne hall). Geunjeongjeon Hall is where important national ceremonies were held. It was the core of the Joseon Dynasty's royal palaces and represented the center of the Jamiwon recreated on land. Gyeongbokgung Palace and Geunjeongjeon Hall in particular were primarily decorated with jaju purple. On the railing of the woldae (a raised stone platform with steps leading up to Geunjeongjeon Hall), the four guardian creatures and the 12 zodiac animals are carved in stone, with the exceptions of the dog, boar, and dragon. As the king himself was regarded as the dragon, there was no need for a statue—but the reason for the missing dog and boar is yet to be confirmed.

Despite the official reason remaining unknown, it makes sense if the presence of the pair of dogs at the gate of Gwanghwamun and the boar at the Geumcheon stream are taken into account. Two golden dragons also keep watch from the ceiling of Geunjeongjeon Hall, representing both the Heavenly Emperor and the center of all things. This is the same as the wall paintings found in the Great Tomb of Gangseo from the Goguryeo Dynasty. The wall paintings display the four gods in their respective four directions and include the gold dragon on the ceiling. These five creatures of the four cardinal directions and the center are known as the Five Gods.

The four-legged golden dragons of Geunjeongjeon Hall in Gyeongbokgung Palace have seven talons on each of their feet, giving them the name of chil-jo-ryong (chil is a word for the number seven). With 28 talons each, the total number of a golden dragon's talons matches the number of constellations that surround the Jamiwon, and the pair of dragons forms a taeguk symbol (like the yin-yang symbol) with the Yeo-ui-ju (the wish-fulfilling jewel) in the center. The interior of the hall is painted jaju purple and holds the king's throne, behind which is the famous folding screen known as the Painting of the Sun, Moon, and the Five Peaks: the Il-wol-o-bong-do.

The chil (seven) in chil-jo-ryong is the same as used in the Chiljeong, or the governing seven. This was the name for when the Heavenly Emperor left his residence in the Jamiwon to make his yearly journey by chariot. Each of the four seasons was designated its own set of seven constellations from the 28 su, and the Seven Stars of the Northern Dipper commanded these sets in their corresponding seasons according to the Heavenly Emperor's mandate. Each set was believed to be active during its assigned season, and its activity during this time would spread to affect all of the universe, even impacting our solar system—the Sun and the Moon (yin and yang) as well as the five main planets of Jupiter, Mars, Saturn, Venus, and Mercury. The Sun and these five planets traveled through space under the command of the seven constellations designated to be in power that season, affecting how all living things could come and go on Earth.

As the Heavenly Emperor ruled the universe from the Jamiwon, the king ruled the people of the land with the divine right bestowed

Figure 5-14 The golden dragon decorations on the ceiling of Geunjeongjeon Hall of Gyeongbokgung Palace / The number of their claws are a total of 28 with seven claws.

upon him from the heavens. Naturally, generation after generation of Korean kings built up a branch of the government dedicated to examining changes and transformations in the cosmos and had court officials record the movements of the five planets and the stars every single day of the year.

He sought to understand the will of Sangje who resides in Jamiwon Constellation in order to exercise the power he has received through the 'divine right'. Since the heavens does not speak nor can they gesture, the King sougt to examine the signs of heaven to understand the will of heaven. So during the Joseon dynasty, the king had a separate government office known as the Gwansanggam within his palace and had them observe and record the heavens and report any major issues direcly to the king.

Figure 5-15 Il-wol-o-bong-do behind the dragon throne where the king seats in the Geunjeongjeon/ This painting is only found in Korea and is also painted on the 10,000 won bill. The painting is based on the philosophy of the samjae of Heaven, Earth, and humanity. The moon and the sun symbolizing the yin and yang is in the sky, and the five peaks symbolizing the five elements are on the earth. The harmony of the samjae(the heaven, earth, and humanity) occurs when the king takes his seat in front of the painting. It is a painting that always follows the king wherever he goes, so when the king passes away, the painting is also buried inside his tomb.

It has been said that, since ancient times, a wise and holy king who wanted to govern the land would lift his head to read the writing of the cosmos (astronomical phenomena) and lower his head to examine the lay of the land and its meaning (geomancy). Enlightened by the principles of Heaven and Earth, the king would bring human affairs, or the core principles of humanity, into harmony and make right the Chiljeong (governing seven or seven governance). In other words, he would bring into alignment spring, summer, autumn, winter, the heavenly principles of astronomy, the earthly principles of geomancy, and the core principles of humanity.

Korean societies stretching back into antiquity kept a watchful eye on these cheon-mun or "heavenly writings" so that they could manifest the principles of nature in their everyday lives, living and governing the land properly in accordance with the will of the heavens. The movements of celestial bodies and the changes that occurred throughout the 24 solar terms of a year were vital pieces of information that affected not just the king but also commoners like fishers, hunters, livestock farmers, seasonal plant foragers, and agricultural farmers. When astronomical phenomena were examined and disseminated on a national scale, the information was of great help to the common people. This is why the Cheon-sang-yul-cha-bun-ya-ji-do was made—for the Heavenly Son and his subjects.

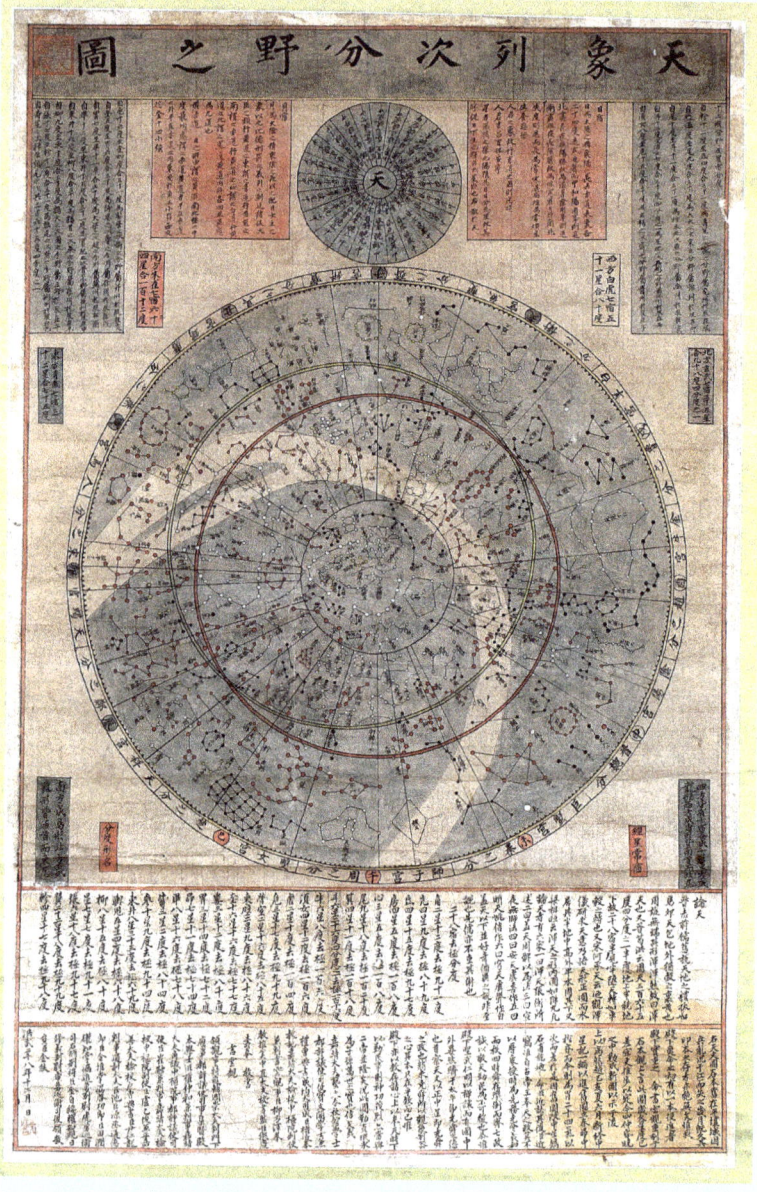

Figure 5-16 A rubbed copy of the Cheon-sang-yeol-cha-bun-ya-ji-do. printed on paper (National Museum of Korea)

08

Goguryeo astronomers draw the world's oldest constellation

The Cheon-sang-yeol-do-bun-ya-ji-do was created during the Joseon Dynasty by making corrections to constellations that had been observed during the Goguryeo Dynasty, which means that it contains depictions of the skies of both the Joseon Dynasty and the Goguryeo Dynasty—two different time periods. Its form also differs from traditional Chinese astronomical diagrams. Astrophysics professor Park Changbeom published a fascinating study on this in 1995. The central section of the Cheon-sang-yeol-do-bun-ya-ji-do features stars observed from the 37th to 38th parallels of the Northern Hemisphere during the early Joseon Dynasty. The place of observation has been estimated as Hanyang (modern Seoul). Most of the stars outside this central area were observed about 2,000 years ago in what has been estimated as the 39th to 40th parallels, where Pyeongyang, the capital city of Goguryeo, was located. It is incredible that one cheon-mun-do could hold observations made during two different dynasties and in two different cities.

Another impressive aspect of ancient Korean astronomy is Goguryeo's level of astronomical observation technology. The world's oldest extant cheon-mun-do carved into stone is the Sunwu Cheon-mun-do, made during the Song Dynasty of China* Like the Cheon-sang-yeol-do-bun-ya-ji-do, it is a stone carving, and it was completed in 1247 by Wang Chiwon; a person by the name of Hwang Sang drew the original astronomical chart in 1190. Yet the basis for the Cheon-sang-yeol-do-bun-ya-ji-do, Goguryeos's cheon-mun-do, has been officially dated back to the first century.

At one point in time, scholars were embroiled in controversy over the relationship between the Cheon-sang-yeol-do-bun-ya-ji-do and the Sunwu Cheon-mun-do. When the Cheon-sang-yeol-do-bun-ya-ji-do began to attract international attention, Chinese academics responded by claiming that the Cheon-sang-yeol-do-bun-ya-ji-do was a copy of the Sunwu Cheon-mun-do and asserted that the Joseon Dynasty lacked the advanced technology necessary to make a more scientific and accurate cheon-mun-do than its contemporary counterpart in China. Their argument was based on the similarities of the two astronomical charts. Indeed, these charts can seem similar at first glance because East Asia has a history of sharing advances in astronomy, but closer comparison reveals clear differences between the two.

Among the numerous notable differences is the fact that the four-star Jongdaebu constellation appears in the Cheon-sang-yeol-do-bun-ya-ji-do, but it does not appear in the Sunwu Cheon-mun-do. Similarly, the size of each star was recorded differently based on its brightness, a detail not reflected in the Sunwu Cheon-mun-do, while the Western zodiac system that was not yet in use by contemporary neighboring nations also appears solely on the Cheon-sang-yeol-do-

---

* Sunwoo Cheonmundo - Made in 1241 during the Southern Song Dyansty(1127 CE - 1279 CE).

Figure 5-17 King Suk-jong's stone sculpture version of Cheon-sang-yeol-cha-bun-ya-ji-do / It is visible even with the naked eye that the size of the holes vary depending on the brightness of the star. (National Palace Museum of Gyeongbokgung Palace)

5-3. Cheon-sang-yeol-do-bun-ya-ji-do and Sunwu Cheon-mun-do Comparison

Cheon-sang-yeol-do-bun-ya-ji-do	Sunwu Cheon-mun-do
• Constellations have the same names but different shapes and locations. Shapes differ because the lines connecting the stars are drawn differently. • Includes Jongdaebu constellation.	• Names are the same but shapes and locations of constellations are different. • Lacks Jongdaebu constellation.
• Distance from Polaris (North Star) to each constellation drawn in direct proportion to actual observed distance.	• Distances from Polaris (North Star) to constellations not expressed proportionately.
• Drawn star size varies per star brightness. Traditional method of expression passed down from Ancient Joseon.	• Star brightness not differentiated. All stars depicted as same size.
• Different shape and location of Milky Way compared to Sunwu Cheon-mun-do.	• Different shape and location of Milky Way compared to Cheon-sang-yeol-do-bun-ya-ji-do.
• Applies Western zodiac system (12 signs, 12 directions, and 12 divisions recorded around constellation circle).	• Uses traditional Eastern system.
• Central constellations estimated as observed from 38th parallel (fourteenth-century Hanyang, capital of Joseon).	• Presumed point of observation is 34th parallel during Song Dynasty, from capital city Gaebong.

bun-ya-ji-do. These and other research results have affirmed the genius of the Cheon-sang-yeol-do-bun-ya-ji-do while putting to rest the claims of Chinese scholars. There is no doubt that the astronomical findings captured by the Cheon-sang-yeol-do-bun-ya-ji-do are a significant cultural heritage that we are lucky to encounter in the present day.

12 Zodiac Signs

- The 12 zodiac signs are 12 constellations that can be observed by following the Ecliptic Plane (the general plane through which planets orbit the Sun) for a year: Sagittarius, Capricorn, Aquarius, Pisces, Aries, Taurus, Gemini, Cancer, Leo, Virgo, Libra, and Scorpio. The 12 signs of the zodiac were named and came into usage around 3,000 BCE in Mesopotemia's Babylonia, passing on to Greece around 2,000 BCE by way of the Phoenicians to become the foundation of Western astrology (note that the West began to differentiate between astronomy and astrology around the seventeenth century).

09

Goguryeo's conception of the cosmos through astronomy

Goguryeo's astronomers may have laid the foundation for the Cheon-sang-yeol-do-bun-ya-ji-do, but sadly, accurate texts or artifacts that might have shed light on Goguryeo's own cheon-mun-do no longer exist. Still, the wall paintings of Goguryeo's ancient burial mounds can offer us a glimpse of its highly advanced astronomy.

Designated as a UNESCO World Heritage site, the Goguryeo tombs have murals of culturally significant scenes and creatures as well as the 28 constellations. There are about 80 Goguryeo-style wall paintings in total and no less than 24 of the mounds feature depictions of the 28 su. The 28 su painting found in the Deokhwari mound even includes the names of the constellations, and the 28 su of Jinpari mound No. 4 are painted gold.

The Goguryeo-style mounds are unique in that the burial chamber within each mound is constructed as a square, but the ceiling is rounded into a dome; the constellations are drawn in the murals on the walls. Structuring a tomb in this way is a reflection of the Gaecheon theory, which is an ancient theory on the structure of the universe.

According to *Goguryeo's Constellation Myths* (2009), a book by professor Kim Ilgwon of the Academy of Korean Studies, 25 Goguryeo burial mounds have constellation paintings, with a combined total of 800 stars. Goguryeo wall paintings of the constellations were first discovered in Hwanghae-do Provinces's Anak Tomb No. 3, built in 357 CE. This tomb's murals have the same characteristics as the stars on the Cheon-sang-yeol-do-bun-ya-ji-do and vary in size according to brightness. The constellations found in the the ancient burial mounds of Deokheungri, Pyeongannam-do Province depict the Seven Stars of the Northern Dipper according to the actual brightness of each star. Even bo, the eighth star, makes an appearance, though this star can barely be seen in the sky with the naked eye.

A stone slab bearing the Jeoncheon Cheon-mun-do, which shows the entire sky, was found in the ceiling of the Jipari mound No. 4, built around 590 CE in Pyeongyang (the former capital of Goguryeo and the current capital of North Korea). According to research by North Korean scholars, the stars of Jipari Mound No. 4 total 136 and are differentiated into six grades of brightness. Mention of the Jeoncheon Cheon-mun-do appeared in Chinese historical records beginning around eighth century CE, but Goguryeo had already incorporated this chart of the entire sky into wall paintings for its burial mounds by the sixth century.

Goguryeo's Jeoncheon Cheon-mun-do was also found across the sea in Japan. In 1998, a Goguryeo-style cheon-mun-do of this type was discovered in the Kitora Tomb, a burial mound located in the village of Asuka in Japan's Nara Prefecture. The ceiling of the tomb is drawn in the Goguryeo style with images of the Sun, the Moon and the 28 su constellations. As with the Jinpari Mound No. 4, the stars are expressed in gold leaf (a form of finely hammered gold). The Kitora Tomb cheon-mun-do is remarkably similar to the Cheon-sang-yeol-do-bun-ya-ji-do. While the tomb itself was built during the seventh century, the stars depicted there are estimated to have been observed from the 39th to 40th parallels of the Northern Hemisphere, where Goguryeo's capital Pyeongyang used to be, with an estimated observation date between 300 BCE to 300 CE.

Gaecheon and Honcheon theories of Goguryeo cosmology

- Gaecheon theory: This is the oldest cosmic theory in the East. According to this theory, the heavens are shaped like a conical "sat-gat" hat that covers the land, and the land is shaped like a square beneath the dome of the sky. This was also known as the Heaven-Circle-Earth-Square, and it is the reason the stone chambers of Goguryeo tombs were built as squares with the tops of the burial mounds forming half spheres.

- Honcheon theory: This theory perceives the relationship between earth and sky as egg and eggshell. The heavens are the eggshell, and the land is the egg yolk which floats in space or water, which means that the land is the center of the universe. This was the popular theory during the time period when the Cheon-sang-yeol-do-bun-ya-ji-do was completed.

10

Astronomy in Shilla, Baekjae, and Goryeo

Goguryeo was the only nation among the three neighbors of Goguryeo, Baekjae, and Shilla that left tangible traces of its heavenly map, the cheon-mun-do. Although there would have been numerous books documenting observations of the heavens, the majority of them have been lost. This leaves today's scholars with no other choice but to rely on the *Samguk Sagi* (*History of the Three Kingdoms*). According to a collection of papers published in 2005 through the workshop "Ancient Korean Astronomy and the Cheon-sang-yeol-do-bun-ya-ji-do," Goguryeo, Baekjae, and Shilla observed and recorded astronomical phenomena on a national level. Their records include a total of 225 observations of phenomena such as solar eclipses (67), comets (59), meteors and meteorites (41), and lunar eclipses (20).

Although constellation paintings from Shilla and Baekjae did not survive to today, the use of the names of the stars and constellations in other surviving records of theirs indicates that they observed the stars keenly. Records show that a monk who spent time in the Tang dynasty returned to Shilla in 692 CE to present a cheon-mun-do to the king of Shilla, which proves that Shilla had an astronomical chart. Moreover, the capital of Shilla was home to the famous Cheomseongdae astronomy observatory (located in the modern city of Gyeongju), which makes it likely that they had a fairly rigorous astronomical theory to match their astronomical devices. It is a well-established fact that the architectural design of the Cheomseongdae astronomy observatory incorporates the 28 su, 12 months, and 24 seasons.*

More recently, it was scientifically proven that the city of Gyeongju itself was built according to the shapes of the constellations. It seems as if every person who lived in those older eras was dedicated to the effort of recreating the lay of the heavens on land.

Though the Shilla's Cheomseongdae astronomy observatory is fascinating, what do we know about Baekjae's relationship with astronomy? The text *Nihon Shoki* details the travels of a monk named Gwanreuk who left Baekjae to go to Japan in 602 CE to offer the Japanese, books about a calendar system, theories on astronomical principles, and the occult art of shapeshifting. These three books were all based on astronomical phenomena, so it is safe to assume that Baekjae also had an astronomical chart at the time.

As for the astronomy of Goguryeo's successor Goryeo, there are countless records of astronomical observations during the Goryeo Dynasty. There are even records of astronomical phenomena that could not have been observed without a precise observational device. In Goryeo, over 30 different astronomers and officials engaged in this work in various national institutions. The observations recorded during the 475 years of the Goryeo Dynasty can be found in books

---

* 24 seasons - Also known as the 24 solar terms and used throughout East Asia, each of the 15 day seasons are closely related to yearly farming. Matteo Ricci(1552-1610), a Catholic priest, restructured the 24 season to match the solar calendar during his mission work to establish Christianity in China.

such as *Goryeosa*,* *Cheonmunji*,** *Yeokji*,*** and *Ohaengji*.**** Among the 6,500 natural phenomena recorded, there are 138 solar eclipses and 87 comets — celestial movements which are relatively easy to observe — but there are also 38 sunspot observations that indicate a superior level of observation. One such record of a sunspot recorded on March 2, 1151 describes a black object inside the Sun that was about the size of an egg. But despite the evidence that suggests the existence of a Goryeo Dynasty cheon-mun-do, none has been found. The only clue is in the *Goryeosa*, which states that a person named Oh Yunbu created an astronomical chart. At the very least, we can infer that Goguryeo's cheon-mun-do was probably inherited by its successor Goryeo, which then passed it on to Joseon. This fits with the records that describe an astronomical chart that existed in Pyeongyang in the early days of Joseon's founding.

Though historians haven't yet found a copy of Goryeo's astronomical chart, there is a notable depiction of the constellations on the ceiling of the burial mound of Goryeo's King Heejong. The Seven Stars of the Northern Dipper are in the center, surrounded by the 28 su. This picture features the Sun and the Moon as well as Polaris, which is accurately expressed as a system of three stars at the center. Additionally, pictures of the constellations have been discovered in nine other Goryeo Dynasty burial mounds.

The three-star system of Polaris, the North Star, is a feature that was passed down from the Goguryeo Dynasty. It is found in Goguryeo

---

* Goryeosa - History of Goryeo. Book written from 1392 to 1451.
** Cheonmunji - originally known as Goryeosa Cheonmunji Annals of Heavenly writing in Goryeo history - Observation records of the celestial body during the Goryeo dynasty.
*** Yeokji - original title is Goryeosa Yeokji - Goryeo Calendar in Goryeo history - A unique calendar system that was developed during Goryeo dynasty. They had already deveoped 5 calendar methods during the regin of Goryeo.
**** Ohaengji - originally titled Goryeosa Ohaengji - Annals of the Five Elements. Recordings of extraordinry phenonmenon occuring in nature or in living things to predict the blessings and disasters coming from the heaven.

wall paintings such as the Gagjeochong (which depicts a traditional Korean wrestling match) in Ji'an, Jilin province (China), the Sashinchong, the Muyongchong (which depicts a dance), and the Jinpari mound No. 4 in Pyeongyang, North Korea. During the same time period in China, the five-star Polaris was a trend.

The constellation wall paintings of Goguryeo include the Sun and Moon, the Seven Stars of the Northern Dipper, and the Six Southern Stars (nam-du-yuk-seong). The Sun is positioned in the east, the moon in the west, the Seven Stars in the north, and the Southern Stars in the south. There is also a three-legged crow standing inside the Sun, and a toad in the Moon. This layout is found on the ceilings of 10 burial mounds including the Gakjeo-chong, Anak mound No. 1, Dukheungli, Muyonchong, and Samshilchong tombs.

There is another constellation system unique to Goguryeo that was passed down to Goryeo: the Cassiopeia constellation. It can be found in Goguryeo's tombs (as seen in the Dukheungli mound in Nampo City, Pyeongannam-do Province), but the W-shaped Cassiopeia is missing from astronomical charts of that same period in neighboring countries. The stone chamber from Goryeo on display at the National Central Museum in Seoul takes this one step further and includes the W-shaped constellation with the Seven Stars of the Northern Dipper. The discovery of the Cassiopeia constellation is yet another piece of evidence pointing to the excellence of Goguryeo's astronomy.

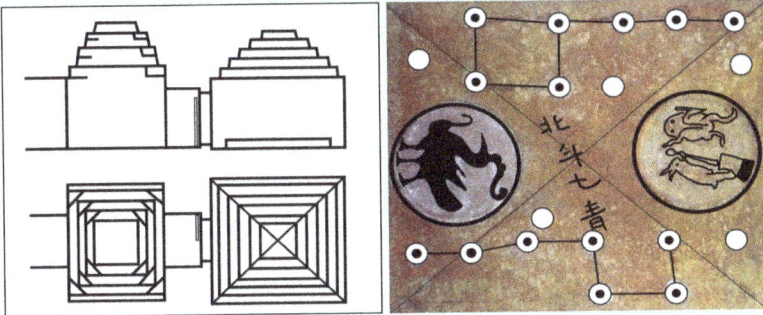

Figure 5-18 (left) The actual map of the tomb of Jangcheon Tomb No. 1 in Ji'an, Jilin Province, China/ (right) The arrangement of the constellations on the ceiling stone of the burial chamber / The tomb features wall paintings of two Big Dipper stars, three-legged-crow symbolizing the sun, and a rabbit and toad symbolizing the moon instead of the Southern Six Stars.

Figure 5-19 The Goguryeo mural paintings of the ancient tombs found in Deokheung-ri, Nampo-si, Pyeongannam-do / The wall painting has Gyeon-woo, Jik-nyeo, the celestial body and the Southern Six Stars. Replicated by the Hanseong Baekje Museum

11

Astronomy inherited from Ancient Joseon

There are countless dolmens in regions that were formerly Ancient Joseon (2333 BCE-239 BCE), and many are carved with constellations. But it was only recently discovered that the patterns of holes on these dolmens resembled the stars. In South Korea alone, there are over 300 dolmens with constellations carved on them.

In 1978, a stone slab carved with approximately 60 stars ranging from big to small was found among dolmen remains in Ahdeuk-ee Village, South Korea (Cheongwon-gun County, Choongbuk-do Province). Researchers compared this stone slab to constellations on the fifteenth-century BCE dolmen in Jiseok-ri and the sixth-century CE Jinpa-ri mound No. 4 (Pyeongyang, North Korea). Then, using a computer simulation, they examined how closely the marks on the stones matched the actual locations of stars and constellations surrounding Polaris in fifth century BCE. They concluded that the

5-4. Dolmens carved with constellaitons (More dolmens carved with constellations are continuously being discovered.)

Region	Features	Era
Dongchon-ri, Bookmyeon Haman-gun	· Seven Stars of the Northern Dipper and the Pleiades confirmed	Neolithic - Bronze Age
Yachon Village, Yegok-ri, Haman	· Six Southern Stars and the Pleiades	Neolithic - Bronze Age
Norgbatjae, Buk-gu Chilpo-ri, Pohang City	· Seven Stars of the Northern Dipper confirmed	Neolithic - Bronze Age
Shinheung-ri, Young-li, Gyeongbuk	· W-shaped and Y-shaped constellations etched into Ojoombawee Rocks	Neolithic - Bronze Age
Geochang Museum, Gyeongnam-do Province	· Constellations including Seven Stars of the Northern Dipper and 3-tae stars	Neolithic - Bronze Age
Ahdeuk-ee Village, Gaho-ri, Munuimyeon, Cheongwon-gun, Chungbuk-do Province	· Excavated stone slab with constellations	Middle Bronze Age
Yongdeok-ri, Joongsan-gun, Pyeongannam-do Province	· Over 10 constellations surrounding Polaris	Dated around 2,900 BCE based on constellation movement
Wunhwa-ri, Pyeongwon-gun, Pyeongannam-do Province	· Seven Stars of the Northern Dipper and other constellations confirmed	Around 25th century BCE
Jiseok-ri, Hamju-gun, Hamgyeongnam-do Province	· Seven Stars of the Northern Dipper and other constellations confirmed	Dated around 15th century BCE based on constellation movement
Yonggok-ri, Sangwon-gun, Pyeongannam-do Province	· Stars carved into top slab of dolmens	Around BCE 30 - 1st century BCE
Unyeong-dong, Jeongdo-ri, Oncheon-gun, Hwanghae-do Province	· Seven Stars of the Northern Dipper carving	Prehistoric - Bronze Age

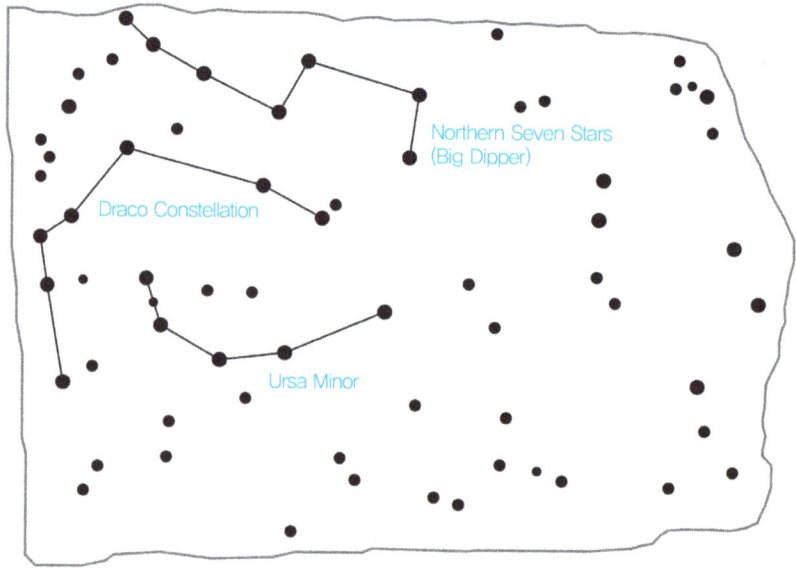

Figure 5-20 A copy of the constellation map excavated from the Ah-deuk-ee dolmen site of Cheongwon-gun County, Chungcheongbuk-do Province. The map is 23cm wide, 32cm long, and 3.5cm thick.

placement of the stars on the stone slab bore a strikingly close resemblance to their calculations, making the stone slab a true relic of ancient astronomical charts from fifth century BCE—a real cheon-mun-do.

While this stone slab's main claim to fame is that it is an ancient yet accurate map of the heavens, it also is notable in that it follows the Korean tradition of expressing the brightness of stars with the size of their carving. When this slab was carved long ago in Ancient Joseon, its makers varied the size of the stars according to each star's brightness. While Koreans today might think nothing of this tradition of adjusting the size of a star according to its brightness—carving the star bigger when brighter and smaller if not as bright—it is a tradition that began as far back as Ancient Joseon.

The people of Goguryeo who made the Cheon-sang-yul-cha-bun-ya-ji-do inherited this art of observing astronomical phenomena from Ancient Joseon, which left behind records of its observations like the stone slab. The Cheon-sang-yul-cha-bun-ya-ji-do is indeed an accumulation of several thousand years of scientific observation and competence that began in Ancient Joseon before being passed on to Goryeo and eventually to the Joseon Dynasty. It is a masterpiece created by the Korean people and a source of pride for humankind.

PART 06

A Trip to the Museums in Korea

The Fantastic Beasts, the Five Elements, and the Drawing of the Five Deities

01 Creating the turtle ship
02 The sacred beast that rules the water
03 The many tales of the turtle ship
04 Everyday life long ago with the Four Gods
05 The greatest of the fantastic beasts
06 The central figures of the Golden Dragon, the Golden Bear, and the Dokkaebi

Korea's cultural heritage is filled with mythical creatures like the ones that dominate scenes from fantasy movies. The Dragon, Phoenix, Tortoise, and Tiger that appear in the Sashindo, or Drawing of the Four Deities, that you encountered earlier in this book are just the beginning. There are also the haetae from Gyeongbokgung Palace, the heavenly horse of Shilla, the numerous creatures on the gilt-bronze incense burner of Baekjae,* and the mythical girin in Gyeongbokgung Palace that originated in the ancient wall paintings of Goguryeo** burial mounds. These creatures were believed to have been sent from the heavens, and while some are regular animals found in everyday life, like dogs and turtles, most of them exist only in paintings and statues. Others serve in functional and historical roles, such as the Geobukson, the famous "turtle ship" that decided the outcome of crucial naval battles, which was built with its namesake in mind. Our first step into the world of Korea's fantastic beasts will begin with the story and symbolism of this special Korean warship.

---

* Baekjae (18 BCE-660 CE) - One of the Three Kingdoms of Korea. Baekjae succeeded Mahan, one of the major nation states found by migrants of Ancient Joseon.
** Goguryeo (58 BCE-668CE) -One of the Three Kingdoms of Korea.

Figure 6-1 Fantastic animals painted on the ceiling of the entrance to the Gwanghwamun Square Arch / Top) Hyunmoo, (Center) Kirin, (Botten) Phoenix

01

Creating the turtle ship

"What do we do about such grief?" This pivotal line comes from the movie, *The Admiral: Roaring Currents* (known as *Myeong-ryang* in Korean), a historical dramatization of a sixteenth-century naval battle between Korean and Japanese forces. Long after the credits rolled, Admiral Yi Sunshin's line lingered in my mind, seeming like an unusually accurate reflection of modern life. The film not only renders the famous historical figure of the admiral as unapologetically human in a rancorous war filled with hatred, but it also paints a vivid picture of the difficult lives of the Joseon people. With this imagery, the film reminds us that war is not something suffered by soldiers alone; civilians are victims, too. The eleventh-hour appearance of armored turtle ships, which are a personification of Admiral Yi Sunshin, takes place in the movie's final moments to foreshadow the impact of Admiral Yi's victory in this battle on future naval battles. The arrival of the warship is a twist on how actual history played

Figure 6-2 Turtle ship built in 2015, anchored at Tongyeong Port.

out. The turtle ship did not make an appearance in the actual Battle of Myeongryang because another admiral, Won Kyoon, had suffered a terrible defeat and lost nearly every ship in Joseon's fleet. This brought about the legendary last words of Admiral Yi Sunshin before he left for battle: "Your Majesty, I still have 13 ships left." The turtle ship made its debut in the naval Battle of Sacheon on May 29, 1592 by the Korean lunar calendar. From this battle on, the armored turtle ship came to be seen by Japanese soldiers as an object of fear.

At the time of the Japanese invasion of the kingdom of Joseon in 1592, there were only three turtle ships. Records show that this grew to five; eventually, the number appears to have reached a total of eight ships. According to a book titled the *Dong-guk Mun-heon Bi-go*,* which was produced a few hundred years later, there were 40 turtle ships in total in eighteenth-century Joseon. While only two turtle ship designs have survived to the present day, historical records tell us that there were up to ten different classes of turtle ships, including the multi-deck panokseon. The turtle ship served as a model for Joseon's warships until the late Joseon Dynasty.

Due to Admiral Yi Sunshin's close association with the turtle ship, many people presume the admiral himself designed the turtle ship as a force to be reckoned with. Unfortunately, the true identity of the inventor remains unknown. Some sources inaccurately attribute the invention to Na Daeyong, an officer who served under Yi Sunshin, due to the officer's experience building other battleships. Another historical figure under discussion in recent years is a scholar of Joseon dynasty, Lee Deok-hong, whose book *Ganjaejib*** features the world's oldest depiction of the turtle ship. According to one popular narrative, Lee Deokhong went to Andong, his hometown, and gave this image to Ryu Seongryong***. Ryu Seongryong then passed it to Admiral Yi Sunshin.

While there are many different theories on the identity of the turtle ship's inventor, Admiral Yi Sunshin is a key consideration in every theory. Countless entries about Admiral Yi building turtle ships fill the pages of *War Diary*, his famous journal that he kept during the war with Japan. Further details can be found in the official records

---

* Dong-guk-Mun-heon-Bi-go - literal meaning Book of all things and policies of the Eastern Nation. King Youngjo ordered Hong Bong-han and others to record and list tradition, policy, material, writing, and other things from Joseon's past.

** Gan-jae-jib - Compliation of Lee Deok-hong's poems and writings. Gan-jae was his nickname.

*** Ryu Seongryong - Joseon's scholar, author, and doctor. He is considered one of the 5 greatest ministers throughout the entire Joseon dynasty. He is the one who recommends Admral Yi Sunsin to King Seonjo just before the Imjin Wars.

that were presented to King Seonjo (1552-1608 CE). Even though Admiral Yi may have not invented the armored warship's design himself, he was undeniably responsible for overseeing the building, completion, and strategic implementation of turtle ships in battle.

Notably, records of the turtle ship extend as far back as the early Joseon Dynasty. In the *Veritable Records of King Taejong*, which come from the *Veritable Records of the Joseon Dynasty*, it reads, "The king was passing the docks at the estuary of the Imjin River and saw a fight between the turtle ship and the Japanese battleship."* Though this refers to a mock battle that took place as a training exercise, not an actual battle, it still offers an astonishing revelation about the age of the turtle ship's design. The record comes from King Taejong's thirteenth year of reign, which means that it was written only 20 years after the establishment of Joseon in 1392. *Volume* 30 of the *Veritable Records of King Taejong* shows that a mere two years later, in King Taejong's fifteenth year of reign, a court official sent him a formal appeal, writing, "The armored turtle ship is the best strategy to achieve the ultimate victory in battle, for our enemies are no match for it. We must make the ship sturdier and with even greater skill so that we are properly equipped for victory in each and every battle."

Pirating by the Japanese was a significant issue for the Korean people beginning in the late Goryeo Dynasty (918-1392 CE). Records detailing how the turtle ship was used in practice maneuvers against a Japanese battleship indicate that the original turtle ship may have been developed to repress Japanese naval forces. This timeline implies that the turtle ship may have been developed as early as the beginning of King Taejong's reign (1367-1422 CE)—or even earlier. The calm and composed tone of the records themselves is another, more subtle clue. If turtle ships were invented during King Taejong's reign, the court historians surely would have written about them with excitement. The turtle ships either must have been developed during

---

* Imjin-do - Imjin-do is the name of the dock at the lower estuary of Imjin River

the late Goryeo Dynasty or at least made with Goryeo's shipbuilding technology because the new nobility who drove the founding of Joseon were a land force and would not have invested heavily in developing such a ship. Interestingly, after King Taejong's royal records, there is no mention of the turtle ships until the reign of King Seonjo (1552-1608 CE), when the ships once again make an appearance in historical records. It remains uncertain whether these are the same as the early Joseon-era turtle ship, or gwiseon, used during the period that Admiral Yi Sunshin made his stand against the Japanese invaders. There is also the intriguing story of Choe Museon, a military commander who used gunpowder weapons to destroy hundreds of Japanese navy ships during the reign of King Wu of the late Goryeo Dynasty. When all of these historical pieces are taken into consideration, it seems likely that the turtle ship was built long before the series of Japanese invasions in the late sixteenth century. As the turtle ship and its many iterations were developed and began to leave a mark on history, it gained a new moniker as "the charging warship" because it would ram enemy warships in close quarters to break their formations and even sink them. Not only was the armored turtle ship highly advanced for its era, but it has been recognized as the first armored warship design in the world.

Despite factious conflict on the domestic political front, Admiral Yi Sunshin fought and won 23 battles during the Japanese invasions of Korea from 1592–1598 CE, a record that earned him proper recognition in history, if not by his contemporaries. As a result, the turtle ship came to personify him, almost as if it carried him aboard through the raging currents of history to today. Together, they are a major part of Korean heritage that testifies to the ingenuity and tenacity of earlier generations of Koreans. For this reason, the turtle ship was previously printed on South Korean currency. At the time, it was depicted on both the 500-won bill and the 50-won coin; Admiral Yi Sunshin also appeared on the 500-won bill. While neither the admiral nor his armored turtle ship can be found on South Korean currency today, there is an exhibition on Admiral Yi in the museum located directly beneath the impressive statue of the Great King Sejong in Gwanghwamun Plaza, Seoul. There is also a small-scale replica of the turtle ship at the War Memorial of Korea located in Yongsan. At the Korea Naval Academy Museum in Jinhae, Gyeongsangnam-do Province, tourists can explore a turtle ship built to scale as well as many exhibits about Admiral Yi.

Places to see turtle ships

- War Memorial of Korea, located in Yongsan
- he Yi Sunshin Exhibition, located under the statue of Great King Sejong in Gwanghwamun
- Tongyeong Port
- Port of the Republic of Korea Naval Academy, located in Sacheon

Figure 6-3 The old 500 won note with the images of the Admiral Yi Sun-shin and the Turtle Ship.

02

The sacred beast that rules the water

"On this month, this day, this hour, we face the southwest with the northeast at our backs and perform the Ipju-Sangryang (erect the pillar and raise the crossbeam). May the sun, the moon, and the stars in the sky bestow upon us humans the Five Blessings* according to the fate of the master of this house."

When you first read these lines, you may think that it has nothing to do with an ancient class of warships that were shaped like turtles. But in fact, this text provides an important cultural clue as to why Admiral Yi Sunshin and Joseon's navy concentrated on building ships shaped like turtles: the water energy of the five elements. We can also see this principle at work firsthand, at the Folk Museum on the eastern side of Gyeongbokgung Palace and Gyeongbokgung's Ancient

---

* Five Blessings - Shi-jing states the five blessings as follows. 1. Longevity 2. Wealth 3. Health 4. Doing good on to others and accumulating virtue 5. Dying without pain.

襲
년월일입주상량
응천상지오광
비지상지오복
귀

應天上之五光
備地上之五福
龜

Palace Museum. The Folk Museum displays Joseon Dynasty-style construction and information about Sangryang, which is the phase of construction when the crossbeam is placed at the center of the main hall when erecting the pillars and raising the roof during the construction of a house; the beam is above the space that will be the living area. Sangryang is the most difficult part of building the frame of a building, so Koreans traditionally would hold a special Sangryang ceremony when a Sangryang inscription is written vertically from top to bottom. The word Yong (dragon) is written upside down at the top of this inscription; the word Gu (turtle) is written at the bottom. This seats the two gods that govern water at the highest point in the building, from which they can protect the house from fire. This is an example of a Sangryang inscription.

Sangryang is not exclusive to regular Korean houses—there are fire-prevention talismans at the Ancient Palace Museum of Gyeongbokgung Palace, too. The museum displays a talisman with the char-

Figure 6-4 A dragon talisman made with the characters 龍(dragon) and 水(water) in small letters./// Made during Emperor Gojong's reign, it was discovered during the maintenance construction of the Geunjeongjeon Hall in 2001.(Gyeongbokgung Ancient Palace Museum)

acter Su (water) written by connecting numerous small Yong (dragon) characters as well as a talisman that depicts a dragon. These talismans were originally placed on the main crossbeam of Geunjeongjeon Hall.

But what is the origin of this idea that dragons and turtles guard against fire? If you recall the wall paintings of Goguryeo that were described in previous chapters, this will be easier to understand. In Goguryeo burial mounds, each wall of a tomb was adorned with the same four gods: the Left Blue Dragon, Right White Tiger, South Red Phoenix, and North Black Tortoise. These sacred creatures were placed there as guardians. If you look at the North Black Tortoise, you will realize that it is no mere tortoise but rather a creature with the body of a turtle, the head of a dragon, and the feet of a beast, all of which are entangled with a snake. Koreans have associated turtles and dragons with water for thousands of years.

The Black Tortoise protects the north, which also stands for the water energy from yin-yang and the five elements. According to these principles, water has the ability to bring about growth in wood

Figure 6-5 Hyunmu diagram drawn on the Goguryeo mural paintings

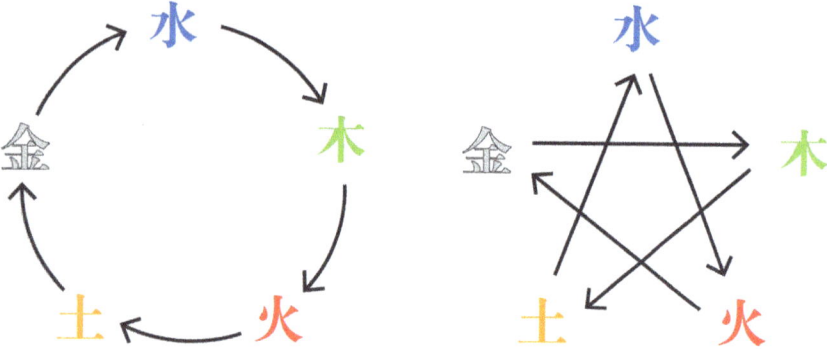

Figure 6-6 (left) Mutual life betterment cycle of the five elements, (right) Mutual restraining cycle of the five elements

energy. This is a perfect example of the symbiotic nature of the five elements, and it can be understood in the same way that we know watering a tree or plant will help it grow. Wood represents the east and is represented by the Blue Dragon. Aided by the Black Tortoise, the legendary Blue Dragon summons water up to the heavens and sends it back down as rain upon the earth. In other words, a dragon brings water in the form of rain, and the turtle is the sacred creature that controls water. This is why the characters for dragon and turtle are used in the Sangyrangmun; both of their divine roles are intended to prevent fire. In the past, any Korean person who was educated enough to read and write could be expected to know the four gods that are found in yin-yang, the five elements, and feng shui.

This is also why historical experts on the Joseon Dynasty navy assert that it was only natural for the turtle ship to have the head of a dragon but in the bodily shape of a turtle. The cultural and historical context makes it clear that the turtle ship was built based on yin-yang, the five elements, and legends.

In a mid-Joseon Dynasty record titled *The Complete History of Lee Chungmugong*, there is a drawing of the "Jwasuyeong region turtle ship" that depicts the ship with the head of a dragon and the body of a turtle. This class of warship could swiftly change directions thanks to its flat bottom that resembled a turtle's stomach. This, combined with its strong armor on top that resembled a turtle's back, gave it a solid defensive structure. The head of the dragon at the front of this ship belched toxic gas and fire, and the ship's cannons blasted the enemy as it maneuvered in embattled waters. It seems likely that Japanese invaders at the end of the sixteenth century were not only surprised by the outward appearance of the warship, but also frightened and demoralized by its seemingly unstoppable advances.

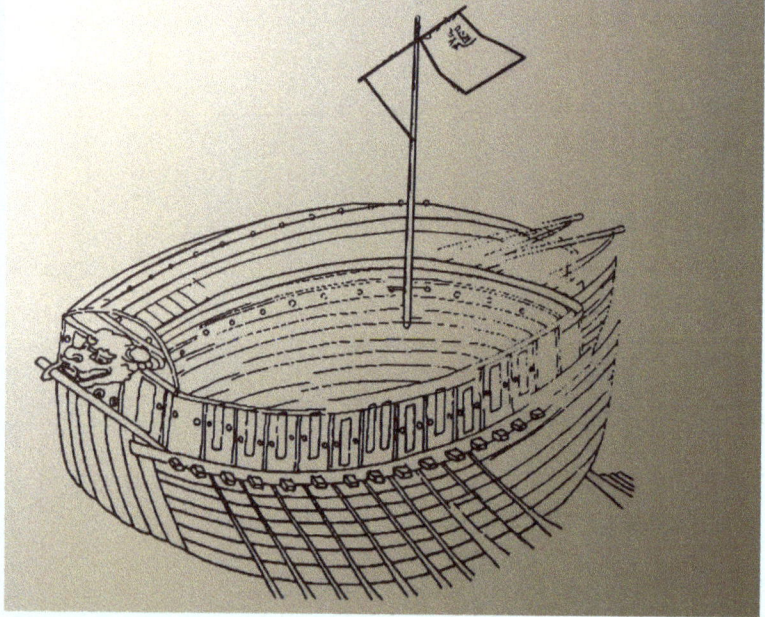

Figure 6-7 (Top) Turtle ship of Jeolla Jwasuyeong, (Bottom) Turtle ship of Tong-jaeyoung

Figure 6-8 Turtle Ship on display at the Yongsan War Memorial Hall

03

The many tales of the turtle ship

Previously in this chapter, we explored the symbolism and basic history of the turtle ship, but there are many other tales about this fascinating warship that offer us a deeper glimpse into Korean history.

One of these tales describes a mysterious man named Song Gubong who lived prior to the Japanese invasions of 1592 to 1598. According to this story, Song Gubong saw a child named Yi Sunshin playing wargames with his friends, and so he asked the boy to visit his house. But when Yi Sunshin obediently went to pay Song Gubong a visit, Song Gubong did not say a word to him; instead, he went to sleep. Song Gubong's house is where the future admiral saw the drawing of a ship shaped like a turtle. Years passed, and the young Yi Sunshin became an admiral who built turtle ships, but he did not know the purpose of one of the holes that he had seen in the original drawing. He asked Song Gubong about it, and the old man told him that the hole was called Sa Cheong Mok, meaning it was placed there as "the snake's eye" so that soldiers inside could more easily hear sounds from outside the warship.

Another legend tells of how Admiral Yi saw the turtle ship in his dreams. Beset with worries about issues of national importance, he fell asleep. As he slept, he had a mysterious dream that planted the seed for the blueprint of the turtle ship in his mind:

"I went out to sea to find food for the soldiers. Though I went a great distance from the shore, I could not find anything to eat. But suddenly there came a massive turtle surging to the surface of the ocean, coming from deep below. I wanted to catch it to eat, so I spent all my arrows and weapons, but could not catch the turtle. And from the mouth of the turtle came flames. It was a fearsome sight to behold." Admiral Yi awoke from this dream and started to design a specialized warship in the shape of a turtle.

Each of these tales likely carries at least some kernels of truth, but we cannot know for certain how much of it is true among any of them. But regardless of the stories that surround the turtle ship, we do know that the ship's design is closely entwined with the principles of yin-yang, the five elements, and the legend of the four gods of the Blue Dragon, White Tiger, Red Phoenix, and Black Tortoise—principles that have been passed down from antiquity.

---

* Sa Cheong Mok literally means "a snake hears with its eyes." Because snakes do not have ears like humans do, they rely on other senses to check for prey or predators. The Sa Cheong Mok was incorporated into the turtle ship's design to enable people inside the ship to see and hear what was happening outside.

04

Everyday life long ago with the Four Gods

The terms used in Korean feng shui to refer to the four gods—the East Blue Dragon, West White Tiger, South Red Phoenix, and North Black Tortoise—are found throughout Korea's cultural heritage. Dragons and phoenixes are so numerous and prominent in Korean museums that we could even dub them "dragon and phoenix museums."

During the Goguryeo Dynasty, dragons and phoenixes were divine creatures that guarded royal burial mounds. It was not until the

Goryeo Dynasty that these creatures made their debut in the daily life of commoners. Depictions are often found in temples and on bronze bells, pottery, and even stirrups that were used for horse riding.

As the Joseon Dynasty rose to power, usage of dragons and phoe-

Figure 6-9 Bronze mirror with the image of four divine animals (National Gyeongju Museum)

Figure 6-10 Geum-dong-dae-hyanh-ro, which shows the exquisite level of Baekjae dynasty artistry / A phoenix symbolizing fire is on the top and a dragon symbolizing water is supporting the incense burner. (Hanseong Baekje Museum)

nixes became increasingly widespread. They featured in everything from folk paintings to pottery and appeared on household items as basic as sewing needle boxes. Even the flag on display at the National Folk Museum of Korea next to Gyeongbokgung Palace is emblazoned with a massive dragon. This flag was made during the Joseon Dynasty to plead for a year of plenty from the dragon god, who was believed to create rain in farming villages. Dragons and phoenixes also dominated everyday life in the royal palace, as seen by the many artifacts and even architecture exhibited at Gyeongbokgung Palace, appearing on buildings, inkstones, dishes and tables used for meals, table covers, bi-nyeo hairpins, uniforms, and utensils used for ancestral rites. The ruler of the land was symbolized by both the dragon and the phoenix, and so these were put on everything from the king's royal garb to nearly anything used in the royal palace.

Figure 6-11 Bronze bell of the Goryeo dynasty, decorated with a dragon (National Museum of Korea)

Figure 6-12 Chilghap Case / A container used by the royal family during the Joseon dynasty has a carving of a dragon and a phoenix on top of the lid which symbolizing the king (National Palace Museum of Korea)

05

The greatest of the fantastic beasts

The four guardian gods, which include the dragon and phoenix, were venerated as the guardians of the king during his life and even after his passing. A classic example of this can be seen in the Goguryeo Dynasty exhibition on the Great Tomb of Gangseo in the National Central Museum, which depicts the four guardian deities in all their majesty, emanating the vigor and life of the people of Goguryeo long after the end of their dynasty. But according to Korean cultural heritage, the guardians of the king numbered not four, but five. As determined by the principle of the five elements, the four guardian deities watched over each of the four cardinal directions while the fifth and most important one stood guard at the center: the Golden Dragon. Although the museum did not choose to display the Golden Dragon in its traditional place on the ceiling of the exhibit, a replica is displayed on the museum wall for better viewing by visitors.

Figure 6-13 The wall paintings of the four deities decorating the Gangseo Great Tomb of the Goguryeo dynasty. Blue Dragon, White Tiger, Red Phoenix, and Black Turtle. (National Museum of Korea)

The Golden Dragon can be seen most clearly at Geunjeongjeon Hall in Gyeongbokgung Palace. The four guardian deities protect Geunjeongjeon Hall from the outside, and two golden dragons watch over the hall from inside, on the ceiling. These golden dragons symbolize the king, the Son of Heaven protected by the five guardian deities even after death.

Although the four guardian deities are found on artifacts from Han Dynasty China, the full set of five has not been found in Chinese ruins. Most ancient Chinese burial mounds only include the Blue Dragon and the White Tiger in the passage that leads to the inner stone chamber. However, all four guardian deities can be found in every burial mound in the regions that once belonged to Goguryeo. This can be seen in Mound No. 4 in Ji'an, the Sashin-chong tombs from Tong-gou, and the Great Tomb of Gangseo, all of which include the fifth and final god, the fierce Golden Dragon, at the center.

If the people who once lived and built their burial mounds in China had fully grasped the principles of yin-yang and the five elements before they drew the four guardian deities, they probably would have included the central fifth divine guardian. Long after sixth- and seventh-century Goguryeo began depicting golden dragons at the center of the group of guardians, there were still no artifacts that featured this fifth deity in China. Was this because they were vassal states of Goguryeo when Goguryeo was in power? Was Goguryeo perhaps seen as the nation of the Heavenly Son and so its neighbors were states run by feudal lords who dared not draw the Golden Dragon?

The five guardian deities are based on the principles of yin-yang and the five elements (wood, fire, earth, metal, and water). In terms of directions and locations, these are reflected by the north, south, east, and west (water, fire, wood, and metal respectively) and the center (earth). When the five directions are expressed as colors, north is black, south is red, east is blue, west is white, and the center is the color of gold. The central earth energy is the place known as the seat of the Heavenly Son, or the Hwanggeuk. This is called the Five Hwanggeuk Ideology, which refers to the concept that the Heavenly Emperor rules heaven and the Heavenly Son rules the human world in his place. The Heavenly Son, who is the fifth Hwanggeuk, therefore is placed in the center of everything. He is the fifth element, the earth energy that is symbolized by the splendor of the golden dragons painted at the center of the ceiling.

The concept of the Hwanggeuk is a vital part of Korean heritage, playing a role in several truly ancient records still extant today. About 4,000 years ago, King Wu of the Xia Dynasty (near present day Henan) tried to overcome a devastating nine-year flood. He sought advice from Crown Prince Buru, who would later become the second Dangun of the High Nation (Ancient Joseon). Crown Prince Buru entrusted King Wu with the knowledge of how to control water us-

Figure 6-14 Among the five deities, Yellow Dragon is painted on the ceiling of the burial chamber of Great tomb of Gang-seo.

ing the five elements.* This secret knowledge is also what Gija** gave King Mu to govern the world, a secret known as the Hongbeomguju.*** There are nine sets (guju) of these widely used rules (Hongbeom). The fifth is the Five Hwanggeuk, which validates the king's authority. The Five Hwanggeuk of the Hongbeomguju also dictated the design of Gyeongbokgung Palace itself. When Jeong Dojeon built the palace during the Joseon Dynasty, he followed the mandate of the Five Hwanggeuk, which is why the jeon-gak (the place in the palace where the king used to live and sleep) is called Gangryeongjeon.**** Gangryeong is the name of one of the five blessings described in the Five Hwanggeuk. The king had to be healthy and well to ensure the Hwanggeuk was maintained, so gangryeong (the well-being of the king) was the most essential blessing of the Five Hwanggeuk, one that the king could not do without. When the palace was built, this became the name for the jeon-gak where the king spent his daily life.

---

* Crown Prince Buru was the heir apparent to the throne of Ancient Joseon. He was the first of Dangun Wanggeom's four sons. Crown Prince Buru ascends to the throne as the second Dangun after the passing of his father. Dangun is the title of the Emperor in Ancient Joseon.

** Gija - A wiseman who lived at the end of Shang dynasty, he originally served as the teacher to King Zhou, the last king of Shang dynasty, until he was imprisoned by King Zhou. After King Wu overthrew King Zhou and released Gija, King Wu asked about the way of the heavens to Gija. This is when Gija taught him about the ways of Hongbeomguju.

*** Hongbeomguju - Crown Prince Buru passed down the method of controlling water using the five elements and a book called Hwangjaejoong-gyeong to King Yu (known as Yu the Great). This is the same Hongbeomguju that Gija taught King Wu a few centuries later.

**** Jeong Dojeon(1342- Oct 6th, 1398) - The First Prime Minister of Joseon. He is considered the principal archtect of Joseon dynasty's policies, laying down the kingdom's ideological, institutional, and legal frameworks which would govern it for five centuries.

06

The central figures of the Golden Dragon, the Golden Bear, and the Dokkaebi

Folklorist Jo Jayong discovered old paintings of the five guardian deities that replaced the Golden Dragon with the figure of the dokkaebi. But why was this mythical figure chosen? Long before Goguryeo started depicting the five guardian deities on the inner walls and ceilings of its burial mounds—even before Ancient Joseon (2,333-239 BCE) existed—the Korean people paid homage to a god of war and victory. Ancient records identify this god as an actual person, the Emperor Chi-wu, who was the fourteenth Hwanung of the nation of Baedal (3,897-2,333 BCE). Eventually, Emperor Chi-wu came to be symbolized by the dokkaebi in local folklore and in neighboring civilizations. As the god of war, the Dokkaebi, Emperor Chi-wu became a cultural symbol in Northeast Asia, which is why some early folk art depicts him as the king dokkaebi at the center of murals with the other four guardian deities, taking the place where later paintings depict the Golden Dragon. The Golden Dragon itself, which symbolizes the emperor, actually originated from the Hwanung who ruled the ancient Baedal Dynasty. Hwanung means "Supreme Divine Regent Bear" and is a term that refers to the king of all kings who ruled over numerous civilizations in ancient East Asia.

Another important cultural symbol originates from the ancient folk tale of Naban and Aman. According to this story, Aman and Naban were the first human beings in the world, and they met in a place called Aisabi, which some historians theorize was Lake Baikal or the Songha River. One day, Aman and Naban held a marriage ceremony after receiving a revelation from the Heavenly God. They set out a bowl of clear water and offered a prayer of gratitude to heaven for making them husband and wife. In return, the Heavenly God sent the guardians down to the earthly realm to watch over the two humans. A red phoenix descended on the south side of the mountain, flapping its wings in delight at their marriage, while a divine black tortoise arose from the waters of the north to bestow them with auspicious energy. A white tiger came out of the west of the nearby hills to guard the boundaries of the mountains, and east of the stream, a blue dragon soared through the sky. Throughout the ceremony, a golden bear sat at the center of all of this, watching over them.

In this tale, the divine creature guarding the center was neither the king dokkaebi nor a golden dragon—it was a golden bear seated at the center. For many Koreans, mentioning a bear brings to mind the story of the queen of the bear totem tribe, the Woongnyeoh.*

The golden bear is the same color as the central Golden Dragon. In the

Hongshan civilization ruins found in Niuheliang, China, where Korea's ancestral people lived during the Neolithic period, archaeolo-

---

* The first empress and consort of the first Heavenly Emperor of Baedal dyansty. She meditated in a cave by only feeding on garlic and mugwort for 21 days.

gists found Goddess statues in meditation, numerous bear-shaped jade pieces, the actual jawbones of bears, and clay figurines shaped like bear feet. This is because the golden dragon, the king dokkaebi, and the golden bear all have taken turns embodying the earth energy at the center. Though the center's guardian has changed with time, the center itself has always been the ruler's rightful place.

Despite the sheer number of figures, totems, and creatures found in the Hongshan civilization, Goguryeo wall paintings, or throughout the Joseon Dynasty, few are properly represented in modern Korean culture. This is a loss for today's society, but perhaps the success of the dragon and the phoenix will lead to a variety of fantastical creatures receiving recognition in everyday life in Korea once again.

PART 07

A Trip to the Museums in Korea

Taegeukgi:
the Universe Spread on Cloth

01 Glory and agony in recent Korean history
02 The first Taegeukgi
03 The many forms of the Taegeukgi
04 The Taegeuk alive within the history of the Korean people
05 Contextualizing the Taegeukgi's white background
06 The geon, gon, gam, and ri trigrams
07 The universal principles of the Eight Trigrams
08 Four, not eight: the trigrams of the Taegeukgi
09 The Taegeuk as the "Great People of Korea"

01

Glory and agony in recent Korean history

The 2015 film *Assassination* by director Cheo Donghoon follows an assasination operation planned against pro-Japanese Imperialists by Korean independence activists. When it was released, it brought in a record-breaking 12 million views by domestic audiences (roughly one quarter of South Korea's total population of 50 million). One of the scenes that lingers with viewers long after the movie ends shows the three agents of the operation smiling brightly in front of the Taegeukgi, the national flag of South Korea today.

The Taegeukgi has been with the Korean people throughout the ups and downs of Korea's modern history. For example, the actual Korean independence activists who fought fiercely for the freedom of their people were known for keeping drawings of the Taegeukgi folded and tucked inside their clothes, close to the heart. Although many Taegeukgi were stepped on, burned, dirtied, and ripped apart

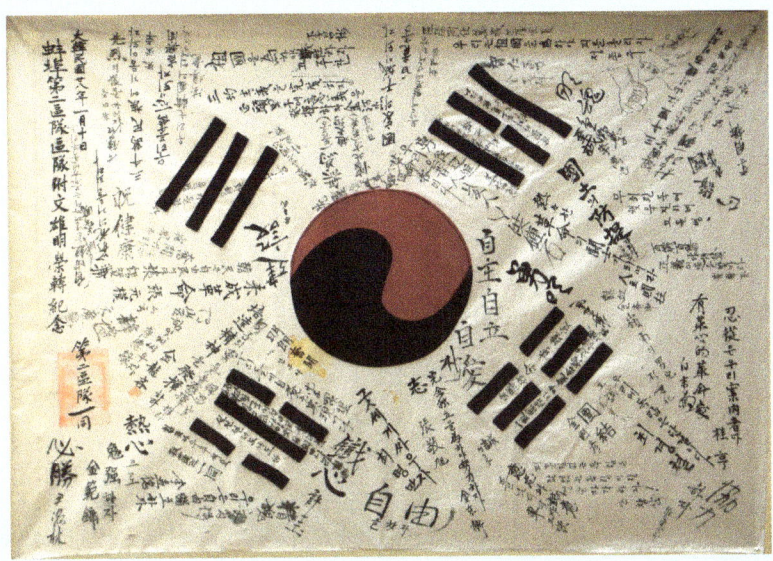

Figure 7-1 Copy of the Taegeukgi signed by the Korean Liberation Army expressing its commitment to the independence of Korea / February, 1945 (History Museum of Korea)

Figure 7-2 An imitation of the Taegeukgi used during the Korean Independence Movement in the 1930s and 1940s (Korea Museum of History)

by Japanese soldiers, the Korean flag was tirelessly reproduced, like a fire that rekindled itself again and again.

Many Koreans are familiar with the story of the patriotic martyr named Yu Gwansun, who was one of the organizers of the Manseh independence movement (also known as the March 1ˢᵗ Independence Movement). On March 1, 1919, Yu drew and shared copies of the Taegeukgi in secret.*

When people marched through the city, calling for independence, the streets were filled with copies of the Taegeukgi that had survived despite the oppression of Japanese imperialism. People also held the Taegeukgi aloft when Korea finally gained independence from Japan on August 15, 1945, and during the Korean War when South Korea took the capital city of Seoul back from North Korea. The Taegeukgi is a sign of the unshakeable resilience of the Korean people.

Thanks to the rise of South Korea's recognition on the world stage, the Taegeukgi has spread across the globe. It is not unusual to see people of other ethnicities and nationalities cheering and waving the Taegeukgi for South Korean athletes at competitions in other countries. Fans of the Korean Wave can be seen waving the Taegeukgi on TV, and I have even met Hallyu fans in Europe who initiated conversations about the Taegeukgi with me. While most South Koreans may have not yet noticed the spread of this familiar symbol, the Taegeukgi is rapidly becoming emblematic of Korean culture.

Romania-born Catholic priest Constantin Virgil Gheorghiu, the famous author of the book, *The Twenty-Fifth Hour*, also wrote about the Taegeukgi.**

---

* March 1ˢᵗ Movement - An independence movement lead by 33 of Korea's most prominent leaders. Many Koreans were captured, beaten, tortured, and killed for standing up for Korea's Independence on this day by the Japanese Imperialists..
** Constantin Virgil Gheorghiu (1916-92) was a Romanian-born writer and diplomat who denounced Nazism and Communism in his best-selling novel, The 25th Hour. He was ordained a priest in 1963 and became the Patriarch of the Romanian Orthodox Church in France in 1971. He continued to write, publishing "Christ in Lebanon" in

According to him, the Taegeukgi represents the universe, and no other country in the world embodies the fundamentals of the universe in its national flag like this. While other countries seem to rely on an overall similar flag form and function, the Taegeukgi stands out with a unique design and message.

The fundamental meaning of the Taegeukgi is "embracing all the world"—but where does this meaning come from? How does the Taegeukgi signify this universal embrace? The next section will explore how the Taegukgi design came about and delve deeper into its symbolism.

1979 and "God in Paris" the next year. His last work, in 1987, was about South Korea.

02

The first Taegeukgi

In their long and storied history, the Korean people have used other flags beside the Taegeukgi. The Taegeukgi's many predecessors include flags that signified the commander in a war, raised soldiers' morale, showed a unified front, or even announced the presence of the king.

While the history of these flags can be studied to understand when and how Koreans first came to use an official national flag, the origin of the symbols used can be traced even farther back. The Taegeukgi flag itself was first created during the turbulent times of the late Joseon Dynasty and implemented by a man named Park Youngho. It has been rumored that he made this flag on the ship on his way to Japan as a Korean diplomat in August 1882, but the Taegeukgi was actually made after an extensive discussion led by King Gojong. The flag was not something made casually; it was an invention born from the king's discussions with his ministers and insights garnered from foreign diplomats, a process that was carefully recorded in many diplomatic records. The following is the true story of how the Taegeukgi became the official flag of Korea on March 6, 1883.

In 1875, the Japanese battleship Woonyo landed illegally on Ganghwa Island at the mouth of the Han-gang River (between modern North and South Korea), leading to bloodshed with the Joseon garrison. Japan used this incident to force Joseon into signing the Treaty of Ganghwa in 1876, which opened long-protected Korean ports to Japanese and other foreign trade. During the meeting, Japanese representatives criticized their Korean counterparts for attacking a ship with the Japanese flag, though the Japanese had entered Joseon's naval territory without permission after a series of provocative incursions by foreign powers in recent years. Then the Japanese representatives demanded to see Joseon's national flag. Taken aback, translator Oh Gyeongseok went off-script to respond that the Taegeuk symbol drawn on the gates of Gaeseong Castle served as the flag. After this incident, Joseon's ruling elite debated over the choice of a national flag. Translator Oh later talked with Kim Kyeongsu about a version of the flag where the four trigrams* were positioned around the Taegeuk, and this was presented to King Gojong.** King Gojong felt the need for a national flag as well, so he had been examining the long-used diagram of the Eight Trigrams and the Taegeuk. After reviewing their proposed flag, King Gojong began using the Taegeukgi with the four trigrams and central Taegeuk during his official state visits. The Taegeukgi was therefore chosen as the national flag in 1883, but its symbolism had been in use since long before.

---

* The four trigrams - Read Ch. 7 Taegeukgi: The Universe Spread on Cloth, Sect 6 Geon Gon Gam Ri.
** Kim Kyeong-su - In Kim Du-bong's book 'The history of unexpected enactment of Taegeukgi (Tae-geuk-gi-ui-chang-jol-gan-je-jeong-dwen-yeok-sa)', Kim Gyeong-su is depicted as a fellow interpreter of Oh Gyeongseok. Kim is the one who suggests that they use 4 of the 8 triagrams for the national flag. King Gojon chose this flag as the official Korean flag in 1882 and 1883. (Chosun Ilbo newspaper, Dec. 27th 1997)

Figure 7-3 This is a reproduction of the original form of Taegeukgi with the eight trigrams. It was known as the Dook-shin-gi Flag. This was a re-creation of a flag used at the Dook-shin-sa spirit temple which honors the Heavenly Emperor Chi-u. Emperor Gojong simply used the Taegeukgi with the four trigrams of geon-gon-gam-ri instead of the more complicated version with the eight trigrams.

The United States-Korea treaty of 1882 was signed on May 22 in Jemulpo (modern Incheon) between the U.S. and Joseon. Prior to the signing, the U.S. ambassador plenipotentiary Commodore Robert W. Shufeldt requested to see Joseon's flag, telling Joseon official Kim Hongjib that an independent nation must have an independent flag. This was a year prior to the official adoption of the Taegeukgi as the national flag of Joseon.

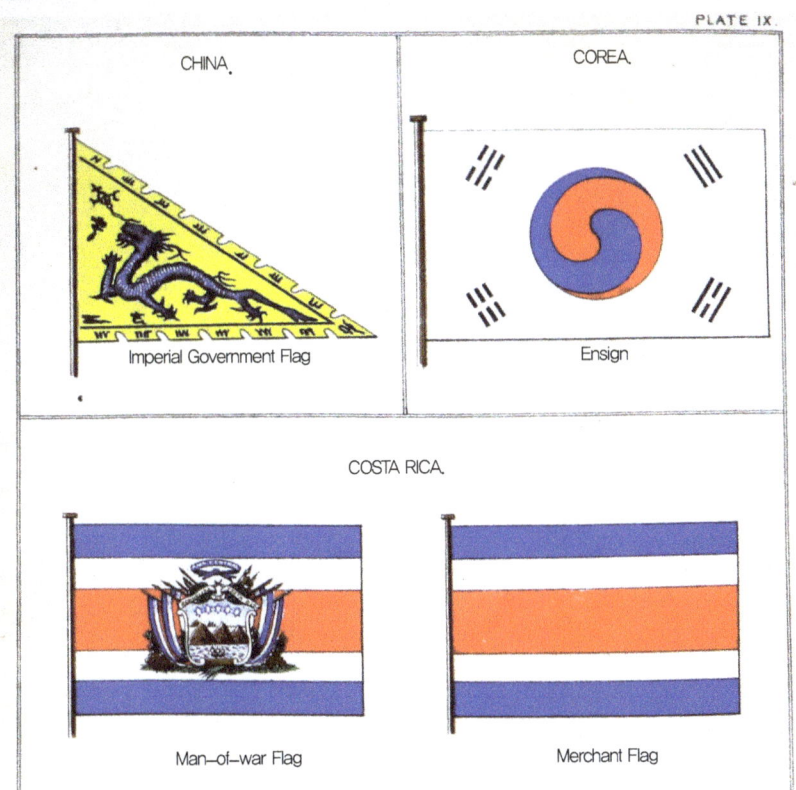

Figure 7-4 This version is known as the Schufeldt Taegeukgi or Lee Eung-jun Taegeukgi as well. It can be found in the maritime national records of the 1880s. The national flag of the Qing Dynasty is next to the Korean flag (Preserved at the History Museum of Korea)

Around that same time, Qing China diplomat Ma Geonchoong met with Kim Hongjib to ask Joseon to use a modified version of Qing's national flag (a yellow dragon flag), as its national flag. But if Kim Hongjib had agreed to China's demand to fly a blue-colored flag with a blue dragon, this would have signaled that Joseon agreed to be a subordinate nation to China. The blue dragon flag was first conceived during the reign of Ju Wonjang,* the founder of the Ming Empire (1368~1644). Ju Wonjang alone dressed in gold while his children, siblings, and feudal lords dressed in blue. Ordinary people were prohibited from using gold colors, and the first king of Joseon, Lee Seongkye, was asked to wear his royal robes in that same shade of blue. Approximately five centuries later, King Gojong, the emperor of Korea, knew that to use blue was to agree that Joseon was a vassal state of Qing China, so he swiftly declined and had his officials make the Taegeukgi as discussed (from Japan's Sisa Shinbo report, October 2, 1882). Accordingly, Kim Hongjib told translator Lee Eungjoon to draw the Taegeukgi, and thus the Taegeukgi was used in a diplomatic meeting for the first time in history.

This flag was sent with Shufeldt when he returned to the United States, making an appearance as the "Corea Ensign" in the U.S. *Navy's Flags of the Maritime States* (1882). This is also known as the Shufeldt Taegeukgi or the Lee Eungjoon Taegeukgi.

Park Youngho, who was sent to Japan in 1882 as a Korean diplomat, received detailed orders from King Gojong on how to create the national flag. He described this in his diary: "With a white rectangle as the base, I drew the Taegeuk in the center, two-fifths as wide as the rectangle, and colored the Taegeuk blue and red with the four trigrams placed at the corners, each facing the center. I flew this flag over our temporary living quarters, thereby completing the mandate bestowed unto me by the King." The Taegeukgi described here, which

---

* Known as 'Hongwu Emperor' Zhu Yuanzhang. His reign began in 1368 and lasted until 1398.

was flown by the group of diplomats that arrived in Japan in September 1882, was later rediscovered in the National Archives in England and revealed to the public. Around that time, a diplomatic document sent by Japan's Vice Foreign Minister to Sir Harry Smith Parkes, the British diplomat to the Empire of Japan in the mid- to late-1800s, included a copy of the Korean national flag and an explanation of its design.

Based on these historical records that show how and when the Taegeukgi was used in treaties with other nations, we know that the Taegeukgi became the official flag of Joseon on March 6, 1883.

03

The many forms of the Taegeukgi

Unfortunately, no one knows exactly what shape the first Taegeukgi took. When King Gojong officially adopted the flag in 1883, he did not clarify the exact details of its design, so many different kinds of flags were made over the years. The various forms of the Taegeukgi include the Shufeldt flag and the Park Youngho flag, to name a few.

In *Tong-sang-jo-yak-jang-jeong-seong-in-hwi-pyeon*, a Qing Empire diplomatic document, the Taegeukgi was introduced as the "the national flag of Goryeo, vassal state of the great Qing Empire." The flag known then as the Goryeo flag had a yellow background, a different Taegeuk shape, and four blue trigrams.

The oldest extant Taegeukgi is called the Denny Taegeukgi and is named after an American citizen. Owen N. Denny, who was the U.S. consul to Korea and diplomatic advisor to King Gojong himself, is

Figure 7-5 The Denny Taegeukgi displayed at the National Museum of Korea / It is known as the oldest Korean flag to exist, which was taken by Denny (1838-1900), an American who served as Emperor Gojong's diplomatic adviser, when he returned to his homeland in 1890.

this flag's namesake. The Denny Taegeukgi differs from the current Taegeukgi in that the Taegeuk symbol in the center is divided from side to side, not from top to bottom, and it is drawn in a dynamic whirlwind shape. The four trigrams of heaven, earth, sun, and moon are blue. The flag is 263 centimeters wide and 180 centimeters long, and it is believed that this flag was used during official state visits by King Gojong.

According to one story, even though it was common to draw the Eight Trigrams before the creation of the Park Youngho flag, it was also too complicated, so this was changed to the four trigrams of today's design. However, this anecdote has not been corroborated by historical evidence, and all of the remaining Taegeukgi flags feature four trigrams.

04

The Taegeuk alive within the history of the Korean people

Since antiquity, the Taegeuk has been used as a symbol by the Korean people. Although some people incorrectly assume it came from China simply because the word "Taegeuk" first appeared in the Chinese book *I Ching*, the history of this Taegeuk symbol among the Korean people reaches much further back.

A Taegeuk symbol on a rectangular stone found at the Gameunsa temple site from the Shilla Dynasty (57 BCE-935 CE) — a temple built in the year 682 — was carved 400 years before the Taegeuk symbol of Ju Don-ee,* a Neo-Confucian** of the eleventh-century

---

* Ju Don-ee(Zhou Dunyi) was a Neo-Confucian. He conceptualized Neo-Confucian Cosmology by explaining the reltatationship between human conduct and universal forces.
** Neo Confucianism is known as the supreme synthesis of Song-Min dynasty(960-1628 CE) redefined by Zhu Xi. Through this movement, Confucianism acquired a universal dimension beyond a concern for society and social duties.

Figure 7-6 Sugun Joryeondo(Navy Maneuvering and Training) The Jwadeukgi flag(A general's flag usually raised on the left side of the general) is located in the center of the ship where the commander with the title of Samdo Daewonsu is riding.(National Museum of Korea)

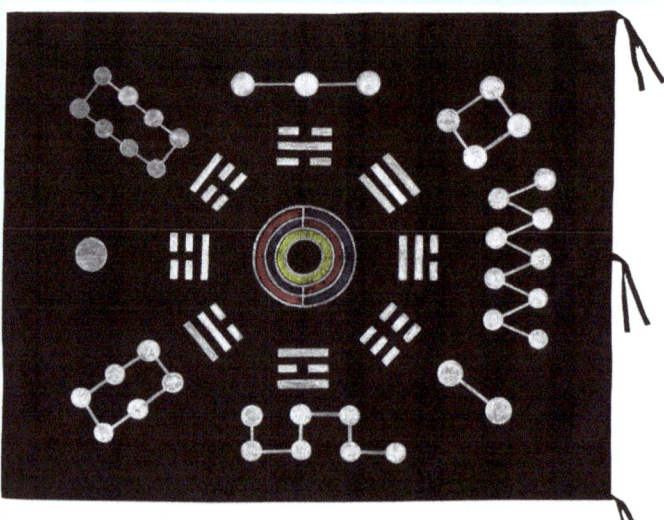

Figure 7-7 Jwadeukgi Flag / The most important and colorful military flag of Joseon dynasty representing the dignity of the commanding general (Preserved at the National Palace Museum)

Song Dynasty. The Korean people used this symbol throughout the Baekjae (18 BCE-660 CE), Goryeo (918-1392 CE), and Joseon dynasties (1392-1897 CE), and even the royal mounds of the King Gongmin (May 23rd, 1330-Oct. 27th, 1374) from the Goryeo Dynasty are decorated with the Taegeuk symbol. The Jwadokgi, a Joseon Dynasty military flag emblazoned with the Taegeuk and the Eight Trigrams, can be seen in places like the Ancient Palace Museum, the Story of Chungmugong memorial hall for Admiral Yi Sunshin beneath Gwanghwamun Plaza, and the National Central Museum.

Despite the occasional claim that the Taegeukgi was made hastily in preparation for entering into commercial treaties with foreign powers during the late Joseon Dynasty, the Taegeuk symbol—the basis for the Taegeukgi—is a shape that has been in use by the Korean people for an extraordinarily long time. Several thousand years before the emergence of Neo-Confucianism in China, the principles of yin-yang, the five elements, and the ideology of the Eight Trigrams were the universal philosophy of the Korean people. The Taegeukgi is a modification of a cultural symbol that Koreans have used for about 5,000 years, one that was carefully revised and reviewed for about a year during the late Joseon Dynasty before it was officially circulated as the national flag.

05

Contextualizing the Taegeukgi's white background

Traditional Korean philosophy is embodied in every detail of the Taegeukgi, down to its white background. Some might leap to the conclusion that this white background was chosen because Koreans came to be known during the Joseon Dynasty as the people garbed in white.*

Others might interpret the flag's color to mean that Koreans value purity and peace above all else. However, the assumption that the white of the Taegeukgi symbolizes purity and peace indicates a thoroughly Eurocentric bias. The Korean people used the Taegeukgi to defend and declare themselves a sovereign and independent nation, effectively cutting ties with the Qing Empire. Throughout its history, the Taegeukgi was deployed as a symbol and shield to protect the nation from foreign imperialism, Western superpowers, and Japanese

---

* Commoners in the Joseon Dynasty were restricted to white clothing except on special occasions.

incursions. There was no time for the Korean people to think naively and idly of peace when the Taegeukgi was created. Instead of serving as a symbol of peace and purity, the color of the national flag of Korea was chosen for a different reason.

The real reason for the Taegeukgi's white background is that white represents light. Previous chapters in this book referenced "the nation of Baedal," and for 5000 years, from this Baedal nation to the last Korean Empire (Daehanjeguk), Korean nations were ruled according to values such as "observing the world and ruling with the truth to enlighten the people," "ruling the world through light," and "benefiting the world far and wide." Immersed in such ideologies, the Korean people wished to benefit the world by revering the sun and praying for its radiance to shine upon all of heaven and earth and enlighten the people. The name Baedal literally means "the land of light." This collective identity as a country of bright and radiant light was passed down from Baedal (3897-2333 BCE) to Jushin (Joseon; 2333-239 BCE),* Buyeo (239-58 BCE),** Balhae (668-926 CE), the Korean Empire (1897-1910 CE), and the Republic of Korea (1948~). This is why the names of the Korean dynasties all were chosen to mean "brilliant radiance."

The four-character phrase for "ruling the world with light" is Gwang-Myeong-Ee-Se (광명이세, 光明以世). The two characters of Gwang and Myeong are a combination of "light" and "brightness." The character Myeong (明) uses the characters for both sun (日) and moon (月) side by side, meaning "brightness regardless of day or night." Gwang Myeong expressed in pure Korean spoken language is "hwanhada," or "to be bright." Brightness also stands for righteousness because it does not allow a person to hide things from others or

---

* Jushin - "Dan-jae" Shin Chae-ho wrote in his book Ancient History of Joseon (Joseon-sang-go-sa) that Joseon, Sukshin, Jusin and Jushin were different names to describe Joseon, basing his claims on the book Man-ju-won-ryu-go
** This time period is referring to Northern Buyeo

engage in hidden matters of any kind. The Taegeukgi's white background therefore signifies a nation without lies—a people of brightness and justice.

According to the principles of yin-yang and the five elements, white is symbolized by the element of metal. Metal also symbolizes west and autumn, and the virtue that it represents is righteousness. Choosing white as the background for the national flag represented the Korean people's aspirations for a brighter and more righteous world and a fair nation.

06

The geon, gon, gam, and ri trigrams

The four trigrams marking the corners of the Korean flag are known as geon, gon, gam, and ri.

7-1. Understanding the trigrams

Shape	Name	Meaning
☰	Geon	Heaven
☷	Gon	Earth
☵	Gam	Moon and Water
☲	Ri	Sun and Fire

The concepts of geon, gon, gam, and ri are rooted deep in ancient Korean history, when Taeho Bokhee first illustrated the concept of the Taegeuk and the eight trigrams 5,700 years ago. The four trigrams on the Taegeukgi come from these eight trigrams of ancient times, but few Koreans today have heard of Taeho Bokhee. Fewer still know anything about him.. Of the few that recognize his name, most are under the mistaken impression that he was a mythic figure.

There is a portrayal of Taeho Bokhee exhibited in the Central Asia Hall of the World Culture Exhibition on the third floor of the National Central Museum, a painting known as a Bokhee-Yeowa-do. This is one of a number of Bokhee-Yeowa-do that were found in the collective burial mounds of the Xinjiang Uygur Autonomous Region in Northwestern China, near the Silk Road. Both the man (Bokhee) and woman (Yeowa) portrayed in the illustration have human bodies that taper into the tails of snakes or perhaps dragons. The picture also includes the sun, the moon, and the stars. This is the only artifact in the entire National Central Museum that makes a direct and obvious reference to Taeho Bokhee.

According to legend, Bokhee and Yeowa were brother and sister, the sole survivors after a prolonged war among the gods that eventually led to the flooding of the whole world. Their marriage birthed the world's first humans, and the Bokhee-Yeowa-do portrays this. The depiction of their lower bodies as snakes comes from the Chinese offensive practice of drawing the ancient heroes of the Korean Dongyi people as inhuman animals or monsters. Other examples of this incendiary practice include drawings of Emperor Chi-wu with the head of a bird or ferocious beast, with weapons instead of human hands and feet.* Shinnong, too, was drawn with a distorted face and

---

* Heavenly Emperor Chi-wu - 14th Heavenly Emperor of Baedal Dynasty. Read 'Ch. 16 Dokkaebi, the God of War Sect 5. Emperor Chi-u: ancestor of the Korean Dongyi or Chinese Zhonghua?' of this book.

horns.* Even Seowangmo was drawn bizarrely, as an old woman with a gruesome face made more frightening with a sharp tongue and teeth.**

Putting this creation myth aside, what might Bokhee have been like as a person? Around 7,000 years ago, the people of Baedal rose to power in East Asia, and their ruler was called the Hwanung. In a mythology related to Dangun found in the Samguk-yusa, which offers a mix of historical accounts and legends of Korea, there is a tale about the Hwanung who established a nation with 3,000 of his people prior to the rise of Ancient Joseon (2333-239 BCE).***

According to this legend, Baedal was then ruled by generations of Hwanungs. Of these Hwanungs, the fifth Hwanung was Tae-wu-ui, who had many sons, and his twelfth son was Bokhee. Bokhee took a position called the Usa, a role that manages the rain, and he was also in charge of livestock farming.

---

* Shinnong - Considered to be the primogenitor of the surname Kang or Gahng. He is also known as the god of agriculture, medicine, and trade.
** Seowangmo - An immortal who is traditionally believed to be living in the summit of Kulun Mountains. She is also known as the one who helped the Yellow Emperor in his war against Heavenly Emperor Chi-u.
*** Samguk-yusa is a record of Korean history written during the Goryeo dynasty by a Buddhist monk named Il-yon. Samguk-yusa portrays Korean history from a Buddhist perspective.

Figure 7-8 The images of Bokhui and Yeowa displayed at the National Museum of Korea. They're Holding a right-angle and a tool to draw a circle. A painting found in the Astana tomb, Turpan, Uiguhr Autonomous District of Xinjiang, China. Astana means capital city in Uighur language as well.

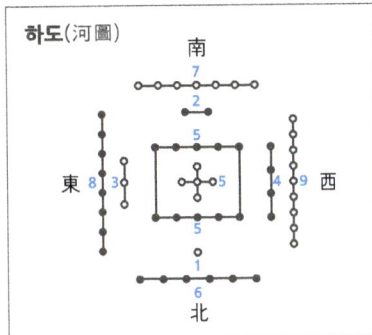 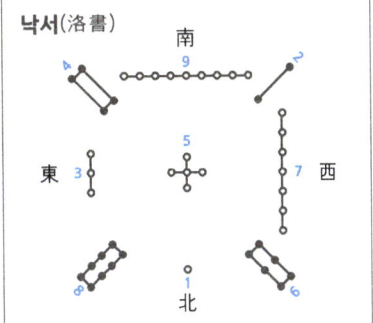

Figure 7-9 Hado, Nakseo

Despite his many duties to the people, Bokhee sought to learn and understand the laws of the universe. He closely studied the Cheonbugyeong, which was passed down from even more ancient times, and he performed the heavenly ritual with utmost devotion.*

This heavenly ritual was an offering to the Heavenly Emperor at Samshinsan Mountain. Bokhee prayed earnestly and with immense dedication to bring about great things, and as a response to his vows and prayers, he received the Hado in a place known then as the Cheonha River (Songha River today). The Hado was a secret code to understanding the universe, and it was drawn on a dragon horse (a creature with the head of a dragon and the body of a horse).

Bokhee studied the Hado intensively. One day, he observed the Dragon God in flight following the sun. As Bokhee watched, the

---

* Cheonbugyeong - Choe Chiwon, a Korean Confucian official, philosopher, and poet of the late Unified Shilla period, discovered a memorial stone containing an 81 character scripture which is known as Cheonbugyeong. According to Hwandangogi, Cheonbugyeong was was only passed down orally during the times of Hwanguk, but Hwan-ung ordered Shinji Hyeok-deok to write it in to Nokdumoon letters. It contains the essence of Eastern philosophy and numerology.

Dragon God changed the color of its body 12 times throughout the day. It is said that by observing these changes and the deep meaning behind the Hado, Bokhee was able to come to an intimate understanding of worldly principles.

07

The universal principles of the Eight Trigrams

The constantly changing universe is so complex and difficult to understand that even a person who has grasped its principles can find it challenging to explain it to others. This is precisely why Taeho Bokhee created the symbols called the Eight Trigrams. His goal was to enable others to more easily understand the various principles and phenomena of the universe's natural transformation.

The oldest design that uses the Eight Trigrams in their original form is a wall painting found in a Goguryeo tomb dating back to the early sixth century. The painting depicts an immortal being who draws the Eight Trigrams while astride a lotus flower. This painting was discovered in the Wuhuifen tomb No. 4 in modern Ji'an, China.

The Eight Trigrams had a significant influence on scientific development in the West, an influence which is demonstrated by the German thinker Gottfried Wilhelm Leibniz. Leibniz was born in Leipzig in the seventeenth century, and he came to be regarded as a genius in many areas. He was particularly exceptional in math and philosophy, and he was known to be skilled in physics, engineering, and still other fields as well. Leibniz's study of the 64 hexagrams that come from the Eight Trigrams helped him discover the theoretical principles of computational machines. Using the philosophical concept of yin-yang as a springboard, he created the binary code system of ones and zeroes and used this as the foundation for one of his inventions, a mechanical calculator. The principles of this early calculator are much the same as the basic principles of modern technology, such as the computer and the smartphone.

But Leibniz was not the only European influenced by the Taegeuk. Niels Bohr, the father of quantum physics and creator of the first atomic model, made the first atomic model based on the basic patterns of the I Ching.*

Famously, this Danish physicist was recognized with the highest honor of Denmark, the Order of the Elephant, which bestowed him with peerage for his achievements. On the day of his induction, he wore the Taegeuk symbol on his ceremonial garb.

By creating the Eight Trigrams as a coded system for philosophical cosmology, Taeho Bokhee provided the foundation for a great turning point in the history of human civilization, greatly influencing society as we know it.

---

* I Ching – I ching is translated as Book of Changes or Classics of Changes. I Ching is a compilation of Bokhee's 8 trigrams and 64 hexagrams, King Wen's explaination of the 64 diagrams, Duke of Zhou's explaination of the 384 lines and Ten addendum written by Confucius.

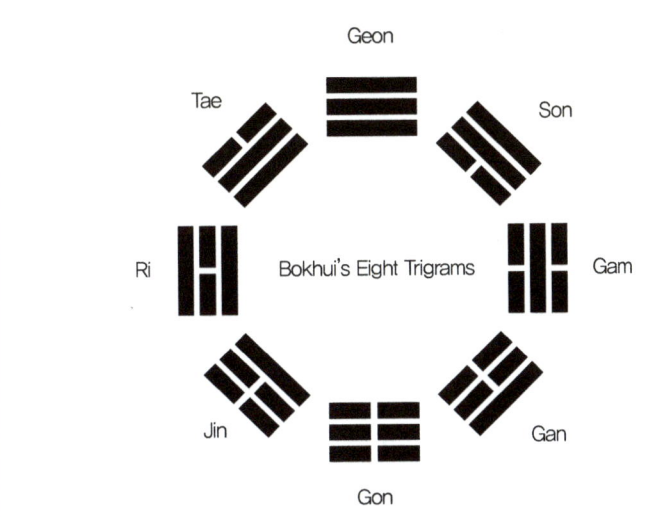

Figure 7-10 **Bokhui's Eight Trigrams**

08

Four, not eight: the trigrams of the Taegeukgi

The modern Taegeukgi features only four of the eight original trigrams, an interesting and intentional choice by its makers. But why did they choose these four, and how?

Historically, Koreans have favored simplicity. This can be seen in traditional painting styles that use copious amounts of space and other artistic methods for simplicity. The choice of the four trigrams instead of eight likewise was based on this desire for simplicity, where only the essentials were incorporated. The four trigrams of geon, gon, gam, and ri are the unchanging foundation of life as it is known to humankind: heaven, earth, sun, and moon. By choosing these key symbols, the Taegeukgi's creators were able to represent the entire world using just four trigrams on their flag.

The picture in Diagram 7-11 how the four trigrams were developed from the original eight.

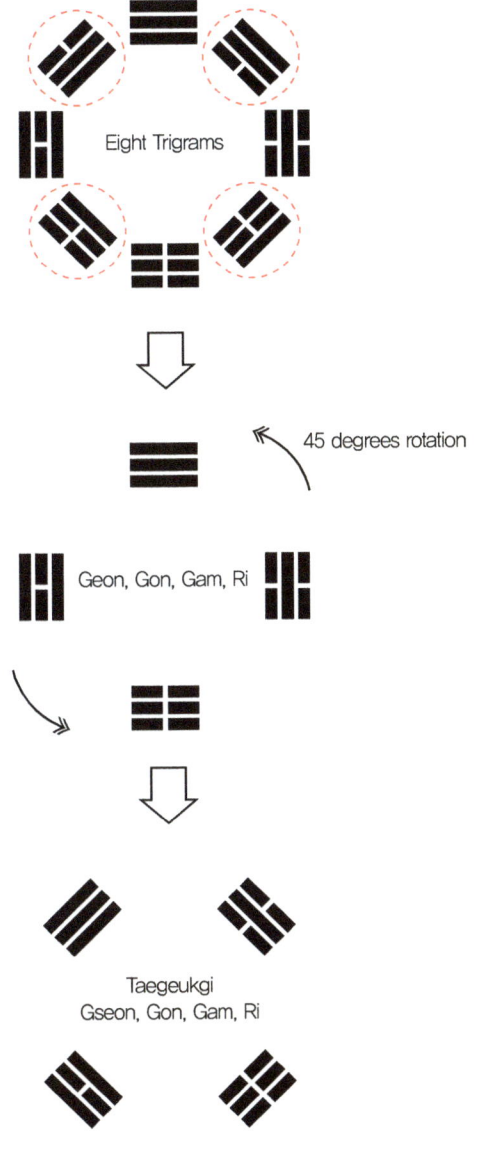

Figure 7-11 The process of Taegeukgi being left with only four trigrams from the Bokhui Eight Trigrams

09

The Taegeuk as the "Great People of Korea"

When the ancestors of modern Korea made the Taegeukgi, they shifted the four trigrams from their original positions. This is because the geon, gon, gam, and ri, while important, are not the main focus of the Taegeukgi. That role falls to the Taegeuk at the center, yet another manifestation of the ideology of the Samjae (heaven, earth, and humankind). This ideology does not merely divide the world into three separate categories. Rather, its true meaning comes from the concept that the parents of humankind are heaven and earth. Heaven is the father, and earth is the mother, so humankind is like a child raised by heaven and earth. This makes the geon, gon, gam, and ri of the Taegeukgi (heaven, earth, sun, and moon) the joint caregivers of the Taegeuk; together, they raise the Taegeuk as parents raise a child.

As explained above, the Taegeuk is protected and fostered by the Taegeukgi's four trigrams, but what about the Taegeuk itself? The Taegeuk represents the "Daehan Saram," or the "Great People of Ko-

Figure 7-12 The passageway between Ichon Station and the National Museum of Korea / Lamp in the shape of Geon-gon-gam-ri is lit on the ceiling and the floor has a painted image of the gon trigram which symbolizes the land.

rea." Even in the Aegukga, the national anthem of South Korea, the lyrics exclaim, "God protect and preserve our nation, Manseh* to our nation," and "Great Korean people, stay true to the Great Korean way!"**

The Aegukga is not the only modern tribute to the Taegeuk and the Great people of Korea. Walk through the underground passage for the subway at Eechon Station near the National Central Museum in Seoul, and you will feel like you are tunneling through Korean history. The walls, ceiling, and even floors of this route are covered with traditional symbols described in this chapter.

All four trigrams (geon, gon, gam, and ri) decorate the ceiling, and the gon trigram can also be found on the floor, which is fitting because this trigram symbolizes the earth. The walls are patterned with a Taegeuk motif, and Taegeukgi designs are found throughout the long passageway. Public incorporation of the Taegeukgi like this is an excellent way to weave history and culture into everyday life, and it may herald a future filled with many more tributes of this nature.

Even distilled to its very essence, the Taegeukgi represents Korea. After all, it carries the wisdom, philosophy, and ideology from the past 5,000 years of Korean civilization. It has also been carried by generations of Koreans through days of glory and humiliation alike. Perhaps what the modern person needs to survive in this complex world is the ideology of the Heaven, Earth and Humanity as one, and the mindset described in the four-character idioms of Je Seh Ee Hwa (observing the world and ruling with the truth to enlighten the people), Gwang Myeong Ee Se (ruling the world through light), and

---

* Literal translation of Manseh means ten-thousand years. Its English equivalent is the phrase "Long Live."
** Dae Han means "Great Hahn." The origin of this term goes back to the time of Ancient Joseon or Dangun Joseon where the nation was divided in to three states of Han or Hahn. Hanguk being the most popular term used in reference to the Republic of Korea, Great Hahn here can be understood as Great Korea and Great Korean people.

Hong Ik In Gan (benefiting the world far and wide). When the proud Taegeukgi flag is raised aloft, used as a motif on public transportation, or even featured on merchandise, it serves as a reminder of the spirit of the Great People of Korea.

PART 08

A Trip to the Museums in Korea

The dolmen, an evidence of a systematic society

01 UNESCO World Heritage at the Ganghwa Dolmen Sites
02 Megalithic culture around the world
03 The era of stone tombs
04 Ancient civilization as told by Korean dolmens
05 The mystery of the Seven Stars on dolmen capstones

01

UNESCO World Heritage at the Ganghwa Dolmen Sites

Gwanghwa Island has seen an increase in visitors in recent years, welcoming everyone from hiking enthusiasts to vacationing families. While the island has many great sites to visit, there are two that I particularly recommend. The first is Manisan Mountain, with its pyramid-like appearance when seen from a distance, and the second is undoubtedly the park of the Ganghwa Dolmen Sites. Even in this park of massive dolmens, one particular megalithic structure stands out: an enormous dolmen in the shape of a huge table. Everyone, including visitors without much initial interest in dolmens, pauses in amazement when they encounter this awe-inspiring feat of human genius and grit. There is also a music box near the site's information board that plays the Gwanghwa Dolmen song; a press of its button plays a melody familiar to many Koreans due to its association with Children's Day. This is known as the Ganghwa Dolmen song.

The translated lyrics include the following lines: "40,000 of the

Figure 8-1 Dolmen song of the Ganghwa Island/ The song contains key information about dolmens in Korea.

world's 60,000 dolmens are ours / And of those, 160 are the pride of Ganghwa." As the lyrics describe, Korea does in fact have 66% of the world's dolmens. Dolmens have been discovered throughout Asian countries like China and Japan as well as in European countries such as France and England. Yet all these dolmens combined still do not come close to the number of dolmens found in Korea, which has strengthened the theory that Korean civilization is the origin of dolmen culture.

Ganghwa Island is one of numerous sites throughout South Korea where dolmens can be found, and there are an additional 10,000 dolmens in North Korea. That number could increase even more if we were to factor in the dolmens that were probably unwittingly destroyed by people who did not recognize them for their historical significance. The dolmens of Ganghwa Island (Incheon) and the

Figure 8-2 Table-style dolmen in Ganghwado Dolmen Park is a classic form of dolmen found in Korea. Although it is tilting about 30 degrees, it is safe according to experts. A technique known as the Geu-reng-ee technique was used to trim the supporting stones that were in contact with the cover stones to mesh them together. The cover stone alone weighs 53 tons, and it is estimated that about 1,000 people were mobilized to create the dolmen.

counties of Gochang and Hwasun (Jeollanam-do Province) were designated UNESCO World Heritage sites, with each location containing anywhere from a few dozen to several hundred dolmens.

The direct translation of the Korean word for a dolmen, "go-in-dol," is a propped or supported (go-in) stone (dol). This style of tomb was typical during the Bronze Age (roughly 3,300-1,200 BCE), but there are dolmens around the world that date within a range of 6,000 to 2,000 years ago, with Korean dolmens among the oldest. While we know that some dolmens were built during the Bronze Age 6,000 years ago, the Bronze Age is actually Western classification for ancient human history, and this Western standard is not a one-size-fits-all for the rest of the world. It differs from Korea's standard, which is based on pottery and other artifacts that date the development of human culture in Korea on a different timeline. Pottery dating from the late Neolithic period (around 12,000 years ago), and even early Iron Age artifacts have been found in Korean dolmens. It remains unclear when exactly these Korean dolmens were built or precisely why such massive rocks were used. As for the time period, it is generally assumed that this particular tomb style was used for a long time in Korea, from the late Neolithic period to the early Iron Age.

When the first of these dolmens were discovered, their staggering size led many to believe that these were the tombs of chieftains and rulers. Subsequent discovery of the remains of women and children in these tombs has led experts to assume that this type of tomb was actually used broadly, rather than used exclusively by a specific rank or gender. This is true of the clusters of dolmens found on Ganghwa Island and in the Gochang and Hwasun counties that were designated as World Heritage Sites.

Dolmens are like guideposts to the past, marking sites filled with important clues to what life was like long ago. In addition to entombed bodies, many artifacts have been found in dolmens, including earthenware, stone tools, Ancient Joseon bronze daggers, bronze mirrors, and bronze bells. A high concentration of dolmens in a specific region indicates that a similarly large population of people lived in the area. It also shows that these people—the people of Ancient Joseon—had a socially stratified society that enabled them to coordinate the construction of massive stone tombs. The society of Ancient Joseon was building not just dolmens, but the structure of a state.

Thus far, we have learned that Ancient Joseon was beginning to develop the structure of a state by the time civilization on the Korean peninsula reached the Bronze Age. However, there were giant dolmens already in existence on the Korean peninsula by the Neolithic period. We find similar evidence when we study Hongshan culture.

Hongshan culture, as mentioned in the chapter on golden crowns, was a civilization that was older than the four cradles of civilizations of the world, and it was the crowning achievement of the Gulf of Balhae civilization.* Hongshan culture was brought to light thanks to a massive excavation site in Niuheliang, which is located in the Liaoning Province of modern China. The ancestral Korean people, the Dongyi, established the Gulf of Balhae civilization and the Hongshan culture.

Evidence unearthed in Niuheliang shows a well-developed religion and culture of spirituality. The three key pieces of evidence for this are the chong, myo, and dan: the stone tomb, the goddess temple, and the altar for ritual rites.** The combination of this evidence, along with the sheer scale of the excavation, makes it likely that a nation of reasonable size was actually established prior to the start of the Bronze Age.

---

* Gulf of Balhae civilization is a vast culture that began before or around 7,000 BCE with the rise of Xinglongwa culture, Xiaohexi Culture, Zhaobaogou culture succeede by the Hongshan culture. These cultures established themselves along the costal lines of Gulf of Balhae.

** The significance of this chong, myo, and dan is that it was found in the shape of heaven-circle earth-square formation which is the essence of Korean cosmology. Also, the altar had been bulit in three layers. This represents the Triune God culture.

02

Megalithic culture around the world

40,000 of the 60,000 dolmens scattered around the world are found in North and South Korea. With about 10,000 of its own, France follows Korea as the next country with the most megaliths. While other European countries have megalithic structures, many of these are simply standing stones, or megaliths that were planted vertically in the ground, rather than dolmens. A dolmen is a more complicated structure with an inner chamber composed of multiple vertical megaliths that support a large horizontal slab.

The Carnac stones found in France's Brittany region are typical of megaliths found in this part of Europe. The number of these sprawling alignments of standing stones is astonishing—there are approximately 3,000 stones, each taller than an average adult, spanning a distance of four kilometers. The Brittany region, a small peninsula that juts toward the Atlantic Ocean, is located in northwestern France.

Figure 8-3 Tunnel-type dolmens on the island of Moen, Denmark.

While we still do not know who raised these stones or why, the sight of them is undeniably breathtaking.

Many of France's dolmens have similarities to dolmens found in Korea, and some are even connected to form tunnel-like structures. These passage grave dolmens have been discovered throughout Europe. European dolmens are unique in that multiple bodies are entombed in a single chamber. In contrast, Korean dolmens are individual tombs, with one body per chamber.

Another notable dolmen site is located between southeastern Europe and Asia, at the eastern end of the Black Sea and northwest of the Russian portion of the Kavkaz (also known as the Caucasus) Mountains. This region near the city of Sochi, where the 2014 Winter Olympics were held, is still under excavation.

Another proud home to megalithic culture is the small Mediterranean island nation of Malta. Malta is an archipelago famous for its many megalithic temples.

Figure 8-4 The dolmens found in the Caucasus region of Russia/ Their cover stone had constellations carved on it, and one side of the finishing stone had a round hole. Estimated to be built around 1800 BCE~1300 BCE, seventy remains were found under the dolmen. It is on permanent display at the State Historical Museum located in Moscow's Red Square.

Figure 8-5 The inside of the temple of Ggantija (meaning "A Giant woman") on the Gozo Island of the Republic of Malta / The temple was built around 5,500 years ago and is built in the formation of rubbles of rock surrounding it. If you look at it from the mid-air, you can see that it is shaped like two clovers.

The origin of the word "dolmen"

- French origin. Dolmen means "stone table" and is believed to come from the Celtic word tolmen of the western Brittany region of France. Henri de La Tour d'Auvergne, an officer during the Napoleon era, used the word "dolmin" in his writing in 1796. Later, dolmen became the standard spelling in France, replacing dolmin. British writers then followed suit and started using dolmen as well. Although the word dolmen originated from France, it is nevertheless intriguing that the pronunciation of the word sounds like the Korean word dolmeng-ee, meaning rock.

Figure 8-6 The entrance of the megalithic temple 'Hagar Qim' on the Gozo Island of the Republic of Malta / The temple, Hagar Qim (meaning standing stone) was built about 5,600 years ago.

Figure 8-7 Part of the megalithic temple "Imnadra" on Gozo Island of the Republic of Malta / The site is estimated to be from 5,600 years ago

03

The era of stone tombs

Koreans long ago used sizeable stones to build the tombs where they buried their dead. The Korean term dol-mu-deom, which directly translates to stone grave, comes from the Korean word "dol" for stone. There are many variations on this structure, each with its own name.

For example, a stone mound tomb (jeokseokchong) is the name for a burial method where stacks of rocks are placed on top of the body. A stone coffin tomb (seok-gwan-myo) is a structure built by digging into the ground to arrange stones into a box-like shape. Another type uses an outer stone coffin and an inner stone coffin. In this stone-lined tomb, the body is placed inside the inner stone coffin while accessories are placed in the outer stone coffin. The stone chamber tombs (seok-shil-myo) of the Four Kingdoms period (42-562 CE) were made famous by the Muyong-chong and Ssangyong-chong

Figure 8-8 Types of dolmen / By type, (left) the table type, (middle) the go-table type, (right) the unsupported capstone type

tombs of the Great Tomb of Gangseo (Goguryeo Dynasty). These have a stone chamber covered with a mixture of soil, charcoal, ashes, and rocks, which is then covered with an additional top layer of soil.

Stone tombs are a traditional burial method that was passed down from the Neolithic era of the Korean peninsula. Like stone coffin tombs, dolmens are a style of tomb typical of the Bronze Age elsewhere in the world, but Korean dolmens date from the Neolithic all the way to the Bronze and Iron Ages.

The oldest stone tombs were made by the Dongyi people, dating back to the Hongshan culture of the Gulf of Balhae civilization (about 4,700~2,900 BCE). These stone coffin tombs are the same type that is found on the Korean peninsula, dating back approximately 5,500 years. The dolmens, a more developed form of stone tomb, are widespread in the Yodong peninsula, Manchuria, and the Korean peninsula.

Dolmens can also be categorized based on shape. The three shapes are called the table type (tak-ja-shik), checkerboard type (ba-duk-pan-shik), and open chamber type (gae-seok-shik). Table dolmens have four aboveground stone pillars with a slab of stone to form the roof of the tomb; these are found throughout the Yodong peninsula all the way to Gochang in Jeollanam-do Province. Checkerboard dolmens are tombs dug into the earth with three to four pillars that

Figure 8-9 Single-chamber type dolmen located in Yongdam-dong, Jeju City

are mostly belowground, with the pillars supporting a capstone. Checkerboard dolmens are usually found south of the Han-gang River, which runs through Seoul. Lastly, the open chamber type has two different subtypes. One is an underground burial chamber dug into the earth with a capstone on top, while the other includes a stone coffin placed within the burial chamber.

Any discussion of Korean megalith culture is incomplete unless it includes the wi-seok dolmen, which is a type of dolmen unique to Jeju Island. These dolmens are constructed from a circle of several support stones topped by a capstone. While a wi-seok dolmen is exposed aboveground much like a table dolmen, a wi-seok dolmen also includes a number of support stones wedged together that block the view of the inner chamber.

Categorizing dolmens by structure over location

- In recent years, more table dolmens (also known as the northern type in Korea) have been found in Jeolla-do Province, a region south of the Han-gang River in South Korea. At the same time, more checkerboard dolmens (also known as the southern type) have also been found in North Korea. Given these discoveries, it makes more sense to differentiate Korean dolmens by their structural design, like the table or checkerboard type, rather than categorizing them based on location.

04

Ancient civilization as told by Korean dolmens

The dolmens found on Ganghwa Island and in Gochang County, Jeollabuk-do Province and Hwasun County, Jeollanam-do Province were recognized as valuable cultural remains back in 2000, when they were inscribed on the UNESCO World Heritage site list. Of all the dolmens in the world, dolmen sites in Korea are noted for their unparalleled density and variety of dolmens, characteristics that earned them a place on the UNESCO list. The way these dolmens dot the land in Korea is certainly an incredible sight to behold.

The Hwasun ruins alone number approximately 13,000 dolmens, the highest concentration of dolmens anywhere in the world. The number of dolmens is not the only impressive feature, however—there are dozens of checkerboard dolmens that weigh more than 100 metric tons each. The dolmen found in the village of Ungok-ri in Gochang County is the biggest in Korea, its capstone weighing 297 tons and standing at a height of four meters. It is hard to even imagine the number of people that would have been needed to move these massive stones. In the modern era, Korean people in Jindo tried to recreate the scene by constructing their own dolmen with a rock that weighed 6.8 metric tons. The effort took 73 people. How many people would it have taken to move the dolmen in the village of Ungok-ri? Several thousand? Constructing a dolmen of this size would have been impossible without a systematically organized, structured society.

The word dolmen makes most people think of prehistoric times, but it also tends to lead to the mistaken assumption that the people who built dolmens were uncivilized human beings. Perhaps this is why many dolmen parks and museums tend to use imagery and descriptions that portray the builders as primitive people wearing crude clothing. The builders of the dolmens are described not as members of a systematic society but as a primitive community of just a few dozen people living in groups.

But the societies that made these dolmens were far from uncivilized: They had the technology to cut and shave massive rocks. The stones that form the dolmens that they left behind were not natural stones, and so they had to develop a variety of techniques, like methods for cutting a certain size of rock from a much bigger one, or for shaping the pillar or supporting rocks to fit a capstone by cutting and drilling the stone.

Another example can be found in the step pyramid of the Niuheliang ruins left behind by the Hongshan culture, which was established by Korea's ancestral Dongyi people around the time the dolmens were built. The Niuheliang step pyramid stands 100 meters tall—a total of seven floors, which might not sound very high in the modern era. But in its time, it would have been an architectural marvel—like a skyscraper. These dolmen- and pyramid-building ancestors were a civilized people who had markedly scientific methods of

Figure 8-10 The dolmens of Osang-ri, Ganghwa-do Island / 12 dolmens are gathered in a group and the finishing stones are preserved intact. Comb-pattern pottery pieces from the Neolithic Age and stone arrowheads and stone swords from the Bronze Age were excavated from this site

Figure 8-11 The dolmen of Gochang, Jeollabuk-do Province/top plate weighs 150 tons and is located just below a quarry.

stone-working and the technology and community organization to move even something as heavy and unwieldy as a 100-ton stone. Recent attempts to recreate these efforts have shown that it is extraordinarily challenging to move stones of this size even with heavy-duty equipment.

Cutting a stone that is roughly the size of a small house from an even bigger rock requires anywhere from several days to several weeks just to work the stone, and hundreds—if not thousands of workers—to move it a few meters. The stones used for dolmens were moved dozens of meters from their original locations; many were moved several hundred. Who could succeed at this kind of project if not a leader capable of coordinating thousands of physically-fit men? The fact that these societies made the dolmens means that they were already organized into different classes, such as a ruling class and a working class. Society had to have been sufficiently stable to allow a leader to dedicate several thousand men to a single project.

The Hongshan cultural region, Ancient Joseon, and regions like Ganghwa, Sooncheon, and Gochang were populated by this ancient civilization. Dolmens are generally found near sunny rivers, river banks, flat coastal regions, mountain ridges, and ravines; the stone tombs from Hongshan culture are no exception to this, commonly sitting along sunny and warm coastal areas or rivers. These locations meet the requisites for an agricultural society as well as the conditions necessary for early civilization. People settled in places made livable by natural environments that were conducive to agriculture, which enabled them to develop civilization.

Dolmens in the village of Daesin-li in Hwasun County were discovered to contain stone tools, red earthenware, and patternless earthenware. A piece of charcoal found with these artifacts was confirmed by carbon dating to be from 4,500 years ago. Sarah Nelson, an American archaeologist who studied artifacts found in dolmens in Yangsu-ri

Village in Gyeonggi-do Province, estimated that these dolmens were created about 4,260 to 4,680 years ago. Examinations of various dolmens like these show that they correspond to a time period ranging from Baedal (3,897-2,333 BCE) to Ancient Joseon.

Dolmen ruins found on the two islands of Joongdo in Gangwon-do Province also revealed the sites of ancient houses, with around 1,400 Bronze Age artifacts that included an Ancient Joseon bronze dagger and a bronze axe. The finding of 101 dolmens and about 900 residential sites, along with valuable artifacts, garnered significant interest in academic circles.

But there was a catch to this excitement. These cultural assets were discovered on land slated for commercial development as a LEGOLAND theme park. Gangwon-do Province originally took the stance that these cultural assets would be moved elsewhere, but after a slow start, the government, the province of Gangwon-do, historical societies, and civic organizations began working together to find a solution to better preserve this cultural treasure. Building a theme park is a natural boost to the local economy, but why not build a one-of-a-kind dolmen culture park? It might be able to attract even more people than yet another theme park would, especially as international tourists continue to demonstrate a great deal of interest in Korea's dolmens. There are better ways to develop the regional economy while keeping Korea's cultural tradition alive.

05

The mystery of the Seven Stars on dolmen capstones

Many Korean dolmens are particularly unique in that they are inscribed with the oldest depictions of constellations in the world. It is not just one or two Korean dolmens that have these constellations. There are approximately 300 dolmens with constellations carved into their capstones in South Korea alone. Dozens of these dolmens feature the Seven Stars of the Northern Dipper, while still more include carvings with the constellations of the Six Southern Stars, Myo, and the Northern Crown. These dolmens with carved constellations tell the story of a highly civilized people whose tradition of observing the cosmos stretches back into antiquity.

The capstone of the dolmen found in the village of Yongdeok-ri in Jeungsan County, Pyeongannam-do Province (North Korea) has a pattern of 80 holes that represent a constellation from 4,900 years ago. Prior to the discovery of this dolmen's constellation, another constellation found on a Babylonian border-marking stone from 3,200 years ago in ancient Mesopotamia was believed to be the oldest of its kind. Also in North Korea, another dolmen capstone with 80 holes dating back 5,000 years was found in Sang-gun County, Pyeongyang. This capstone is caeved with the Seven Stars of the Northern Dipper along with many other constellations. A similarly carved slab of stone from a dolmen located in the village of Ahdeuk-ee in Cheongwon County, Chungcheongbuk-do Province was examined by a variety of experts including South Korean astrophysicist Park Changbeom. They concluded that it was a depiction of constellations that were visible in the ancient night sky.

As explained in the chapter on the cheon-sang-yul-cha-bun-ya-ji-do, scientists have used computer simulations to compare fifth-century BCE Polaris and its surrounding stars with the constellations found on the dolmen in the village of Jiseok-ri, located in Yichun City, Gyeong-gi-do Province (fifteenth century BCE) and in Goguryeo burial mound No. 4 in Jinpa Village (sixth century CE). All were found to be accurate. This means that several thousand years ago, ancient Korean societies were accurately recording cosmic movements.

Why, then, did they carve these accurate movements of the stars on dolmens?
Korean people long ago thought that they were granted their heavenly souls by one of the stars in the Seven Stars of the Northern Dipper. This belief left a linguistic and cultural mark that can still be seen today in modern Korea, where the phrase, "they went back," or "they returned," is used when people pass away. The phrase is significant because it means that when a person dies, they are going back to where they came from: the stars. This is because Korean tradition holds that the human world, the afterworld, and the heavenly realm are all connected.

This is the reason behind numerous Korean traditions associated with the Seven Stars of the Northern Dipper. Though it is more common to be cremated these days, in the past, Koreans used to carve seven holes into a wooden board, each hole representing one of the Seven Stars; this board was placed beneath the body of someone who had passed away. The body would then be tied seven times with hemp.

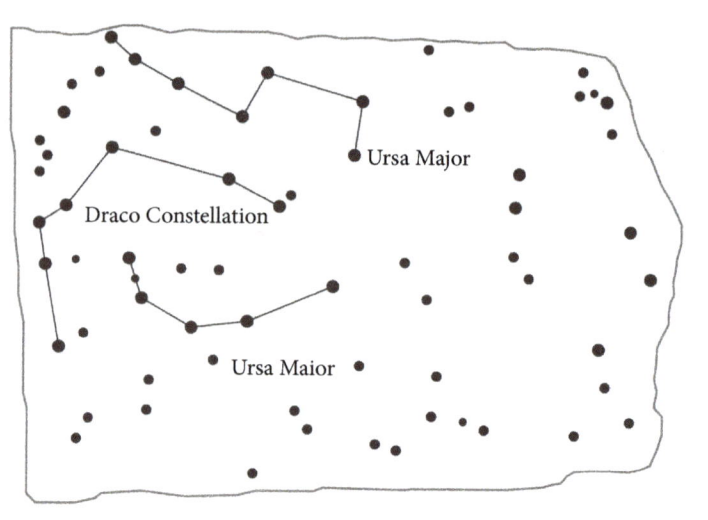

Figure 8-12 A replica of stone plates with constellations unearthed from the A-deuk-ee dolmen site of Cheongwon-gun county, Chungcheongbuk-do Province

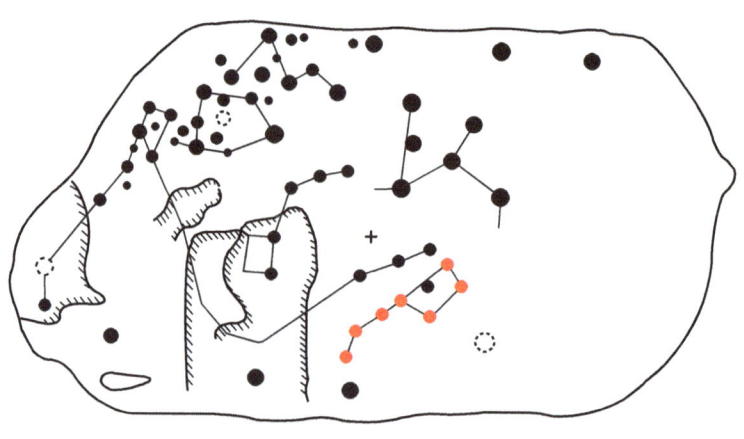

Figure 8-13 A replica of constellations on the dolmen in Jiseok-ri, Hamju-gun, Hamgyeongnam-do Province. / Depicts the celestial body with countless small stars along with the Big Dipper, Little Bear, Cassiopeia, and Cepheus that appeared in the Korean sky about 3,500 years ago.

Mourners used the term "yeom," which means to clean and shroud a corpse, saying it seven times to send the deceased back to the Seven Stars. Essentially, the dolmens with carved Seven Stars can be interpreted as performing the same function as the wooden board with seven holes. The purpose of carving the Seven Stars of the Northern Dipper on their dolmens was to return their deceased back to the stars from which they had come.

The cosmology associated with the Seven Stars is connected to the traditional Korean perspective on religion. Beginning thousands of years ago, Koreans believed that the Seven Stars were the place from which the Jade Emperor ruled the universe and that the Seven Stars served as his chariot. The constellation of the Seven Stars came to be seen as an object of worship because it was viewed as the seat of governance for the ruler of the universe.

The tradition of engraving tombs with constellations continued down through generations of Korean civilization, appearing in places like the Goguryeo tomb murals, which also depict the Seven Stars of the Northern Dipper. These astronomical observations were passed down through Ancient Joseon, continuing during the period of the Three Kingdoms and throughout Goguryeo, Goryeo, and of course, Joseon. As described previously*, the Seven Stars are also famously found in the cheon-sang-yeol-cha-bun-ya-ji-do.

Dolmens are not the remnants of uncivilized times. Dolmens are remnants of an impressive heritage handed down from the people who established a proud civilization thousands of years ago. The sheer number of dolmens concentrated in Korea tells us that the Korean peninsula was inhabited by such a society, and the 40,000 dolmens that mark the land from the northernmost end of the Korean peninsula to the farthest tip of Jeju Island are evidence of this proud and lengthy history.

---

* Seven Stars of the Northern Big Dipper - Read more in Ch. 5 Mapping the Cosmos with Cheon-sang-yeol-cha-bun-ya-ji-doh. Sect.C

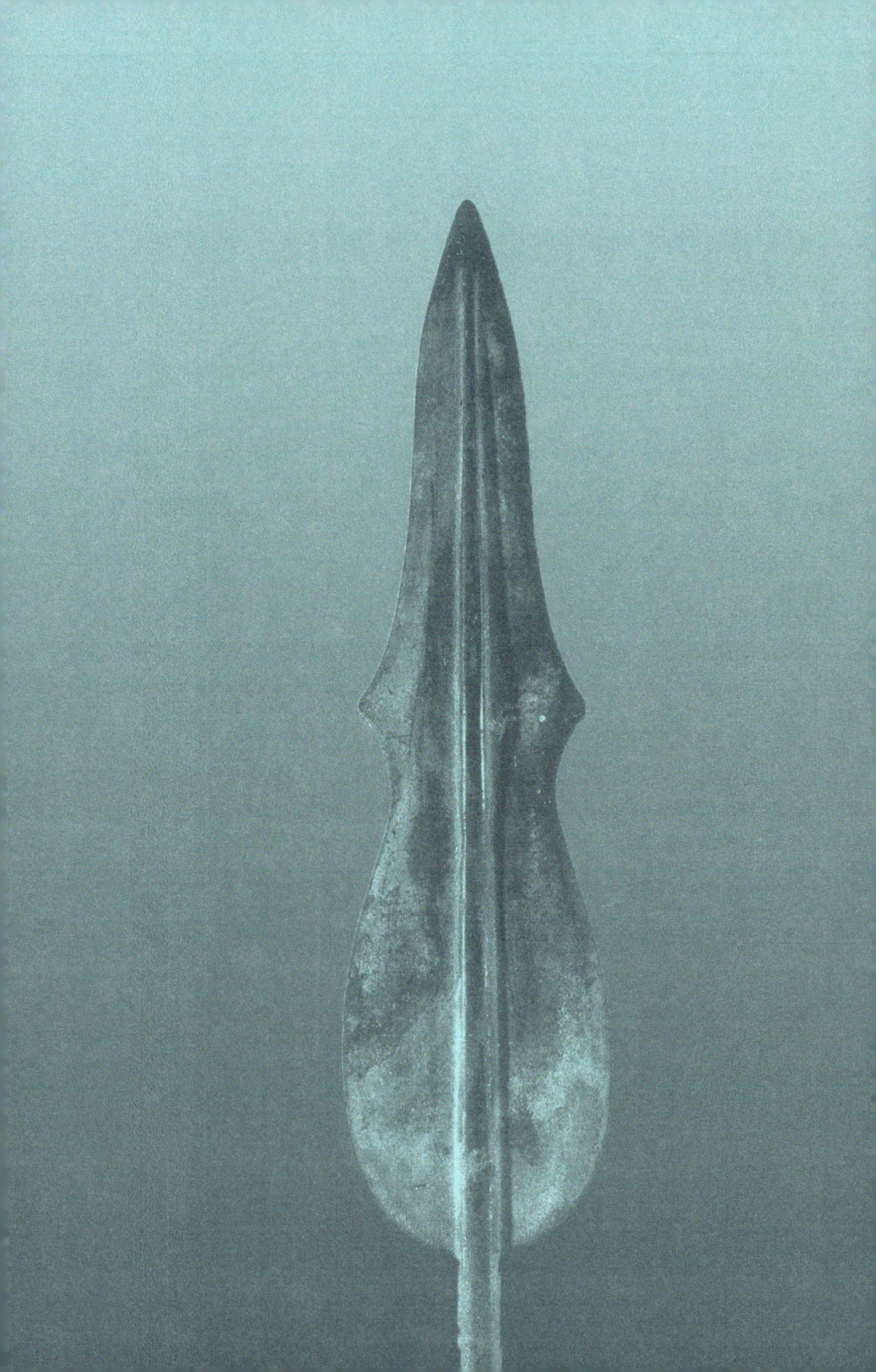

A Trip to the Museums in Korea

A design of flame, the bronze daggar

01 The Bronze Age: antiquity's Industrial Revolution
02 The Ancient Joseon bronze dagger that predates the mandolin-shaped dagger
03 Discoveries from the territories of the Dongyi people
04 The flame of the Ancient Joseon bronze dagger
05 A beautiful and lethal weapon for active combat
06 The ingenious design of the ssembly-type dagger
07 Ancient Joseon bronzeware's copper, tin, and zinc alloys
08 Lightning, symbol of the divine

01

The Bronze Age: antiquity's Industrial Revolution

If the invention of earthenware brought forth the revolution of the Stone Age, the invention of bronze tools was the Industrial Revolution of the prehistoric era. After this, humankind began to progress rapidly, writing the next chapter of history faster than ever before. A Greek poet named Hesiod addressed humankind's development 2,700 years ago, when he was the first to write about the lineage of the Greek gods in the epic poem *Theogony*, which depicts the famous tale of Prometheus and Pandora. He also penned a poem on the morality of labor called *Works and Days*. Hesiod divided world history into five periods or five tribes known as the Golden Age (Golden tribe), Silver Age (Silver tribe), Bronze Age (Bronze tribe), Age of Heroes (Hero tribe), and the Iron Age (Iron tribe). According to him, human beings once lived together with the gods without disease or worry, but after Pandora opened a box given by Zeus, human beings began to face more difficulties that increased not just in number, but

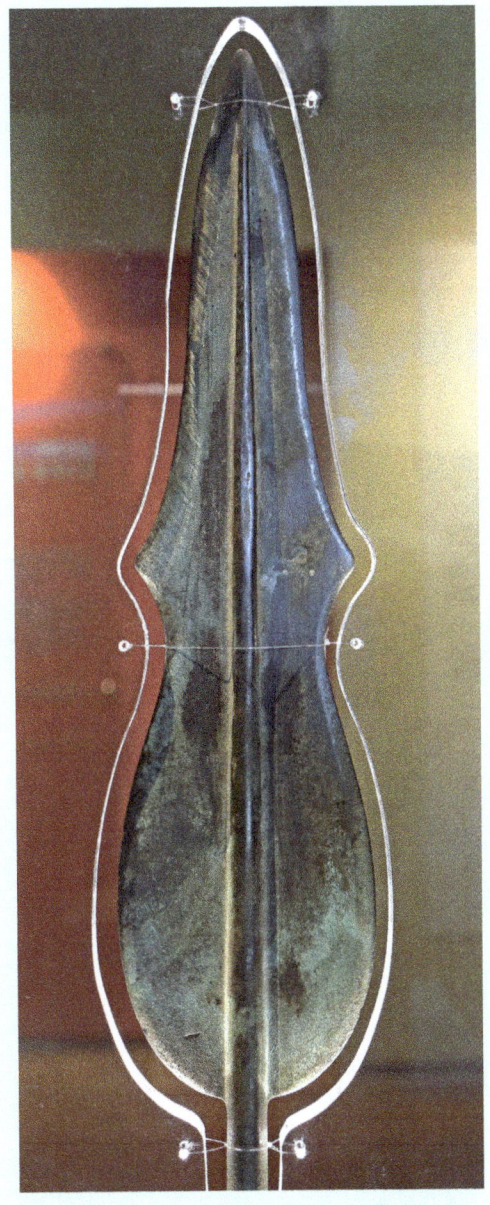

Figure 9-1 The Gojoseon type bronze daggar (madoline type) on display at the Gyeongju National Museum.

in scale.

Hesiod also wrote that, of the Five Ages, the people of the Bronze Age came to power with weapons made of bronze because they were interested in brutal acts and violence like Ares, the Greek god of war.

Ancient Greece was not alone in the effect that bronze had on society. In places around the world, bronze weapons altered the course of history and ushered in a new era. The Bronze Age was a period of nonstop development of weapons for survival and abundance, a time of advanced skills and warfare.

This version of the Bronze Age is true in East Asia as well, where the Bronze Age people who resided in the Gulf of Balhae, Inner Mongolia, Manchuria, and the Korean peninsula left behind helmets, chest armor, axes, spears, swords, and many other weapons. The story of Korean civilization's development of bronze weapons in particular begins with the mandolin-shaped bronze dagger and extends to the slender bronze dagger. The mandolin-shaped bronze dagger, sometimes also referred to as the Liaoning bronze dagger, is a weapon that has come to epitomize the Bronze Age, while the slender bronze dagger is notable for figuring heavily from the late Bronze Age to the early Iron Age.

Figure 9-2 Tools of the Scythian warriors from 4th Century BCE / The emergence of Scythians, the horse-riding people, in Europe was around the 7th century BCE. They were based in modern day Ukraine and the Crimean Peninsula, just north of the Black Sea. (National Museum of the History in Ukraine)

02

The Ancient Joseon bronze dagger that predates the mandolin-shaped dagger

Past the prehistoric era exhibits in the National Central Museum of Korea in Seoul lies the Ancient Joseon display and its trove of Bronze Age artifacts. Even among these many relics, the mandolin-shaped bronze dagger is particularly eye-catching. The weapon's shape invokes the shape of the mandolin, a Chinese musical instrument, which is how the dagger's modern name came to be. But Chinese mandolins did not yet exist when these daggers were produced and widely used, which means that the mandolin-shaped dagger predates its current namesake. More precise scholars refer to this dagger as the Manchurian dagger, Liaoning dagger, or Liaoning curved dagger instead. This is because it has curved edges and is mostly found in the Liaoning area of Manchuria. Another apt name for this weapon is the Ancient Joseon dagger, because it is the artifact that has come to represent Ancient Joseon (2,333-239 BCE).

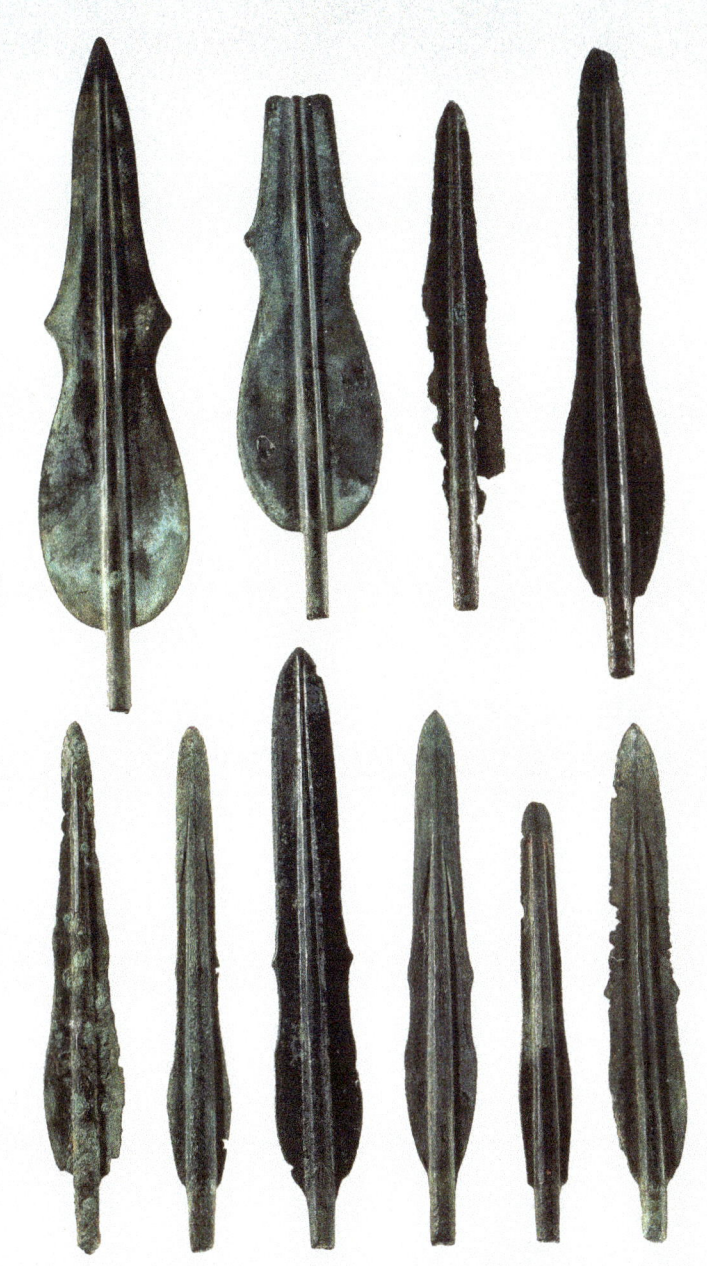

Figure 9-3 Gojoseon type (mandoline type) Bronze daggar (National Museum of Korea)

Korean textbooks and many museums refer to the slender bronze dagger, which arrived after the so-called mandolin-shaped bronze dagger, as the Korean-style bronze dagger. This is because it is fashioned in a style that is almost exclusively found within the boundaries of the Korean peninsula. Regrettably, the nomenclature of the mandolin-shaped dagger leaves a strong but mistaken impression that the origin of the mandolin-shaped bronze dagger has nothing to do with Korea.

Why have scholars not yet standardized it as the Ancient Joseon bronze dagger instead? Associating the mandolin with a dagger that predates the instrument by centuries seems unfair to the weapon. This sentiment has been reflected in a recent movement to name this historically significant bronze weapon after Ancient Joseon. It is important to note that this dagger has been commonly excavated in regions that were formerly Ancient Joseon territory, such as the Korean peninsula, making it not just an artifact of Ancient Joseon, but an emblem. Accordingly, this book will refer to the mandolin-shaped bronze dagger as the Ancient Joseon bronze dagger.

03

Discoveries from the territories of the Dongyi people

Ancient Joseon bronze daggers have been found in a region that ranges from the shores of what formed the Gulf of Balhae to the southernmost reaches of South Korea. This type of dagger has been found along with bronze mirrors in stone tombs like the dolmens.

Bronze daggers in general have been found throughout the Eurasian continent, and they are exhibited in a long list of museums: Natural History Museum of Vienna, Austria (NaturhistorischesMuseum Wien); Hungarian National Museum (Magyar Nemzeti Múzeum); National Museum of the History Ukraine, Kiev, Ukraine; The Hermitage Museum in St. Petersburg, Russia; State Historical Museum, Red Square of Moscow; Museum of History Kazan University, Russia; Siberian Branch of the Russian Academy of Science; Far East State Technical University Museum, Vladivostok; Kazakhstan; Uzbekistan; Tehran National Archaeological Museum in Iran. But the Ancient Joseon style of bronze dagger is found nowhere else but in the former territories of the Dongyi people. Comparisons can be made to the bronze dagger exhibited in the Hungarian National Museum and the bronze spear in the Moravian Museum in Brno, Czech Republic, but there are still clear distinctions that will be addressed later in this book. This section focuses on the fact that no Ancient Joseon bronze dagger has been found south of the Great Wall of China, in Siberia, or in Central Asia.

The Ancient Joseon bronze dagger boasts a design unique even among its peers. The edges of the blade exhibit smooth curves, flaring at the middle. The central stem that functions as the spine or core of the weapon is called the deungbae. Even from a modern standpoint, the design is aesthetically pleasing. Ancient daggers discovered from the remains of other civilizations are usually formed with straight blades, and none are stylized with the exact same design as the Ancient Joseon bronze dagger.

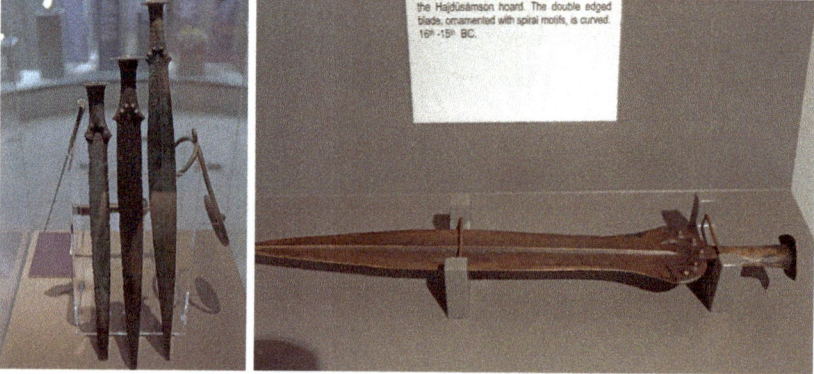

Figure 9-4 (left) The bronze sword displayed at the National Museum of Hungary, (right) Also known as the double curved sword, it is somewhat similar to the Gojoseon type.

Figure 9-5 Bronze spear on display at the Moravian Museum in Bruno, the second largest city in the Czech Republic/ The tip of the spear is similar to the Gojoseon type bronze sword.

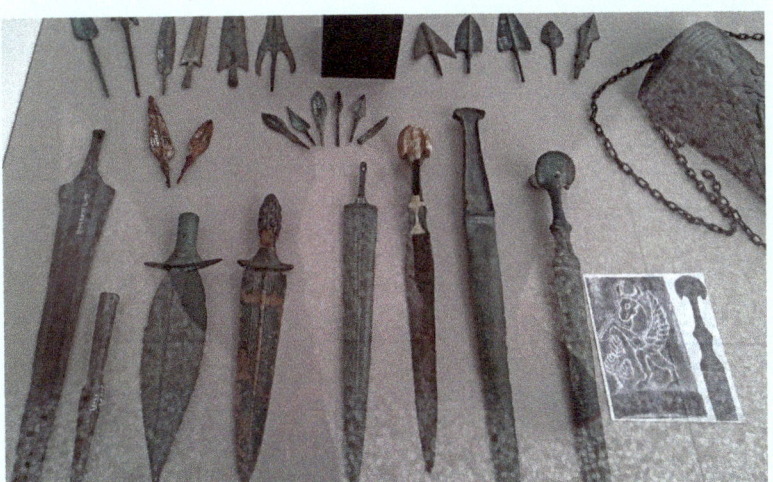

Figure 9-6 Various bronze daggers on display at the National Museum of Archaeology in Tehran, the capital city of Iran.

How was such a unique design for this ancient bronze dagger developed? Clues to this unsolved mystery were revealed in the 1980s when a jade dagger was excavated from Hongshan culture ruins—the Niuheliang ruins in Inner Mongolia (Inner Mongolia Autonomous Region of northern China). This jade dagger was made 5,500 years ago, and its design looked curiously like an Ancient Joseon bronze dagger. The jade dagger was not discovered alone; it was accompanied by a bronze dagger that seemed like an early predecessor of the Ancient Joseon bronze dagger. This bronze dagger was strikingly similar to verified Ancient Joseon bronze daggers that were already on display in Korean museums. The sole exception to the similarities was that this predecessor lacked its successors' unique flared edges.

The discovery of this earlier Ancient Joseon bronze dagger and its complementary jade dagger in the Hongshan culture ruins — ruins from the time and territory of the Dongyi people — was crucial because it confirmed that the Ancient Joseon bronze dagger was indeed a traditional design of the Korean people.

04

The flame of the Ancient Joseon bronze dagger

Now that we understand the relationship between the Ancient Joseon people and the origin and design of the Ancient Joseon bronze dagger, it is time to explore why they developed this unique design. Keimyung University (Daegu, South Korea) professor Kim Yangdong addresses this in *Original Symbols and Explanations of Ancient Korea*.

Kim explains that the people who once wielded the Ancient Joseon bronze dagger were sun worshipping descendants of the ancient Dongyi people. The Dongyi people heavily influenced northern nomad culture and came to be symbolized by fire, another symbol for the sun. This symbolism alluded to their divine right: the right to rule. This is why sun and flame motifs were used for their clothing and tools. The flame-like shape of the Ancient Joseon bronze dagger is therefore a reference to sun worship. It was used to evoke divine power in rituals and ceremonies and represent the authority of the ruler. In his book, Professor Kim suggests that the Ancient Joseon bronze dagger should be called the bronze flame spirit dagger. He also describes how the jade dagger found in the Hongshan culture ruins in Niuheliang was crafted in the same symbolic flame shape.

The ancient Korean people lived according to the traditional values of Gwang Myeong Ee Se (ruling the world with light), Je Seh Ee Hwa (enlightening the people to observe and govern the world with truth), and Hong Ik In Gan (widely benefiting the world). It stands to reason that they also would have shaped their weapons according to their worldview. You can see the Ancient Joseon bronze daggers that were birthed from these ideologies for yourself in museums throughout South Korea.

05

A beautiful and lethal weapon for active combat

The Ancient Joseon bronze dagger has elegant curves from the tip of its blade down to the top of its handle, a beautiful design that led to the misinterpretation that this was not a weapon made for active combat. Many scholars concluded that the Ancient Joseon bronze dagger was used only in ceremonies, ancestral rites, or as a votive offering (an artifact intentionally buried with the deceased). This theory was incorrect.

that was used in real combat. When scholars more closely examined its design, they found all the markers of an active combat weapon.

Perhaps most obvious characteristic to note is that the entire length of the dagger is bladed, with the small exception of its handle. The furrow on its edge is also called the blood groove or blood gutter, a name that comes from the theory that muscles tighten when stabbed,

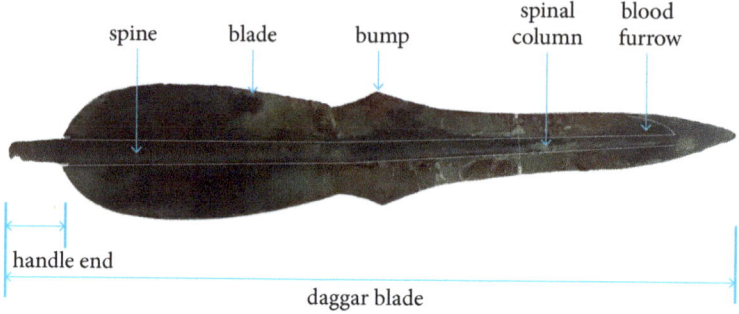

Figure 9-7 The shape and names of each part of the Gojoseon type bronze dagger

making it hard to pull the dagger free. The blood groove allowed blood flow to ease the withdrawal of the blade. The deungbae, or core of the blade, is also designed in this way.

The flared edges at the midpoint of the blade serve multiple functions. The blade would wear down from frequent battles, leaving the edges dull, so the twin protrusions of the blade helped by enlarging the wounds inflicted by the dagger. This made even attacks with a dulled blade more efficient.

There was also the problem of what happened when two blades collided during a fight. In this situation, the protrusions helped by "catching" the enemy's blade, reducing the chance of the enemy's weapon slipping down the blade of the bronze dagger to injure the wielder unexpectedly. This design arrested the enemy's weapon much in the same way that the guard on the top of a sword's hilt was designed to protect its wielder. Later versions of the bronze dagger developed a sword guard that replaced these protrusions. Both were designed to protect the wielder's hand.

Compared to bronze daggers found in other parts of the world, the Ancient Joseon bronze dagger has a relatively short tang, which is part of the handle side of the dagger. This short tang was one of the reasons it was mistaken as a dagger used only for stabbing. However, when we examine the handle of the assembled dagger and the part that connects to the blade, it becomes clear that the handle extends into the curved part of the lower portion of the blade. There, the part at the end of the tang and the end of the handle are fixed tightly together with an iron wire. It is easy to dismiss the short tang as impractical if we only consider the blade and tang, but pressure can be safely applied from different angles when the dagger is fully assembled with its handle. This combination made it easy to stab and cut with the dagger.

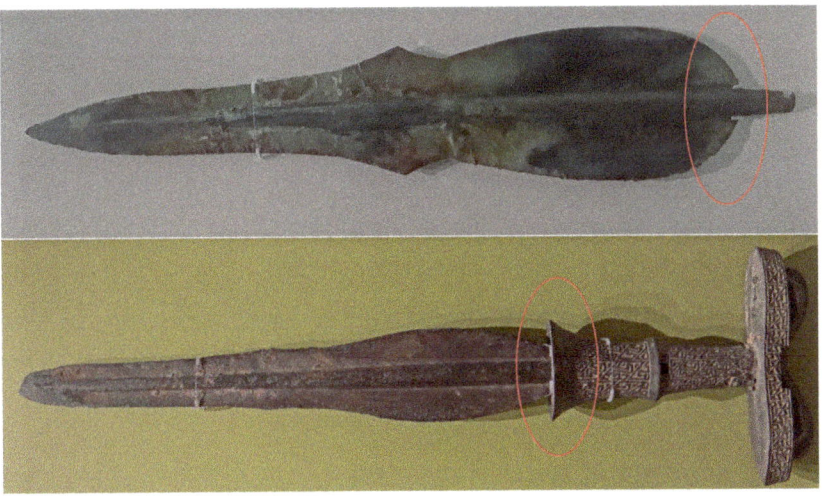

Figure 9-8 (Top) Seumbae part of the bronze daggar before assembling with the handle (Bottom) Body and handle of the daggar after assembly (National Museum of Korea)

Together, the blade and the handle make it clear that the Ancient Joseon bronze dagger was designed meticulously with the wielder in mind. For example, if you were to stab your target too fiercely with a weapon like a dagger, the force of the impact would normally cause your hand to slip, injuring you. The blade of the Ancient Joseon bronze dagger flares out in a bell-like shape to prevent this from happening.

Another piece of evidence that the dagger was a combat weapon is the ga-joong-seok stone. The ga-joong-seok stone looks like a hammer at the end of the handle. It served multiple purposes, such as helping to exert more force when stabbing an opponent. The end of the handle was also thicker to help brace the hand when pulling the blade from a target. Last but not least, the ga-joong-seok stone could have been used as a blunt weapon, allowing a fighter to strike their opponent with this stone even when they were too close to swing their weapon freely.

The dimensions of the bronze dagger have been another cause for debate as to whether it was a combat weapon. But these arguments are like saying that the rifles carried by soldiers marching in ceremonial exercises are not fit for use in battle. Weaponry experts and those who actively practice the art of sword fighting say that the length and width of the Ancient Joseon bronze dagger would suffice to inflict a large wound in actual combat. There are also bronze daggers found in Eastern Europe, Rome, Central Asia, Siberia, and Inner Mongolia's Ordos that are shorter than the Ancient Joseon dagger. Daggers like these were extremely useful during the Bronze Age as well as the Iron Age—they were not merely decoration.

While longer weapons offered certain advantages in battle, they also worked against their wielders. A long weapon was useful for attacking from a distance during an initial clash with an opponent. But once fighters were tangled in close combat, the advantages of a long weapon became all but obsolete.

Terrain and training also played an important role. In a thick forest or a tight space, shorter weapons had the upper hand. A soldier who spent a significant amount of time training with a long spear might have found a smaller weapon difficult to use, but for a person who spent that same time training in martial arts with small daggers, a bronze dagger 20 to 40 centimeters in length was an ideal weapon. In fact, the mighty military of the Roman Empire was predominantly composed of foot soldiers who wielded short swords. We can infer from this that the bronze dagger was probably quite efficient in close combat.

The metal itself is another important element. The assumption that bronze would not have been used to make a weapon for battle because it is a soft metal is flawed. In fact, it was disproved by two masters—one of smithing, and the other of swordcraft. First, Master Blacksmith Yi Wan-gyu, the Living Human Treasure (a special designation by the South Korean government for people with a skillset considered an intangible cultural asset) who restored the Da-nyu-she-moon-gyeong bronze mirror, restored an Ancient Joseon bronze dagger in Yeosu, Jeollanam-do Province. Then, Master Ahn Pyeong-no, an expert in Joseon-style swordcraft, performed a "test cutting" demonstration where he sliced through bamboo and straw bundles with the dagger that Master Yi had restored. This type of demonstration is traditionally used to show not just a person's skill and technique, but the superiority of various weapons. The bamboo was cut cleanly, and when Master Ahn performed a series of consecutive slices on a straw bundle, he reported that he felt no impact to his hand. These consecutive cuts are difficult to perform with an average weapon because the hand has to absorb the impact of each blow. The test affirmed that the bronze dagger was a weapon in its own right, even compared to an iron sword.

The bronze alloy that was used to make a typical Ancient Joseon dagger generally contained approximately 10 to 20 percent tin, proportions similar to the bronze weapons of ancient Greece that were lauded thousands of years ago by Greek poets. It seems likely that the bronze daggers of Ancient Joseon were just as fierce and powerful as the bronze weapons of Greece long ago.

06

The ingenious design of the assembly-type dagger

  The Ancient Joseon bronze dagger was all the more unique among its rivals on the battlefield because it was designed to be assembled from multiple parts. In contrast, integral-type daggers were made as a single piece of metal, with no parts that could be attached or removed. The assembly-type design was particularly useful when part of the dagger became worn or degraded from frequent combat. Weapons would become dull, or they might chip, bend, or even break. Once damaged, an integral-type dagger was useless, but an assembly-type dagger could be used again after the damaged components were replaced. Thanks to this innovation, the assembly-type Ancient Joseon bronze dagger was a practical weapon.
  For example, a damaged blade could be removed and the handle and pommel fixed to a new blade, making weapon upkeep cheaper and easier. During times of peace, blades could be prepared in advance for future battles. Blades could also be changed quickly in the

Figure 9-9 The bronze sword known as the Dossigeom originating from the Spring and Autumn Period of China, currently housed in the National Museum of Korea

immediate aftermath of a battle to prepare for the next fight. This practical production and usage shows that the people who designed the dagger drew on experience in the field of battle.

Most daggers from other societies are integral types. The Dossi sword, which is a type of bronze dagger that was made by a man named Dossi during China's Warring States Period (475-221BCE), is one such weapon; its handle and the blade are formed from a single length of bronze. Likewise, the hilt and blade of the bronze dagger from Ordos (Inner Mongolia Autonomous Region in modern China; Ordos is a Mongolian word meaning "palaces") is also fashioned from a single piece of bronze.

If the theory that the Ancient Joseon bronze daggers were slated for sole use in ceremonies or as grave goods left in burial mounds, there would have been no need for them to be designed as practical assembly-type weapons. Making the dagger from a single piece of bronze (an integral-type weapon) would have been easier, and it might have allowed them to develop a more interesting design.

07

Ancient Joseon bronzeware's copper, tin, and zinc alloys

Bronze is an alloy generally composed of copper and tin. But many of Korea's traditional Bronze Age artifacts include a third component: zinc. The method of including zinc in bronze alloys reached China after the Han Dynasty (202 BCE-9 CE), before which Chinese civilization used an alloy of copper, tin, and lead. Likewise, the alloy used for bronzeware from neighboring Siberia also lacked zinc.

But why go to the trouble of adding zinc to a bronze alloy? Why use such an alloy to make bronzeware? The addition of zinc made heavily used tools less susceptible to wear and rust, so a bronze and zinc alloy was a suitable material for everyday tools and weapons in the Bronze Age. Without zinc, an alloy of copper and tin is softer and more malleable. But when copper, tin, and zinc are mixed, the resultant alloy is easier to cast, and the metal is dense and sturdy. It can be molded into different shapes or carved with symbols, and it resists rust even when exposed to seawater, which is why modern shipbuilders favor copper, zinc, and tin alloys when making ship parts. Like the shipbuilders of today, bronze smiths who lived thousands of years ago in Ancient Joseon skillfully adjusted the ratio of the metal alloys they used to make better and longer-lasting tools.

But the melting points of these materials are all different, which makes the use of this alloy in the Bronze Age all the more surprising. Zinc, copper, and tin melt at 419.5, 1,080, and 231.93 degrees Celsius respectively, and their boiling points are 907, 2,562, and 2,602 degrees Celsius respectively. It is exceptionally difficult to combine multiple metals with different melting and boiling points in the same alloy. A metal that reaches its boiling point could even vaporize. The melting point is further complicated by the ratio of the metals used in the alloy. It is amazing that the makers of bronzeware in Ancient Joseon understood these properties well enough to create complex metal tools. Although they lived several thousand years ago, these smiths knew how to carefully manipulate metals into an alloy that required a high level of skill and an intimate understanding of metallurgy.

Despite the common misperception that ancient China outpaced ancient Korea in terms of technology and other advancements, Korean bronzeware from the beginning of the Bronze Age shows that this was not necessarily the case. Nearly a thousand years after Koreans began to incorporate zinc into their bronzeware, the Han Dynasty started to create its own bronze alloy with zinc. The sixth book of the ancient Chinese text *The Rites of Zhou*, known as *Gogonggi*, lists the proportions of copper and tin used to make bronze tools and weapons, but zinc is never mentioned. This difference in Bronze Age production techniques produced a dagger in Ancient Joseon that was more resilient and powerful than its counterpart in China. The technique of adding zinc to the bronze alloy did eventually reach China, and it seems logical to look to Ancient Joseon as the source, given that it was an immediate neighbor that had already developed the necessary metallurgy.

The Rites of Zhou's Gogonggi

- *The Rites of Zhou* is a Confucian scripture from the Zhou Dynasty (1046-256 BCE) that is traditionally divided into six parts (Heaven, Earth, Spring, Summer, Autumn, and Winter). The original sixth part of Winter was lost, so *Gogonggi* was added in its stead during the Han Dynasty. *Gogonggi* is like an encyclopedia of ancient China, dealing with artisanship, production management, and city building. This book was referenced when the capital city of Hanyang (modern Seoul) was built after the Joseon Dynasty began in 1392.

08

Lightning, symbol of the divine

Even the handles of Ancient Joseon bronze daggers can tell us a fascinating story about Korean symbolism long ago, thanks to the detailed lightning motifs found on the handgrips of these weapons.

While symbols found on ancient artifacts and ruins naturally vary by country and culture, the early states of Korean civilization favored repeated symbols and geometric patterns and shapes in particular. As mentioned in previous chapters, these early states were Ancient Joseon, Buyeo, Goguryeo, Baekjae, Shilla, and Gaya.

Ancient artifact symbols and meanings

- Circle – Heaven, Sun, Male, Father, One, (Heaven one)
- Square – Land (including flowing water), Female, Mother, Two, (Earth two)
- Triangle – Nation, Humanity, People, Children, Three (Humanity three)

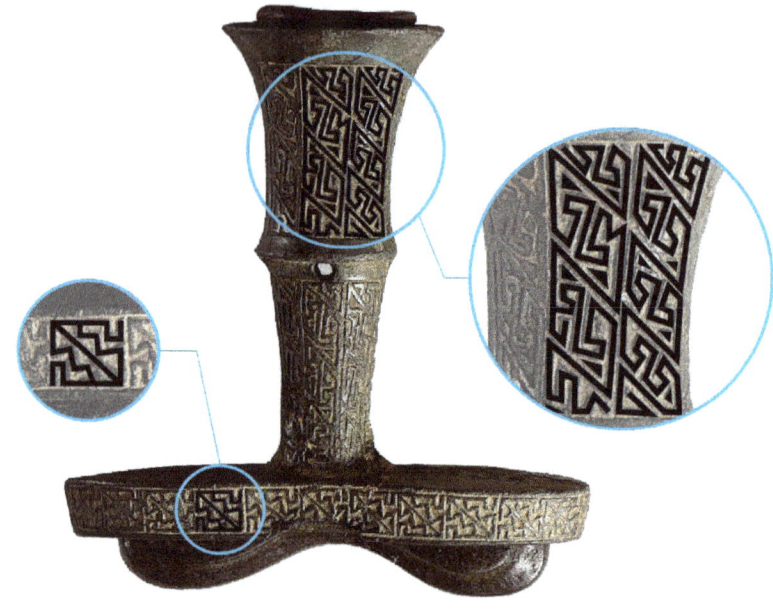

Figure 9-10 Handle of Gojoseon type bronze daggar engraved with lightning patterns(Ulsan Petroglyph Museum)

Types of symbols found on ancient artifacts and ruins

- Writings of heaven – features of the sky such as the sun, moon, stars, lightning, cloud, wind

- Writings of earth – features of the earth such as mountains, fields, rocks, sea waves, trees, animals, tools

- Writings of humanity – things related to human beings such as the face, hands, legs, body, writings, tools, houses

Figure 9-11 Pattern on the handle of mandolin shaped bronze daggar

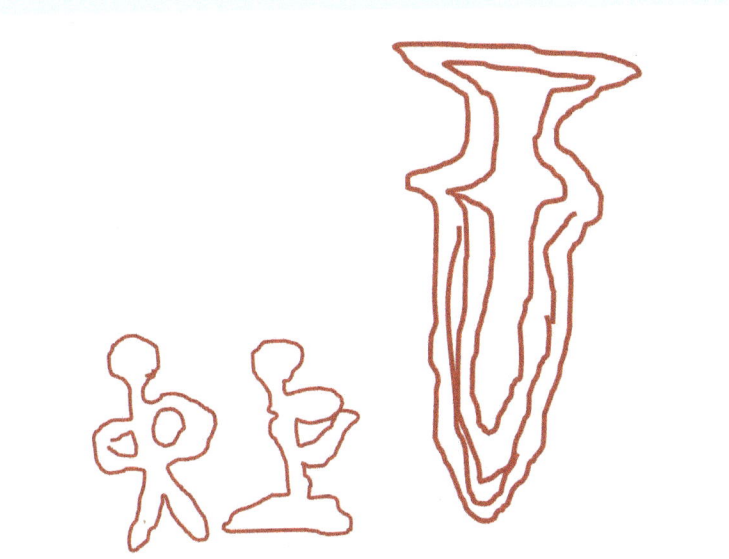

Figure 9-12 Replica of a person kneeling in front of a sword, carved on a stone plate of dolmen in Olim-dong, Yeosu, Jeollanam-do

But before we examine the meaning of lightning engraved on a bronze dagger, we must first understand the symbolism of the weapon itself. In ancient Korean society, daggers represented authority, one backed by a military force. An example of this can be seen in a special carving on the dolmen found in Ohrim Neighborhood in Yeosu, Jeollabuk-do Province, which depicts a stone dagger surrounded by people on their knees, gazing up at the weapon.

To understand why the Korean people of long ago would have put a lightning symbol on a bronze dagger that represented the authority to wield military power, we need to revisit the building blocks of ancient East Asia ideology: the Eight Trigrams. About 5,500 years ago, Taeho Bokhee (the ancestor of the Dongyi people) drew these trigrams, including the trigram Jin, which is symbolized by thunder and lightning. This is described in *I'Ching*, which explains that "Jin is thunder, lightning, dragon, and the appearance of the Heavenly Emperor in the Direction of the Dragon." In other words, lightning symbolizes the strong power (authority and military force) of the Heavenly Emperor. From this, we understand that the lightning on the handle of a bronze dagger was placed there to signify that the Heavenly Emperor had given the person who wielded the dagger the divine right to rule.

From this, we know that the bronze dagger of Ancient Joseon was not only used in battle as an effective and powerful weapon. It was also a symbol of the divine authority that the heavens gave to those in power. In many cases, a bronze dagger, bronze mirror, and bronze bell have been excavated alongside each other. This bronze trio represented the authority of the ruler, carrying the mandate of obeying the will of heaven and governing and nurturing the people. Amazingly, even now, thousands of years later, we still do not know how they possessed this scientific

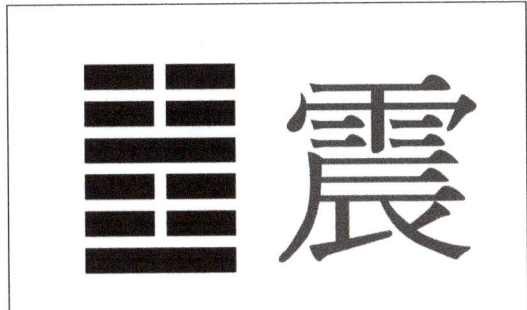

Figure 9-13 The 'Jin' trigram from the "Ten Wings (ten commentaries of Confucius)"

knowledge and technology to craft such high-quality daggers.

The bronze dagger in particular is culturally significant because it embodies the advanced technology, courage, and cultural heritage of its makers. It is also another piece of Korea's proud and storied heritage, proving that the country has earned its place in world history. The appreciation of symbolic and historical artifacts like the Ancient Joseon bronze dagger no doubt will continue to flourish throughout this generation and the generations to come.

Shattering Bronze Age stereotypes

The idea that the Bronze Age was when people began organizing themselves into states and that the Neolithic Age was a purely primitive era fails to capture the bigger picture. We cannot fully explain ancient history only by analyzing the metal tools used by people long ago. While it is a piece of the puzzle of human history, it cannot be used on its own to fully understand the politics, economies, societies, and ethos of an era.

The ancestors of modern Korea started paddy-field (irrigated) farming and dryland (non-irrigated) farming more than 5,000 years ago. They also had unique earthenware and the skills to weave and make textiles, so clothes were woven, not fashioned from animal skins. They built ships for organized whale hunting, coordinated a national system that was in charge of collecting, crafting, and distributing jade, and used an economic system that operated on currency. The organization of their structured society enabled them to move massive boulders to build dolmens—megalithic structures that are difficult to move even with today's heavy-duty equipment. Their Bronze Age society blazed a trail for East Asian culture.

Another type of Bronze Age artifact commonly excavated from Ancient Joseon ruins was a type of bronze ornamental button. A mold for making this sort of patterned bronze button was found in the dolmen ruins in the village of Yonggok-ri in Gangdong-gun County, Pyeongyang (North Korea). This discovery is significant because it means that bronze buttons were made in that region.

The Ancient Joseon bronze spear is another important Bronze Age artifact. Thanks to excavations of daggers, spears, and other artifacts like these, we know that Korea's ancestors were using bronze weaponry more than 4,500 years ago, predating even the establishment of the Ancient Joseon Dynasty.

The widespread use of a eurocentric standard for the Bronze Age has

Major Bronze Age discovery sites by time period

Time period	Dongyi people / Ancient Joseon	Neighboring nations/regions
6,500-4,500 years ago	-	Kavkaz (Caucasus) region of southern Russia. Bronze horse riding bit. Maykop Culture (bronze with arsenic alloy).
6,100-4,900 years ago	-	Uruk, a city state of Sumer, uses a bronze alloy containing tin.
5,500-5,000 years ago	Later Hongshan culture ruins, bronze coin, bronze mold found.	-
4,500 years ago (predates establishment of Ancient Joseon)	Dolmen No. 4 in Yonggok-ri Village, Gangdong-gun County, Pyeongyang (North Korea). Bronze buttons, Ancient Joseon-style spearhead found.	-
4,200 years ago	-	Bronze artifacts found in the Yellow River region. Bronze Age begins in China.
4,000 years ago (after establishment of Ancient Joseon)	Dolmen No. 5 in Yonggok-ri Village, Pyeongyang (North Korea). Ancient Joseon-style spear, bronze ornaments found in Chodo Village, Najin City, North Hamgyeong Province (North Korea).	-
3,400 years ago	Slender bronze dagger found in Seongcheon-gun County dolmen, South Pyeongan Province.	-
3,200 years ago	-	Bronze Age begins in Siberia's Karasuk culture.
3,100 years ago	-	Late Shang Dynasty. Bronze buttons excavated.

led to the common yet mistaken impression that Korea's Bronze Age also began 3,000 years ago. This is why most South Korean textbooks still teach this inaccurate classification, despite the many artifacts and excavation sites that prove Korean civilization developed bronzeware prior to the establishment of the Ancient Joseon Dynasty (2,333-239 BCE). In contrast, museums like the Natural History Museum in Vienna, Austria (Naturhistorisches Museum Wien) assert that the Bronze Age began 6,000 years ago.

PART 10

A Trip to the Museums in Korea

The unsolved questions about an ancient Corean bronze mirror, Danyu- Semungyeong, which is engraved with many fine lines that is virtually unreproducible with modern technology.

01 The taffy seller and the Danyu-semungyeong mirror
02 Ancient technology turned modern marvel:
   the mystery of the Danyu-semungyeong mirror
03 Symbolizing the sun and its brilliance
04 The divine representative becomes both shaman
   and warrior
05 The sophisticated metallurgy of ancient Korea's alloys
06 Bronze mirrors in Ancient Joseon and China
07 The bronze mirror and the eight bells

01

The taffy seller and the Danyu-semungyeong mirror

The National Museum of Korea in Seoul has a collection of excavated bronze mirrors typical of the Ancient Joseon era (2,333-239 BCE) in which they were made. These mirrors are embellished with such intricate patterns that it seems impossible to see your own reflection clearly on the marked bronze surface—at least, that is what many museum visitors think at first glance. Upon a closer look, you will discover that only the back of the mirror is patterned. The other side, which is patternless, was used for reflection.

Back then, there were no mirrors like the ones we use today, and glass was rarer than gold, so water was essentially the only way to see your own reflection. The bronze mirror was a game-changing tool that enabled people to see themselves properly for the first time. The reflective side of an Ancient Korean bronze mirror was made to be smooth, without any pattern, while the other side was usually engraved with geomet-

Figure 10-1 Da-nu-se-mun-gyeong Mirror unearthed from Nonsan, Chungcheongnam-do Province (Korean Christian Museum at Soongsil University)

ric patterns and designs. Bronze was a good material for this purpose because it is particularly reflective, especially when polished. Polished bronze can reflect distinct facial features clearly.

There are two types of Korean bronze mirrors: fine pattern mirrors and rough pattern mirrors. A fine pattern mirror has detailed engravings and is also referred to as a Danyu-semungyeong mirror. The word Danyu-semungyeong consists of "da," meaning many; "nyu," meaning loop; "semun," meaning detailed pattern; and "gyeong," which means mirror. The full translation of its name is therefore "an engraved mirror with a detailed pattern and two loops." As for the rough pattern mirror, which is referred to in Korean as a Danyu-jomungyeong mirror, the engravings are a rougher arrangement of thick patterns.

Given the production dates of these mirrors, it appears there was a change in artisanship from the making of the Danyu-jomungyeong mirrors to the Danyu-semungyeong mirrors. These artifacts were made during the Bronze Age (3,300-300 BCE) and into the Iron Age (1,200 BCE-586 CE).

A Danyu-semungyeong mirror of exceptional craftsmanship was discovered in the 1960s by South Korean soldiers digging a trench at the Nonsan military training camp in Chungcheongnam-do Province. The mirror was excavated along with a Paljuryeong, a type of bronze ring with eight branches that was used like a bell or rattle, and put on exhibit at the Korean Christian Museum at Soongsil University.* The Nonsan mirror is regarded as the most exquisite bronze mirror among those excavated so far.

In 1971, a Danyu-semungyeong mirror of the same production technique and form as the Nonsan bronze mirror was chanced upon at a private home located in Daegok-li Village in Jeollanam-do Province. While fixing a drain in the barn, the homeowner found an assortment of bluish metal objects jumbled together with a pile of stones . Without sparing much thought to them, the homeowner sold these strange bluish metal objects to a taffy seller. The taffy seller rightly guessed that there was something special about these pieces of metal and reported them to the provincial government. Experts evaluated the find and confirmed that the metal pieces were bronze relics from Ancient Joseon, and the relics were designated as National Treasures the following year. If not for the taffy seller's wisdom, these valuable relics might have been thrown away or melted as scrap metal. Instead, they have been preserved in a museum for future generations.

A follow-up investigation by the Cultural Heritage Administration

---

* Paljuryeong Read. Ch. 10. The Unsolved Mysteries of the Ancient Danyu-semungyeong Mirror Sect. 07 The bronze mirror and the eight bells

Figure 10-2 Bronze Age artifacts unearthed in Daegok-ri, Hwasun, Jeolla Proam-do Province / 2 bronze mirrors, 2 Paljuryeong, 2 Ssangduryeong, 3 Sehyung Bronze Dagger, 1 bronze axe, and 1 bronze carving tool (images provided by the National Museum of Korea)

Figure 10-3 Fine patterns of the Da-nu-se-mun-gyeong excavated from Daegok-ri, Hwasun, Jeollanam-do (a replica exhibited at the Hansung Baekje Museum)

revealed that the site where these relics were discovered was actually a stone mound-and-coffin tomb, and the 11 excavated artifacts included two Danyu-semungyeong bronze mirrors, two Paljuryeong bronze bells, and three slender bronze daggers. Another excavation took place at the same site in 2008, during which two more slender bronze daggers were discovered.

Bronze mirrors produced thousands of years ago are certainly not exclusive to Korea; they have also been excavated in many other countries around the world. However, Korea's Danyu-semungyeong bronze mirrors are worthy of special attention due to their refined and complicated engravings. The level of skill required to make such engravings is evidence enough that Koreans had possessed an unparalleled bronze production technique ages ago.

02

Ancient technology turned modern marvel: the mystery of the Danyu-semungyeong mirror

As explained in the previous section, the meaning of the Korean name for the Danyu-semungyeong mirror describes it as a type of mirror that has at least two rings and that is elaborately patterned. But even though a Danyu-semungyeong mirror was crafted thousands of years ago, it is engraved with geometric patterns so intricate that they cannot be replicated by modern technology.

The Danyu-semungyeong bronze mirror on exhibit in the Korean Christian Museum at Soongsil University has a diameter of only 21 centimeters, which is barely the size of a small dish. This tiny surface is covered with approximately 100 circles and 13,000 lines. Each line is 0.3 millimeters thick—roughly the thickness of a single human hair. Three lines side-by-side are a mere millimeter wide. This degree of precision is tricky to achieve even with the latest laser technology; how these intricate patterns were engraved by human hand more than 2,400 years ago remains a mystery.

At the very least, we do have well-supported theories about how the design was created, if not how it was engraved. It is hypothesized that molds of sand, mud, beeswax, or talcum were used. One of the most likely hypotheses is the sand mold.

In 2008, after the excavation of the Danyu-semungyeong bronze mirror in Nonsan, the Korean Christian Museum placed the artifact on display and announced a theory about its production method. It was hypothesized that fine sand had been used as a mold for the pattern, and molten metal poured into this mold. Researchers at the museum had discovered fine sand particles, believed to come from a mold, on the surface of the Danyu-semungyeong bronze mirror, which served as evidence for the sand mold hypothesis. But this met some resistance from other scholars because no matching mold for the Danyu-semungyeong bronze mirror has been found. This is why we still do not have a conclusive answer for how any of the Danyu-semungyeong bronze mirrors were produced. The only other clue is that the Paljuryeong that was excavated with this particular Danyu-semungyeong was produced around 2,400 years ago.

03

Symbolizing the sun and its brilliance

Before modern mirrors were invented, bronze mirrors were a useful way to see your own face. But bronze mirrors were not simply tools that people used to stare at their own reflections; the mirrors had important symbolic and ritual functions, too. This is evidenced by the fact that the excavation sites of bronze mirrors were tombs for leaders from the ruling class. In addition, we have learned that the bronze mirrors were made with such extraordinary skill that we have yet to replicate them with modern technology; clearly, these mirrors were not used for ordinary purposes. Bronze mirrors have been excavated from the Tomb of King Muryeong (426 - 523) of the Baekje Dynasty in Gongju, Chungcheongnam-do Province, and an ancient tomb of the Gaya confederacy in Namwon, Jeollanam-do Province, among other places.* Interestingly, for each discovery, the mirrors were located by the head of the body in the tomb. Scholars

---

* King Muryeong of Baekjae is also an ancestor of the Japanese Imperial line. Former Japanese Emperor Akihito publicly announced that he is a descendant of Baekjae's royal bloodline.

10 • The unsolved questions about an ancient Corean bronze mirror, Danyu- Semungyeong, which is engraved with many fine lines that is virtually unreproducible with modern technology.

Figure 10-4 Exquisite patterns of the Da-nu-se-mun-gyeong excavated from Cho-po-ri, Hampyeong, Jeollanam-do (National Museum of Korea)

believe that the bronze mirrors were placed to cover the faces of the entombed individuals.

The making of a bronze mirror, a quintessential artifact from Ancient Joseon, was no simple task. Copper is the main component of a bronze alloy, and its malleability makes it easy to shape into a tool. However, its malleability also makes it impractical to make tools out of pure copper, because they simply are not strong enough. This is why tin and copper were mixed in the right proportions to produce a new alloy: bronze. The existence of this refined yet solid bronze demonstrates that Koreans possessed an excellent technique for creating a copper and tin alloy. It is believed that only the highest-ranking members of the ruling class owned bronze mirrors due to the high level of skill required to produce them. But why were these bronze mirrors produced in the first place?

These bronze mirrors that reflected sunlight were apparently used to literally and figuratively to reflect the sun in the sky. Leaders hung bronze mirrors around their necks by threading strings through the rings on the mirror's back like a necklace. A bronze mirror hung this way would reflect bright light from its wearer's chest, serving as an emblem of a ruler empowered by the heavens.

The Korean people revered both the sun and light in general, and this reverence is embodied in their many relics and ruins as well as in a founding principle of Ancient Joseon. The principle of "Gwang Myeong Ee Se" means "ruling the world with light." Another example of this is inscribed on the Gwanggaeto Stele, an immense memorial tablet marking the tomb of the Great King Gwanggaeto of Goguryeo. The epitaph describes Jumong, the founder of Goguryeo, as Cheonjejija and Ilwoljija, which means that he was the "Son of the Light of the Sun and the Moon." In the same vein, leaders in ancient times displayed their elite status as representatives of heaven by wearing sun-brightened bronze mirrors on their chests.

10 • The unsolved questions about an ancient Corean bronze mirror, Danyu- Semungyeong, which is engraved with many fine lines that is virtually unreproducible with modern technology.

04

The divine representative becomes both shaman and warrior

Initially, bronze mirrors were exclusive to leaders in the highest echelons of society due to the considerable difficulties surrounding their production. But as bronze smelting techniques advanced, the use and ownership of bronze mirrors spread from the ruling class to other parts of society. This led to the diversification of the patterns used on the backs of bronze mirrors.

Today, historical reenactments and TV dramas continue to pay homage to the important role bronze mirrors played in ancient society, such as the Naadam Festival in Mongolia. Held annually in July, this is a traditional sports festival, with archery, wrestling, and equestrian competitions held throughout Mongolia. During the festival, Mongolians reenact the horsemanship of the Genghis Khan era in which riders hung metal discs on their chests.

In a recent South Korean TV historical drama, soldiers can be seen wearing bronze mirrors on their chests. This part of their warrior attire came about because bronze mirrors were passed down to soldiers to symbolize the Divine Army, or the Army of the Sun. These bronze mirror-bedecked soldiers galloped on horseback across vast plains just as the Huns, Gök Turks, Mongolians, and other nomadic horse-riding cultures also rode from the east of the Eurasian continent to the west, bronze mirrors flashing brightly from their chests.

Light reflected by a shining bronze surface travels farther than silver, which is why bronze mirrors were used to send signals to allies and to distract the enemy on the battlefield. Imagine the mighty Goguryeo cavalry, the Gaemamusa, armed with shining lamellar (char-gap) armor and bronze mirrors. In those days of warfare, if the enemy was located to the west, fighters would move strategically farther to the west. At sunrise, they would charge the enemy from the west. The rising sun would blind the enemy, perhaps even delivering a sense of impending defeat by mighty warriors armed with the light of the sun itself.

At first, bronze mirrors were the sole province of a small and elite number of people who were rulers and chief priests. But as royal authority and divine right were differentiated, bronze mirrors began to be passed down through generations of shamans, too. These shamans were religious leaders who used the mirrors as important ritual tools, and shamans in Asia in particular have been known to wear bronze mirrors on their chests. For example, the depiction of a shaman wearing a bronze mirror in this way can be seen in a museum in the Republic of Buryatia near Lake Baikal, Russia. Even today, Buryatian shamans wear bronze mirrors on their chests when they perform their rites.

Korean shamans also used to hang bronze mirrors in their shrines when they performed rituals. This came from the belief that spirits would descend where the bronze mirror was hung. The sun, the

Figure 10-5 Mirror of a shaman, housed in the Ulan-Ude Folklore Museum, east of Baikal, Russia

Figure 10-6 Bronze mirror of a shaman wearing a Mask(Ulanwoode Folklore Museum)

Figure 10-7 Mirror of female shaman on display at the Irkutsk Museum, west of Baikal, Russia.

Figure 10-8 Myeongdu used by Korean shamans. The words "Ilwol Daemyungdu" and "Sun," "Moon," and "The Big Dipper" are carved on the mirror.(National Folk Museum)

moon, and the Seven Stars of the Northern Dipper are engraved on the backs of some of these mirrors. Shamans called this set of three the Cheon-Bu Sam-In (three holy items given by the Great Spirit), a symbol of heaven itself. The trio of the bronze mirror, bronze bell, and bronze sword also represented the Cheon-Bu Sam-In. In contemporary shamanism, the bronze mirror is called Myeong-du, with "du" meaning the Seven Stars of the Northern Dipper.

Bronze mirrors in Japan

- Historically, bronze mirrors, bronze swords, and curved jade pieces were passed down through generations of Japanese rulers as symbols of absolute authority. A Japanese bronze mirror was typically engraved with the sun and the moon but without the Seven Stars of the Northern Dipper.

05

The sophisticated metallurgy of ancient Korea's alloys

Bronze mirrors excavated in Korea, like the Danyu-semungyeong mirror, demonstrate a surprisingly advanced understanding of metallurgy. This section will discuss two techniques that were key to this high-level production: a bronze alloying technique and a delicate mold production technique.

Bronze relics excavated in recent years appear to have been produced by adding tin to soft copper, which resulted in a hardened bronze alloy. But randomly mixing in tin did not guarantee a good bronze alloy. Bronze is usually made from a mixture of approximately 90 percent copper and 10 percent tin; an increased proportion of tin results in white bronze with improved reflective qualities. The Danyu-semungyeong mirror's ratio is

10 • The unsolved questions about an ancient Corean bronze mirror, Danyu-Semungyeong, which is engraved with many fine lines that is virtually unreproducible with modern technology.

65.7 percent copper to 34.3 percent tin, an optimal ratio for crafting an alloy of the greatest strength and reflectiveness that could have only been achieved by virtue of strenuous artisanship. It likely took many attempts by the master artisans of Ancient Joseon to develop this advanced understanding of metallurgy. The technique itself was necessary, enabling the validation of royal authority and providing advantages on the battlefield through the production of highly-reflective bronze.

Some scholars like to refer to a description of an alloy ratio of copper and tin (66.7 to 33.3 percent) in *Gogonggi* from *The Rites of Zhou*, an ancient record of technology from the Zhou Dynasty (1046-256 BCE), China. But this writing is influenced by imperial Chinese revisionist pseudo-history, and so it disparages the level of metal-working technology that Ancient Joseon reached in producing the Danyu-semungyeong mirror. This Sinocentric perspective insists that the optimal ratio of copper to tin used in Ancient Joseon was borrowed from China. If we set aside *Gogonggi*, however, and look at the ratio used for bronze mirrors produced during the Warring States Period (BCE 770-221), Sui Dynasty (581-619), and Tang Dynasty (618-907), we discover that the copper-to-tin ratio was approximately 75 to 25. The ratio written in *Gogonggi* appears to have been less of a rule and more of a baseline or suggestion. Regardless of this, no other bronze mirrors from anywhere else in the world attained the same optimal ratio as the Danyu-semungyeong mirrors.

It is also interesting to note that the ratio in the *Gogonggi* differs by a minimum of one percent from ratios used by the master artisans of Ancient Joseon. In science and various technological fields, one percent is a significant margin of difference that leads to vastly different results. In addition, Ancient Joseon's master artisans added other elements beside tin, such as zinc and lead, but the *Gogonggi* does not mention any details beyond the ratio of copper and tin. Consequently, it is conjectured that master artisans in China during the time of

Ancient Joseon did not know the technique that was used by their contemporaries in Ancient Joseon to improve the quality of a bronze alloy by mixing in other materials, such as zinc and lead.

The making of molds is another important piece of Ancient Joseon's bronze craftsmanship, and it emphasizes the beauty and ingenuity of the numerous engravings and line patterns. In fact, the line pattern and overall design of the Danyu-semungyeong mirror is so finely done that it is difficult for professional drafters to draw it by hand in the modern era. The Danyu-semungyeong mirror that was excavated in Nonsan has over 13,000 lines engraved on a surface that is just 21 centimeters in diameter. Drawing two or three lines within the space of a single millimeter is difficult even on paper, but the master artisans of ancient times were skilled enough to engrave their lines into a mold first, and then cast it. Many scholars and modern technicians have failed in their attempts at reproducing the Danyu-semungyeong mirror, but it may be possible to reproduce its design if the lines are drafted by computer software and then engraved with lasers.

Wankeu Lee, a South Korean Intangible Cultural Asset from Gyeonggi Province, succeeded in reproducing a Danyu-semungyeong mirror by using a talc mold, which led him to believe that the Danyu-semungyeong mirror was originally made from a talc mold. Talc is a mineral that bears similarities to modern metal molds in three important ways. Firstly, it is soft enough to carve patterns into; secondly, it has high surface quality; and thirdly, it has a semi-permanent lifespan. Lee reproduced the detailed patterns of a Danyu-semungyeong mirror by utilizing a dachigu, a tool like a drawing compass with multiple fine teeth that allows the drawing of many circles at once.

Obviously, sophisticated magnification did not exist 2,400 years ago, and even with magnification, the fine patterns of the Danyu-semungyeong mirror would have been extraordinarily difficult to

10 • The unsolved questions about an ancient Corean bronze mirror, Danyu- Semungyeong, which is engraved with many fine lines that is virtually unreproducible with modern technology.

achieve. Also, it is not clear whether the dachigu or a similar tool had been invented at that time. If such a tool did exist then, it would have required more than twenty fine needles for drawing circles within one centimeter of width. These are just a few of the unresolved questions surrounding the making of the Danyu-semungyeong mirror, which leaves a sense of wonder and admiration of the techniques of artisans who lived 2,400 years ago. With this in mind, Korea Institute of Science and Technology (KIST) scientist Jongho Lee has described the Danyu-semungyeong mirror as one of seven mysteries of Korea.

Figure 10-9 The design of the Danuse Mungyeong from Nonsan, Chungcheongnam-do Province/ It was on display during the Special Exhibition on Conservation Science in 2016 at the National Museum of Korea.

06

Bronze mirrors in Ancient Joseon and China

The Danyu-semungyeong mirror found in Nonsan was made approximately 2,400 years ago during a turbulent time period in East Asia. In China, that era is called the Warring States Period (BCE 770-221 because many states rose and fell then in a seemingly endless series of battles and wars. In Korea, this was the later stage of Ancient Joseon, when a rebellion was suppressed, the capital city was moved, and the name of the country was changed to Great Buyeo. Of particular note during this time period was the war waged between Ancient Joseon and the Yan Dynasty. This fierce war was a fight for control over what is now Liaoning Province in China.

The people of Ancient Joseon preferred geometric patterns while their contemporaries in China during the Warring States Period favored themes of animals, plants, clouds, and mountains, as well as mythological references. In other words, it seems the Ancient Joseon focused on the beauty of geometric lines while China emphasized its understanding of nature at that time. The differences between the two cultures become even more apparent when we look at the divergence in bronze mirror designs. In addition to the bronzeware designs, the bronze itself differed; bronzeware from Ancient Joseon was an alloy including materials like copper, tin, and zinc, while bronze alloys from the Warring States Period only had copper and tin.

Ancient Joseon's Danyu-semungyeong mirror in particular has many geometric shapes including lines, circles, and triangles. From the perspective of the twenty-first century, designs like these may look like a kind of postmodern abstract art, but this type of mirror was conceived more than two millennia ago. It seems highly likely that there was a special reason for making such complicated patterns, which begs the question: What did those patterns symbolize? One of the likeliest functional theories explains that the patterns on a Danyu-semungyeong mirror were a record of the movements of celestial bodies and seasons. Key to this theory are the pairs of circles that are engraved at the top, bottom, left, and right of the mirror's back, numbering eight circles in total. The concentric circles at the mirror's center, where the rings are connected, are called Jung-gung or To-gung, meaning the center. Jung-gung is the center of the light and symbolizes the sun. The other circles represent beams of that light—brilliance—expanding in the eight directions. This is called the Gu-gung Pal-pung movement. The large central circle and its surrounding smaller circles make a total of nine circles (Gu-gung, where gu means nine). Collectively, these eight surrounding circles are used to depict how the light of the ninth and central circle, which symbolizes the sun, expands in eight directions (Pal-pung, where pal means eight). This way of expressing directions is simplified as the Eight Directions, which is similar to that of expressing the change of nature in heaven and earth as the Eight Trigrams.* In summary, this dominant interpretation states that the patterns on a Danyu-se-

---

* Paljuryeong Read. Ch. 10. The Unsolved Mysteries of the Ancient Danyu-semungyeong Mirror Sect. 07 The bronze mirror and the eight bells

mungyeong mirror are a geometric reconstruction of the sun radiating light in all directions.

Ancient societies commonly believed that their deity or deities dwelled on the sun. In ancient Korean society, a person who wore a finely crafted bronze mirror was a ruler who represented the sun god. Accordingly, the bronze mirror was a symbol of the sun and the divine spirit dwelling there. The small circles on the bronze mirror that indicate the Eight Directions signified that the person who possessed the bronze mirror was the ruler of the eight directions. This meant that they were the ruler of everything touched by the light of the sun.

Bronze mirrors and their association with the sun can be seen in many myths, legends, and ancient tales, such as in the following tale. This story was passed down through hundreds of generations and offers a legend of how the bronze mirror came to be.

While on a royal tour, Hwanung and his entourage went hunting and held a heavenly ritual on Mount Taebaeksan. Pungbaek, the god of wind, marched about holding a bronze mirror engraved with the Heavenly Emblems and the Seals, called the Cheonbugyeong. Usa, the god of rain, had his retainers dance around to drum up sound. Unsa, the god of clouds, had many soldiers with swords form into lines to guard the altar where the heavenly ritual was held. Through this ritual, the Heavenly Emperor himself bestowed a gift upon the ruler of the Korean people: the bronze mirror.

Gu-gung Pal-pung movement

- With a complement of eight small circles at the periphery and a ninth large circle at the center, where the rings are attached, the Danyu-semungyeong mirror boasts a total of nine areas with concentric circles. In traditional East Asian thought, these nine locations or positions are known as Gu-gung. The Gu-gung Pal-pung movement is a Korean name that describes how the universe operates, referring to nine positions and eight directions. Ultimately, the meaning of Gu-gung Pal-pung is associated with the Eight Trigrams. Taeho Bokhee, the man who established the principles of the Eight Trigrams, was the Usa of the nation of Baedal about 5,500 years ago. He is regarded as the ancestor of the Korean people. His teachings about yin-yang, the five elements, and the Eight Trigrams were passed down to Ancient Joseon, where the concepts were further advanced. The philosophies then were transmitted not only to Ancient Joseon, but also shared throughout East Asia, and numerous master crafters who lived in eras long ago imbued their comprehension of this into their work. This left us the many artifacts that grace museum exhibits today.

07

The bronze mirror and the eight bells

The Paljuryeong is a piece of bronzeware with eight bells connected to form eight branches. One of these bronzeware pieces was excavated in Nonsan together with Korean National Treasure No. 141, the Danyu-semungyeong bronze mirror. The Danyu-semungyeong mirror of Daegok-ri Village was also excavated together with a Paljuryeong and Ssangjuryeong (another type of bronzeware with two bells connected at the end of a rod-shaped body). The Paljuryeong, which has not been discovered in other countries, is an ancient artifact unique to the Korean people during the Bronze Age.

This remarkable eight-branched bell actually surprised Korean and international scholars at the time of its excavation. This is because there are beads inside the eight bells that experts realized had already been placed there when the bells were extracted from a mold. This signaled a stunning mastery of craftsmanship and bronze-working.

It is thought that the Paljuryeong, like the Korean bronze mirror, was also designed to symbolize the sun. The shape of this type of bronzeware was made to imitate light as it spreads from the sun in the eight directions that symbolize all directions, and that light is symbolized by each individual bell. The eight-belled Paljuryeong, like the bronze mirror, symbolizes the Korean "philosophy of light" that has been passed down over the last several thousand years.

The Danyu-semungyeong bronze mirror and the Paljuryeong bronze bell are stunning relics of ancient Korean history, and although scholars and technical experts have investigated these artifacts, many puzzles remain unsolved. I hope that that one day we might fully understand the depth and breadth of the philosophical, cultural, and technical context in which the Danyu-semungyeong mirror was made.

Figure 10-10 A replica of Paljuryeong (Hanseong Baekje Museum)

10 • The unsolved questions about an ancient Corean bronze mirror, Danyu- Semungyeong, which is engraved with many fine lines that is virtually unreproducible with modern technology.

PART 11

A Trip to the Museums in Korea

Silk and Sil-Kkury

01 Why did ancient Rome import silk thread?
02 Parthia, the intermediary trading empire
03 Nothing but purple silk for the top brass
04 The portable and precise weight of sil-kkury trade
05 Goguryeo invents sil-kkury
06 Ancient Korean silk outshines Chinese textiles
07 The bronze mirror and the eight bells

01

Why did ancient Rome import silk thread?

The Korean word sil-kkury is the name for thread that has been wrapped on a bamboo reel; the reel is then removed, leaving behind a clew, or a ball of thread. Sil-kkury was once a common household item, but it has fallen out of favor as people who sew or mend their own clothes dwindle in number. Still, the story of how sil-kkury came to be is an integral part of human history, and so this chapter will explore some of the fascinating stories tied to this unassuming ball of thread.

In 2014, emeritus professor Jo Hwan of the Department of Textile Engineering at Yeungnam University published a research article about the origin of silk in the *Journal of Fashion*, in which the origin of the word silk was the Korean word sil-kkury. The article had previously been published in a Japanese textile journal in 2013, where it also received attention from Japanese experts. According to the article, sil-kkury was the gold standard for silk products when Europeans began importing silk through the Silk Road. For several centuries, Romans and merchants from countries bordering western China imported sil-kkury from Goguryeo to make silk. Through this exchange, the Korean word sil-kkury was truncated to become the word silk.

Rome, the mighty conqueror of Europe, treasured silk deeply. Silk reached ancient Roman society at a time when Romans knew no fabrics besides stiff linen, woolen cloth, and leather. They were immediately entranced by silk's smooth and supple texture, varied and subdued sheen-bearing color, and overall durability despite being lightweight and thin. When Gaius Julius Caesar, the famous Roman politician and military general who dominated the end of the Roman Republic, attended a performance at the theater, he reportedly wore a toga (traditional Roman outer garb consisting of a roughly semicircular cloth draped over the shoulder and around the body) made of silk. The striking image of Caesar in silk caught the eye of the upper class, catapulting silk clothing to the height of fashion for Roman nobility.

Figure 11-1 A ball of thread known as Silkkuri/ The thread is wrapped around a rod called 'bidae'.(National Folk Museum)

Silk could not be produced in Rome, making it a luxury item supplied only through middlemen who came and went between the East and the West. Silk became a symbol of power, wealth, and status. As demand swelled, prices skyrocketed, prompting the second emperor of Rome, Tiberius (r. AD 14-37), to issue a decree that prohibited men from wearing silk cloth. He even went so far as to completely prohibit the import of silk, too. But silk became fashionable again when Rome's third emperor, Caligula (r. AD 37-41) himself, was seen wearing silk clothes.

According to *Samguk Sagi (History of the Three Kingdoms)*, a historical record of the Three Kingdoms of Korea complied in 1145, Rome was not alone in regulating access to and use of silk. Goguryeo (37 BCE - 668 CE), Baekjae (18 BCE - 660 CE), Silla (57 BCE - 935 CE), and Gaya (1c. BCE - 562 CE) experienced similar issues in controlling supply and demand of this coveted material. In an attempt to curb expressions of extravagance, rulers in each of these dynasties limited silk to members of specific social strata. In other words, silk was a premium luxury item in both the East and the West.

When ancient Rome discovered its love for silk, Korea and China were the top silk-producing countries; Korea had begun to produce silk prior to even the era of the Four Kingdoms of Korea (1c. BCE- 562 CE). Once it left East Asia, silk rose steadily in price as it passed over land and sea through the many kingdoms and empires along the route of the Silk Road. Transportation was expensive due to the great distance that included mountain ranges and deserts, and by the time a load of silk was delivered to Rome, it was as expensive as pure gold. Nevertheless, the Roman people's interest in silk was unflagging. Examples of this can be seen in Constantinople, the capital of the Roman Empire, where everyone used silk regardless of social class, and the remarkable story of how all attendees of the baptism of Theodosius II, the Eastern Roman Emperor (r. 408-450), adorned themselves with silk and jewels. The Roman philosopher Seneca (4 BCE-65 CE) lamented this exorbitant social trend in his dialogue *On the Happy Life*, criticizing how Roman women were tempted into importing silk from a distant foreign country at enormous expense and exposing their figures by wearing revealing silk clothes. Interestingly, the silk obsession in Rome 2,000 years ago can be compared to modern Korean society's preoccupation with luxury goods imported from Italy.

In summary, this obsession with silk and its impact on society was not only a problem seen in the ancient Roman Empire. Similar silk-related issues arose in the East Asian countries that produced silk, as well as among the people in the Central Asian countries that were intermediaries of the silk trade. Everyone from East to West loved this fine fabric, ensuring that silk received both praise and censure as a luxury good no matter where it went.

02

Parthia, the intermediary trading empire

Though the Romans first learned of silk about 2,500 years ago, it made an indelible mark on their memory at the Battle of Carrhae in 53 BCE. The battle was fought between the Roman Republic and the Parthian Empire near Carrhae, a major city in ancient Upper Mesopotamia (modern Turkey). Parthia, a nomadic people introduced in the Ch. 2 "Conquering the Continent: The Stirrup and the Gaemamusa" of this book, was located in a region between modern Iran and Iraq, and their empire dominated that famous trade route between the East and the West—the Silk Road. This section revisits this battle in order to contextualize its connection to silk in ancient Rome.

Crassus, who was a member of the First Triumvirate and the wealthiest man in Rome, was enticed by the prospect of military glory and riches and decided to invade Parthia without the official consent of the Senate. Despite heavily outnumbering the Parthians, the Romans were soundly defeated. The Roman soldiers were stunned by their enemy's outstanding cavalry tactics and further surprised by their flags, having never seen anything like Parthia's silk banners, which were lightweight, glossy, and shone in the sun. The Battle of Carrhae left its mark on the Romans due to the disparity in battle tactics as well as the culture shock.

The Parthian Empire and its successor, the Sasanian Empire, stood directly in the way of the intermediary trade route between Rome and the East. The Sasanian Empire was the last period of the Persian Empire before the rise of Islam, and it was named after the House of Sasan (224 - 651). These empires were major silk-consuming markets

Figure 11-2 Map of the Parthian Empire (BCE 247 - CE 226) / An ancient kingdom founded by the horse-riding nomadic people known as the Parni people after the collapse of the Persian Empire, in the modern day Iran and Iraq. It has benefited greatly from playing a big role in intermediary trade between Rome and the Han Dynasty China

Figure 11-3 A petroglyph with Shapur, the second king of Persia during the Sasanian dynasty, capturing the Roman emperor Valerian as a war prisoner/ It's located near the "Naqsh-e Rostam" in the cave tomb of Persian kings near Persepolis, Iran.

Figure 11-4 A reproduction of a piece of petroglyph of Shapur I, who is riding on a horse. Shapur I wearing a silk dress and a silk scarf that flutters against the wind.

themselves, in addition to being controllers of the Silk Trade. Rome had no choice but to confront them repeatedly because it was unable to access Eastern culture and its products without passing through this region.

Over the years, the Romans made various attempts to obtain the secrets of silk production, but they failed each time. The mighty conquerors of Europe presumed that silk thread was produced from some sort of tree bark, but they never imagined that it was actually harvested from the cocoons of insects.

Because silk came to Rome through intermediaries, it was a commodity high in demand but low in supply, which resulted in an unavoidably high price. This was a key reason for Rome's long-lasting conflict with the Parthian and the Sasanian empires.

03

Nothing but purple silk for the top brass

Part of silk's appeal was its ability to be dyed in a variety of colors. During the Roman Empire, there were silk-dyeing factories in coastal cities like Sidon (a harbor city of modern Lebanon). Although other colors were available, purple was heavily favored by the highest echelons of society. In Rome, only the Roman emperor was allowed to wear cloth of this particular purple, known as jaju purple in Korea (see the "ch.5 - Mapping the Cosmos with Cheon-sang-yeol-cha-bun-ya-ji-do" section of this book). This is how it became known as Imperial purple.

Imperial purple was in such demand that the neglectful and brutal Roman emperor Nero Claudius Caesar (37 - 68) proclaimed a law putting to death anyone who wore purple cloth other than himself. Only Roman generals returning home after winning a war were temporarily exempt from this. A successful general was allowed to adorn himself with a purple toga and gold bands during a parade that celebrated his victory on the battlefield.

Figure 11-5
Imperial Purple

Not all shades of purple are created equal. For example, jaju purple (sometimes called claret in English) is a particular shade of purple that is more reddish than other violet colors. Imperial purple is a darker red than this, whereas violet is a purple that trends toward blue, giving it a bluish hue. In the traditional color wheel used by painters, violet and purple are both placed between red and blue. Purple occupies the space closer to red, between crimson and violet. Violet is closer to blue and is usually less saturated than purple. It is important to distinguish the different shades of purple because obtaining dyes of these nuanced hues was extraordinarily difficult in ancient times.

A shade of purple known as Tyrian purple was invented for the first time in Tyre, an ancient Phoenician city (now a harbor city of Lebanon) in 14 BCE, where it was made from the secretions of sea snails laboriously harvested in this area in a complicated process. Processing the Tyrian purple dye made a terrible odor, so workshops were located in remote areas far from cities. Back in those days, a person who handled things that produced such a foul odor could make a fortune. According to Roman records, ten thousand sea snails were required to make a single gram of purple dye. There is still a 40-meter-high mound of crushed shells in Sidon, Lebanon, evidence of the staggering number of sea snails that were collected at that time.

The smelly, complicated, and laborious production of purple dye resulted in the dye trading at a very high price. According to the *Ancient History Encyclopedia*, an imperial order from 301 CE, during the reign of Emperor Diocletian, revealed that a mere 0.455 kilograms of the purple dye cost 150,000 denarii, which was 1.36

Figures 11-6 Mosaic art from 6th century at the Basilica di San Vitale in Ravenna, Italy / Roman Emperor Justinian I, who made the Corpus Juris Civilis, and his wife Theodora, are both wearing purple silk.

kilograms of gold. This would equal over 6.5 million won in current Korean currency—about US$5,600. As the price of a small amount of a single type of dye, this was a tremendous sum. Given that purple dye was such an exorbitant luxury, it seems reasonable that only the emperor could wear purple clothes.

In Rome, the very first person to wear purple clothing was Gaius Julius Caesar. Purple was synonymous with the emperor in the Byzantine Empire (the Eastern Roman Empire and Byzantium) as well, where the emperor ruled from a purple-curtained room in a palace built of purple stones. Byzantine emperors even granted the title of Porphyrogenitus—"born in the shade of purple"—to their newborn heirs to indicate that the child was born of the imperial bloodline.

04

The portable and precise weight of sil-kkury trade

Silk was traded from East Asia to Rome through the Silk Road in both fabric and thread form. Traders carried it across the desert of death, over the rough terrain of a chain of mountains, and by a grueling sea route. At times, they were robbed of their silk by bands of thieves and even lost their lives. Merchants preferred thread to fabric in these frequent dangerous situations because thread was cheaper, lighter, and not as great a loss if stolen or damaged. Additionally, it was more profitable for the merchant to sell silk as a thread than pre-woven fabric because it enabled the buyer to more easily use the thread as desired.

But transporting silk thread all the way to Rome without any damage to the goods had its own challenges, too. The thin thread easily snapped or tangled, and the damaged thread was unsellable. To combat this issue, thread was wound into a bundle using a spool, but spooled thread presented its own problems. The thread had to be unspooled from its outermost layer first, which was often damaged from travel, resulting in the thread snapping. Additional problems arose during transportation and trading because thread was sold by weight, and the weight of spool added to the weight of the thread when the goods were assessed. Korean sil-kkury was the solution to these drawbacks.

Sil-kkury was an innovative technique for its time. To make sil-kkury, the end of the thread was tied to a wooden stick called a bee-dae, and then the thread was reeled onto the stick. Once a suitable amount of thread had been wrapped around the bee-dae, the stick was removed, leaving behind sil-kkury. Sil-kkury was designed to be unwound from the center, not from the outer layer. This method ensured that the surface of the thread was neither damaged nor tangled when the thread was unspooled. Additionally, it was a better method for trade because merchants were able to accurately measure the weight of the thread by itself.

05

Goguryeo invents sil-kkury

According to Yeungnam University professor Jo Hwan, the word silk came about when textile manufacturers in Europe and the Middle and Near East regions imported sil-kkury from the East to produce fabric as they saw fit. In particular, Professor Jo asserts that sil-kkury originated from Goguryeo. Goguryeo was not the only ancient Korean state that possessed the ability to produce and weave high-quality silk; Buyeo (200 BCE - 494 CE), Okjeo (300 BCE - 244 CE), Naklang (196 BCE - 37 CE), Silla (57 BCE - 935 CE), Gaya (1c. BCE - 562 CE), and Baekjae (18 BCE - 660 CE) also engaged in silk production. Around the time that the silk banners of Parthia astounded the Romans in battle, China was in the Han Dynasty era (202 BCE - 9 CE); meanwhile, Korea was dominated by warring states— Buyeo, Goguryeo, Baekjae, Gaya, Dongye, Okjeo and the Three Han States of Jinhan, Mahan, and Byeonhan (300 BCE-300 CE).*

---

* King Muryeong of Baekjae is also an ancestor of the Japanese Imperial line. Former Japanese Emperor Akihito publicly announced that he is a descendant of Baekjae's royal bloodline.

The idea that silk was only produced in China is a common misperception. In reality, the later era of the Ancient Joseon's silk weaving technique was already more advanced than that of China and produced a greater variety of silk. In a section on Goguryeo in the *Book of Wei*, a historical record from China, it is mentioned that when Chumo-wang (King Chumo or Jumong) founded the state, his people made their own clothes from a material called baek. Baek is a type of silk woven with undyed silk yarn, usually called myeongju. In the states of Buyeo and Okjeo, people used jeong, a type of fine silk woven without pattern. According to *Samguk Sagi (History of the Three Kingdoms)*, King Chumo prohibited the public from wearing clothes made from sa, a type of very fine and lightweight silk. Given that these techniques of silk weaving were developed at such an early stage in history, it is speculated that the thread-storing technique of sil-kkury had already been in use for a significant amount of time.

06

Ancient Korean silk outshines Chinese textiles

Was there a significant difference between silk produced in ancient Korea and silk produced in ancient China? To answer this question, we need to first know what types of silks were produced in ancient Korean states.

Three different types of silks were discovered among ruins near Pyongyang and the Taedong River (North Korea). These silks (Gyeon, Na, and Gyeom) date back to the later period of Ancient Joseon (from the third to first centuries BCE). These three types provided sufficient data for experts to speculate on ancient silk production and weaving techniques.

Gyeon silk was also excavated from Baekjae-era ruins (a tomb in Suchon-ri Village, Chungcheongnam-do Province and the Tomb of King Muryeong in Songsan-ri Village). According to *Samguk Yusa*

(Memorabilia of the Three Kingdoms), which includes both historical records and legends from ancient Korea, silk was used for tax collection in Goguryeo and Baekjae, and in Gaya, Gyogyeon silk (a type of silk embroidered with a fishnet pattern) was used for drawing portraits. Na silk was found in the Tomb of King Muryeong, and evidence indicates that it was produced on a large scale in Silla as well. Gyeom silk was produced by Silla and Samhan (the three states of Mahan, Jinhan, and Byeonhan).

Ancient Joseon silk typically found in Pyongyang and the Taedong River

Gyeon silk	Ancient Joseon silk typically found in Pyongyang and the Taedong River
Na silk	Literally named "basic silk". Thin, white, and coarse silk woven without a pattern from undyed silk yarn.
Gyeom silk	Silk that combines two or more threads, where the raw threads are twisted to make a thick textile.

The silk produced by early Korean states was superior to its counterparts produced in China for multiple reasons. Firstly, the silk thread itself was smooth and refined; the thinner the fiber, the higher the quality of thread. In turn, better thread made better fabric. Multiple thinner fibers could be combined to make a thicker thread that was of higher quality, too, because thinner fibers had a more pleasing texture and aesthetic. Unlike Ancient Joseon, Chinese silk produced from the Shang Dynasty (1600-1046 BCE) to the Han Dynasty (202 BCE-9 CE) did not attain this level of refined silk production. In fact, the silk fiber produced by Ancient Joseon was even thinner than silk produced today by modern technology. To combat problems with friction, modern textile processes use a type of thread that is easily twisted as a stiff warp (vertical threads) instead of a stretchable weft (horizontal threads). Ancient Joseon knew that this produced a better textile, which is why it used thick threads as warp in its own silk production. Ancient Joseon's counterparts in China did not make silk in this way.

Another reason for Ancient Joseon's superior silk was its versatility in taking on color. Silk textile from Ancient Joseon in particular was stretchable and easily dyed. As highlighted in the previous section on the expense and desirability of Imperial purple, silk that was easy to dye was in high demand.

Given the features of Ancient Joseon silk that have been explained in this section, it is easy to see how the quality of this silk was superior to textiles produced by adjacent states. Moreover, it is clear that Ancient Joseon was ahead of its time with its creative techniques for weaving and dyeing.

07

Ancient Korea pioneers silk production

For many years, no one questioned whether ancient China was actually the first to produce silk. But why? Was that assumption true? To examine this issue, we turn to Nujo, the Chinese goddess of silk who has been lauded as the inventor of sericulture, or the farming of silkworms to produce silk. Nujo is recorded as the wife of Huangdi, the Yellow Emperor (2698-2598 BCE) who is regarded as the forefather of Chinese civilization. Nujo is known as Seoreung in Korean, and she was the daughter of Shennong, also known as the Wugushen in China. Shennong was an official of a Baedal nation, an ancient Korean nation.

Baedal was the state that the Dongyi people, the ancestors of modern Korea, founded prior to Ancient Joseon. It was governed by the Heavenly Emperor Hwanung (this was the title of Baedal's ruler). After the eighth Heavenly Emperor Hwanung, Anburyeon, dispatched a man named So-jeon as a governmental official to settle the Gahngsu River region, So-jeon fathered a son named Shennong there. Shennong became the progenitor of the Gahng family. Shennong's daughter Seoreung was also from this ancient Korean ethnic group. According to an ancient Chinese literary work, *Jamsangchewpyeon* (*On Silkworm Breeding*), Taeho Bokhee wove thin fabric with silk thread obtained from silkworms, and Shennong also taught others how to weave textiles with silk thread. As introduced in Ch. 7 Taegeukgi: the Universe Spread on Cloth, Taeho Bokhee was the twelfth son of Taewoowi, the fifth Heavenly Emperor Hwanung. He was also a government official of the state of Baedal. These historical figures-turned-legends came from the same ethnic group as modern Koreans. Even if we reject the details of the stories told in *Jamsangchewpyeon*, we can safely assume that the Korean and Chinese civilizations shared sericulture as far back as 5,000 to 6,000 years ago. Next, we will look at objective archeological evidence of this.

A drop spindle (tool for reeling thread) was excavated from the Heowoowa ruins in modern China's Liaoning Province (formerly known as Manchuria), which are estimated to be about 6,700 years old. The entire territory of former Manchuria was inhabited by the Korean civilization prior to the Ancient Joseon era. Recently, the remains of the ancient civilization of the Bohai Bay (Liao River) region sparked excitement after silkworms made of jade were excavated there. The use of prized jade to produce silkworm figurines is significant because it means that sericulture was considered important work in this expansive civilization. Additionally, excavations in multiple ruins found around Pyeongyang and Hamkyong-do Province in North Korea have unearthed numerous pieces of pottery engraved with mulberry leaves. Silkworms subsist on a diet of nothing but mulberry leaves. There was also a piece of silk cloth, collocated with a bronze helmet, excavated at a site in Ancient Joseon's former

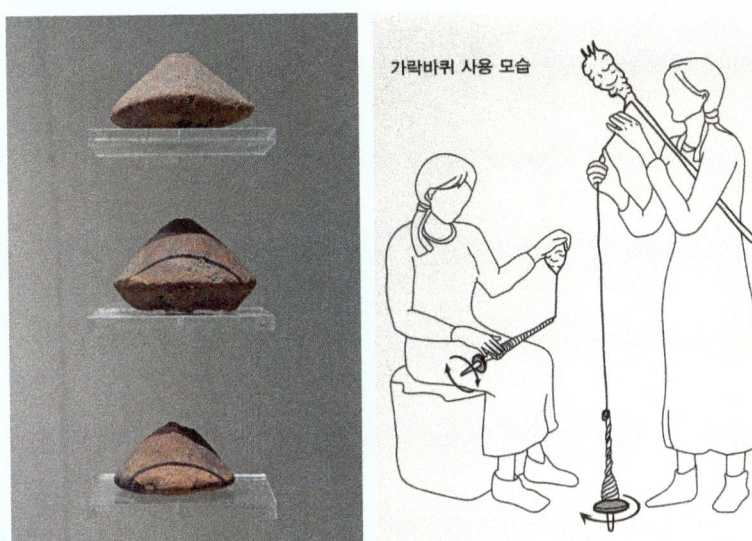

Figure 11-7 Ancient form of spinning wheels and how they were used during the Neolithic Age displayed at the National Museum of Korea

territory in Liaoning Province. It is believed that this silk was used as the helmet's lining. Similarly, it is speculated that the gold accessories for royalty that were excavated from the Tomb of King Muryeong of the Baekjae Dynasty were once attached on either side of a silk hat.

Excavations at another site in China, which dates to approximately 4,700 to 6,700 years ago, have discovered earthenware with patterns made by pressing rough cloth into the material, as well as pottery shaped like a silkworm. Due to the discovery of very small pieces of silk cloth among artifacts from the Shang (1600-1046 BCE) and Zhou ((1046-256 BCE)) dynasties, it is presumed that the popularity of silk production and the utilization of silk were already widespread then. Moreover, when we consider the various artifacts and regional characteristics of East Asia, we can trace the continuous cultural exchange between the ancient Korean people and adjacent groups and states. Sericulture, the silk reeling technique, and silk cloth were also subject to this cultural exchange. Regardless of whether the story of the Yellow Emperor and Seoreung is true, there is no doubt that silk production was a common part of life for both Korea and China.

Although Professor Jo's research on the etymology of silk is promising, it remains to be seen whether it will be established as the official theory. Regardless, it is important to restore the historic status of ancient Korean silk production and trade and to recover the relevant records. One such effort is already underway in Geumseong, the ancient capital of the Silla Dynasty (modern Gyeongju, South Korea), where the restoration of this city's status as a major city of the Silk Road has recently come under consideration.

Silk and numerous other artifacts and historical records are proof that ancient Korea stood at the cultural epicenter of a long-lasting exchange with multiple states. Comb-pattern pottery, jade pottery, dolmens, whale hunting petroglyphs, bronzeware, and many other artifacts and remains suggest that this type of exchange and communication connected the East and the West of the Eurasian continent since long before recorded history. Korean sil-kurry, too, should be recognized as an important cultural icon of this exchange between the East and the West.

PART 12

A Trip to the Museums in Korea

Whale Hunting 7,000 Years Ago in the Bangudae Petroglyphs

01 The world's oldest depiction of whale hunting
02 Estimating when the Bangudae Amgakhwa was created
03 A prehistoric superstar makes waves
04 Prehistoric cinema
05 Secrets of successful whale hunting: sturdy nets and skilled shipbuilding
06 The power of organized community
07 The Bangudae Petroglyphs' Russian cousin: the Zalavruga Petroglyphs
08 A shaman's hunting song

01

The world's oldest depiction of whale hunting

A massive photo welcomes visitors to the prehistoric exhibition hall of the National Museum of Korea. Although it is hung at the entrance, it is easily missed by visitors eager to see what lies beyond it. To the untrained eye, the photo may look like a shot of inconsequential scribbles, but it is an image of a rock panel that is the world's oldest depiction of an organized group of people hunting whales: the Bangudae Amgakhwa. The actual Bangudae Amgakhwa is located in the town of Eonyang-eup in Ulsan. The name Bangudae refers to the shape of a sitting turtle, because the rock on which these petroglyphs were engraved looks like a turtle. In Korean, amgakhwa means petroglyph, which is an image engraved on a rock surface.

The Bangudae Amgakhwa is engraved on a rock surface that is about 10 feet (three meters) in height and 33 feet (10 meters) in width. The initial engraving of these petroglyphs is estimated to have taken place about 7,000 years ago. For a 7,000-year-old picture, it is

Figure 12-1 A picture of a petroglyph hanging at the entrance of the Prehistoric Exhibition of the National Museum of Korea in Ulsan.

surprisingly well-designed. It is an impressive example of ancient artistry, but most people today do not understand its significance.

At a glance, it does seem like a cartoonish prehistoric picture—like nothing special. But these petroglyphs are a treasure trove of clues about the life of the prehistoric people who lived on the Korean Peninsula.

The Netherland archeological journal *Archeologie* featured a story on these petroglyphs in its 2013 special edition. The journal introduced the Bangudae Amgakhwa as the oldest whale-hunting imagery in the world, describing it as an archetypal depiction that tells the story of a mythical subject. With its dynamic portrayal of scenes of whale hunting and the realistic characteristics of its animals, it is highly regarded by archeology experts as a work of art that offers insights into both hunting and religious custom.

02

Estimating when the Bangudae Amgakhwa was created

When the Bangudae Amgakhwa was discovered by Dongguk University professor Moon Myeongdae in 1971, it was originally dated to the Bronze Age due to the inclusion of a whale struck by a harpoon. But in 2010, the remains of whalebones struck by a harpoon were excavated in Whangseong-dong Neighborhood in Ulsan; these were revealed to be about 6,000 years old. The fragment of the harpoon itself was significant because it was fashioned from deer bone, which meant it was not a metal tool that corresponded to the Bronze Age. It was something even older. Further investigation confirmed that, in cases involving sedimentary rock like the Bangudae Amgakhwa, it was possible to engrave images as long as the engraving tool was hard enough; it did not have to be a metal tool to engrave sedimentary rock. As a result, it was concluded that the Bangudae Amgakhwa was actually produced 7,000 years ago when metal tools were not yet available and deer bone was used to engrave stone instead.

Figure 12-2 Bangudae Petroglyph Rocks in Ulju-gun, Ulsan

Figure 12-3 A whale bone relic from a harpooned whale found in Hwangseong-dong, Ulsan. It was displayed as a special exhibit at the National Museum of Korea/ The right part where the arrowhead was stuck is marked with a red dot.

The design of the Bangudae Amgakhwa indicates that different petroglyph skills were used to make it, skills that can be seen in other petroglyphs around the world, such as chipping out the areas of some designs and chipping only the outlines of others. This suggests that the Bangudae Amgakhwa was produced over a long period of time, beginning during the Neolithic Age and continuing to the Bronze Age; as time passed, different engravers added to the image using the skills that corresponded to their specific time period.

03

A prehistoric superstar makes waves

When unknown artists engraved these pictures on a massive rock canvas 7,000 years ago, the art was mainly concentrated on a flat surface of the rock some 10 feet tall and 33 feet wide (three meters high and 10 meters wide)—but there are more than 10 other rocks nearby that also boast engraved images. According to the Ulsan Petroglyph Museum, there are 353 pictures engraved on these rocks. The images add up to a stunning number of petroglyphs concentrated in a single area, a collection unparalleled anywhere else in the world. Perhaps these artists who lived many millennia ago simply had so many stories to tell. The figures of hunters, whales, turtles, sharks, various types of fish, deer, tigers, weasels, boars, and more are realistically articulated alongside other as-yet unidentified animals.

Among these many figures, the creatures that garner the most attention are the whales. While famous petroglyphs in Europe predominantly depict land animals, the sheer number of whales in the Ban-

Figure 12-4 Copy of of Bangudae Petroglyph Rock displayed at the Gyeongju National Museum

gudae Petroglyphs in Ulsan makes it clear that whales are the main subject matter. Of the whales depicted, as many as 58 are carved in significant detail.

The inland location of these rock engravings of whales begs the question as to why sea creatures would be depicted far from their natural habitat. A review of literature from the Joseon Dynasty reveals a sixteenth-century record that states sea levels once reached the upper region of the Taewha River of Ulsan. If the petroglyphs were first engraved about 7,000 years ago, the coastline then would have been even farther inland. The average temperature 6,000 to 10,000 years ago was higher than today, which means that sea levels were higher as well, and so the coastal waters that once encroached on the Bangudae Amgakhwa's location would have been populated by a variety of sea creatures.

There used to be many whales in the East Sea of Korea, although this is no longer the case. A mid-nineteenth-century record from an

Figure 12-5 A Gray whale is carrying a baby whale on its back in Bangudae Petroglyph Rock/ This is an enlarged picture of the petroglyph at the entrance of the National Museum of Korea's Prehistoric Museum

American whaling ship on expedition in the East Sea even described how "numerous humpback whales, blue whales, right whales, and fin whales frolic on all sides." Unfortunately, this sizable population of whales dwindled due to indiscriminate slaughter by whaling ships from America, Japan, and Norway.

Among the whales depicted in the petroglyphs, there is a gray whale with a whale calf on its back. In 1912, American explorer Roy Andrews came to Ulsan's Jangsaeng-po Port and studied whales in the nearby sea; he called these whales the "Korean stock of gray whales." In Korean, these whales were called ghost whales. Andrews observed that these whales came and went between the East Sea of Korea and the Sea of Okhotsk.

The Korean name for the ghost whale comes from the tendency of these whales, which grow up to 50 feet long (about 15 meters) and have a limited lung capacity, to break the surface with just the tip of the head when rising in coastal waters; they do this to breathe before disappearing again like a ghost. While this type of whale is currently referred to as a se-whale in South Korea, most Western countries call it a gray whale. Because whales like these easily vanish from sight, a common whale-hunting strategy revolves around the knowledge that the mother whale will not leave when her calf is wounded or killed. Hunters target the calf first and then harpoon its mother upon her approach. South Korea designated these gray whales as a natural treasure in 1962, but they disappeared from the East Sea without a trace by 1977.

The humpback, fin, and other types of whales depicted in the Bangudae Petroglyphs are also endangered. According to the National Fisheries Research & Development Institute, about 80 species of whales exist globally and an estimated 37 of these inhabit or pass by Korea's coastal waters. In particular, 13 different species of whales are frequently observed in the waters near Ulsan. It is estimated that there are eight species of whale depicted in the Bangudae Petroglyphs.

Although commercial whale hunting has been banned internationally for decades, Ulsan still maintains its long-standing connection with whales. South Korea's sole whale museum is located in Ulsan's Jangsaeng-po Port, where whaling ships once actively frequented the area. Local tours offer trips on whale-spotting ships to watch for the pods of whales that frequently appear in autumn. While it has become more difficult to see whales in Ulsan's coastal waters, the area still teems with several thousand dolphins. Through a variety of exhibitions and tours such as these, Ulsan continues to honor and upkeep its 7,000-year-old relationship with whales.

Following an international treaty in 1986, whale hunting was banned on a global scale. Spurning this agreement, illegal whale hunting has continued to occur in various places around the world. In the seas surrounding South Korea, the main target of these poachers is the minke whale, which they hunt by following their migration pattern in the West Sea (January-March), the Southern Sea (April-May), and the East Sea (June-September). When the animals break the surface for respiration, poachers harpoon them. Even though at least a dozen poachers are arrested every year, it remains difficult to completely eradicate illegal whale hunting because whale meat is traded at a high price—and there are always buyers. Meanwhile, the Ulsan Whale Festival held in Ulsan's Jangsaeng-po Port seems to focus on this interest in whale meat rather than the culture surrounding the creature itself. To truly celebrate the whale through such a festival, the focus should shift from the consumption of whale meat to ecotourism and the preservation of the species.

A Trip to the Museums in Korea

Figure 12-6 The bones of the sperm whale displayed at the Ganghwa Natural History Museum in Incheon. It's length is 14.5 meters long, making it possible to imagine actual size of the whale. Sperm whales are one of the whales featured in the Bangudae Petroglyph Rock.

04

Prehistoric cinema

The left section of the Bangudae Petroglyphs teems with whales while its right section is like an amusement park filled with land animals. The engravings depict dynamic situations with various animals, such as mating hogs and even pregnant tigers and deer. The petroglyphs also portray a beautiful breed of horned deer that once was a common figure in totems from Central and East Asia. In addition, there is a variety of land animals with stripes and spots, and even a bow-wilding hunter wearing a quiver and aiming an arrow at a deer. This grand panorama of wild land animals, sea creatures, and the hunters seeking to catch them all sharing the same space gives a sense of dramatic tension, like the climax of an award-winning blockbuster film.

The ancient artists of these petroglyphs captured the characteristics of whales in impressive detail. Among the engravings is a humpback whale with wrinkles covering its entire belly, a killer whale with a

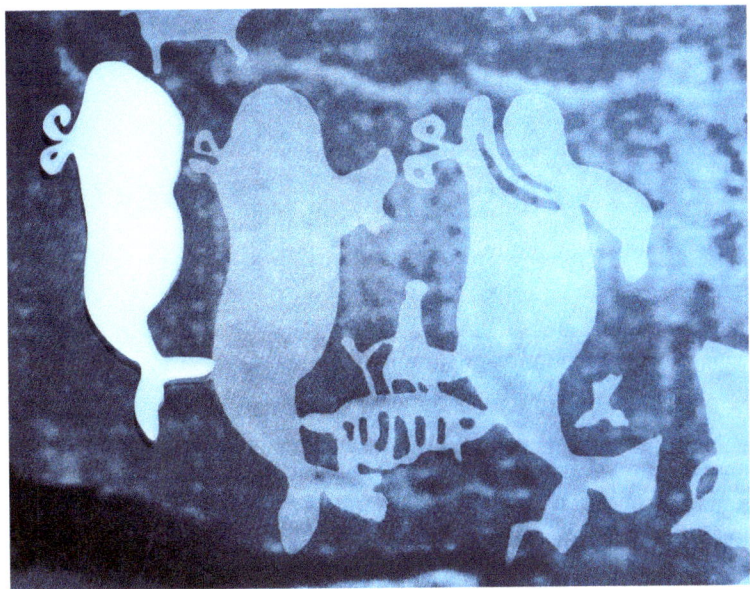

Figure 12-7 A whale that looks like a north pacific right whale spews water / looks like a whale was expressed in three different images.

dorsal fin and white spots, a ghost whale with her cub, and a variety of others. There is even a whale that has been harpooned by a hunter. But the most remarkable depiction is an extraordinary petroglyph of what appear to be North Atlantic right whales spouting water from their blowholes. A French scholar and expert in prehistory appraised this expansive petroglyph scene as the "cinema of prehistoric times." The ability to depict whales with such detail in these petroglyphs is evidence that the prehistoric people who made it had extensive knowledge of different species of whales and ecosystems.

These pictures were engraved by chiseling and grinding the rock surface with stones, an artistic endeavor that was no matter of a few days; in fact, the range of skills used to engrave these pictures indicates that the petroglyphs were completed over a long period of time. As time passed after the first petroglyphs were engraved, new subjects and ideas were added to the empty spaces. Experts praise these petroglyphs in particular for the fact that they portray an evolution of thought and artistic methods throughout the passage of time.

The tools used to make the petroglyphs were inferior and inconvenient compared to what we have access to today, but the artistic result holds its own when compared to modern art. In this collection of engravings, prehistoric artists realistically expressed their own aesthetics, sensitivities, and spiritualities with skillful craftsmanship.

As is commonly found in paintings and calligraphic works, the Bangudae petroglyphs offers clues about the religion, thought, and philosophy of its makers. In particular, the figures of pregnant animals and men with emphasized genitals offer a glimpse into the earnest wishes—like prosperity and fertility—of the people of prehistoric Korea.

05

Secrets of successful whale hunting: sturdy nets and skilled shipbuilding

The Bangudae petroglyphs has drawn scholarly attention because it not only describes animals in detail, but it also has dynamic scenes of prehistoric people hunting animals as well. Marine biologist Daniel Robineau, professor emeritus at the French National Museum of Natural History in Paris, described the Bangudae petroglyphs as "a documentary painting that shows the origin of whale hunting" in his book *A History of Whale Hunting (Une histoire de la chasse a la baleine, 2007)*. Next, we will examine how these prehistoric whale hunters actually caught their prey.

In the Bangudae petroglyphs, whale hunting images are depicted with a range of surprisingly familiar features including nets, boats, and harpoons. Throughout human history, we have typically hunted whales with harpoons. Even 7,000 years ago, whale hunting was not significantly different from today; hunters caught whales by throwing

Figure 12-8 Harpooned whale (second from top) / On the bottom, you can find Humpback whales with wrinkles on their stomach. The picture of the petroglyph in the National Museum of Korea has been enlarged.

Figure 12-9 A whale hunter hunts whales by throwing an arrow with a string attached from a ship with several people on board (a replica of the Bangudae Petroglyph Rock on display at the National Museum of Korea).

harpoons or firing arrows. Figure 12-8 shows a clear picture of a harpooned whale, and Figure 12-9 is an image of people riding a boat with a rope attached to a whale.

During a whale hunt, a group of a dozen or more whale hunters spread across several boats would go out to sea and launch harpoons and arrows at their prey. Ropes were fixed to the harpoons and arrows, and the other end of each rope tied to one of the boats. The hunters then would endure the rushing water and fierce jolts as their prey, struck and tethered by harpoons and arrows, flopped around with the hunters' boats in tow. It is believed that the hunters would wait until the whale was exhausted before dragging it out of the water and onto shore.

In the event that a boat was capsized or damaged during a hunt, many people were in danger of going overboard. In particularly unlucky instances, many of them would have lost their lives. A whale writhing in agony and desperation could capsize or crush a boat, making hunting a matter of life-or-death.

It appears that harpoons were not the sole hunting tool; nets were also used for whaling. At the center of Figure 12-8, a U-shaped fishnet has been cast with the whale below the net. Even if the prey of these nets were only small whales, this indicates that prehistoric hunters were skilled in making whale hunting nets that were surprisingly durable.

Naturally, whale hunters needed boats to go whaling, and several whaling boats are depicted in the Bangudae petroglyphs. Above all else, a whaling boat had to be strong enough to endure a whale's struggle to free itself. The National Museum of Korea exhibits a reproduction of the remains of one such boat that was excavated in Bibong-li Village (Changnyeong-gun County, Gyeongsangnam-do Province). The Bibong-li wooden boat was discovered during reconstruction efforts in an area damaged by a typhoon. When the boat's age was estimated, many scholars could not help their excitement. At 8,000 years old, it is the oldest boat of its type in the world. Made of pine wood, the boat's dimensions are estimated to reach a maximum length of approximately 10 feet (about 310 centimeters), with

Figure 12-10 The world's oldest piece of log boat and a pole excavated in Bibong-ri, Changwon, Gyeongsangnam-do Province / It's preserved in the National Museum of Korea.

Figure 12-11 Model of the World's Oldest Wooden Ship found in Bibong-ri on display at the National Museum of Korea. It is believed that the stone tools and fire was used to dig out the insides of the log.

Figure 12-12 A harpoon made of animal bones used near Vladivostok between 7,000 and 5,000 years ago. Museum of the Far Eastern Federal University in Vladivostok, Russia

a width of about two feet (60 centimeters) and a depth of about eight inches (20 centimeters). Perhaps Ulsan's claim to fame as possessing the biggest dockyard in the world may have its roots in a much older shipbuilding history than we thought—one that is 8,000 years old.

Although it remains unclear how exactly whaling boats like the ones in the petroglyphs would have been built, some details can be extrapolated based on the actual wooden boat remains found in Bibong-li Village and other clues. There is a particularly large boat among the petroglyphs' various whaling boats and fishing tools. With many people on board, it seems to be able to hold about 10 to 20 people, and although the image has worn down over millennia, there are multiple paddles visibly engraved on the boat. Hunting whales in the rough East Sea and towing the catch back to land would have only been possible for a society skilled in building sturdy boats.

What did hunters do with a whale after they fought such a dangerous battle among the waves? One of the scenes in the Bangudae petroglyphs appears to show people taking a whale carcass apart. Hunters would have dragged the whale to shore before cutting it into pieces on the beach. This suggests that organized communities capable of whale hunting had already formed in Korea at least 7,000 years ago.

06

The power of organized community

A whale was a precious source of food for many people, and its bones, oil, and other parts were also used as materials for basic necessities. It is likely that whales were the biggest harvestable resource for the people who settled in the Ulsan area around the period when the petroglyphs were made.

The fact that prehistoric people routinely hunted whales suggests many aspects of life back then, such as the size of such a society. Whaling was vastly different from regular fishing, and it required more than merely one or two people. Depending on the size of the whale, anywhere from dozens to over a hundred people were needed to facilitate a hunt. There were the whale hunters themselves, the people who made tools for hunting and harvesting, and those who harvested the various parts of the whale and distributed these resources to the community. Of course, hunters could have done every

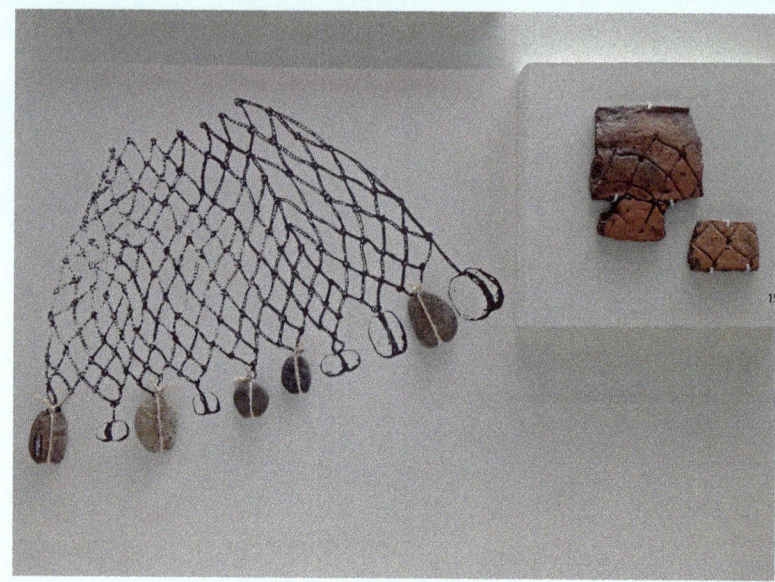

Figure 12-13 Neolithic Age net, net sinkers, and net-shaped earthenware sculptures from about 8,000 years ago (National Museum of Korea)

Figure 12-14 The sinker stone of the Neolithic Age (National Museum of Korea)

part of the process themselves, from making the hunting tools and cutting apart the whales to the distribution itself. However, it does not appear that the hunters who survived the fierce struggles at sea were involved in the complex process of harvesting the whales they brought back. Whaling is a process that needs role specialization such as found in modern society. In the prehistoric Ulsan region, whale hunters likely led the formation of a highly organized society in which those who performed the vital duties of distributing whale meat and other by-products probably became the leaders of their community.

The topic of prehistoric social groups often prompts people to imagine primitive humans living like animals. However, people back then possessed remarkable skills and lived in systemized, structured societies. Museums all around the world exhibit a variety of artifacts from this prehistoric era that allow modern society to learn about the high standards of living achieved by people who lived many millennia ago. These ancestors of ours lived in organized social units and had cultural knowledge that was advanced enough to produce artwork. They developed a spiritual culture that they expressed through religious activities and rituals. They honed tool-making skills, crafting fishnets, harpoons, knives, bows, and arrows strong enough to hunt whales and wild animals. They fired earthenware and stored food, building boats large enough to carry many people and strong enough to haul tethered whales, and they had the skills to produce sizable and durable fishnets that could withstand the weight and force of a whale. Artifacts and relics like these, ones that tell the stories of people who lived and thrived long ago, can be found throughout prehistoric exhibits in South Korean museums.

07

The Bangudae Petroglyphs' Russian cousin: the Zalavruga Petroglyphs

Though the Bangudae Amgakhwa petroglyphs boasts a range and depth of artistic expression that exceeds any other collection of petroglyphs in the world, a collection of petroglyphs with striking similarities was discovered near the White Sea in Russia, a find that intrigued scholars and tourists around the world.

Fittingly named for its frozen appearance in winter, the White Sea in northwest Russia is likely the inspiration for the collection of whaling petroglyphs discovered nearby in the coastal city of Belomorsk. This collection has been estimated as 6,000 years old, placing its production period 1,000 years after that of the Bangudae Amgakhwa, when the White Sea did not freeze during winter because the average temperature then was higher than it is today. These rock carvings are called the Zalavruga Petroglyphs, and they are remarkably similar to the Bangudae Amgakhwa. In June 2015, an Ulsan broadcaster in-

Figure 12-15 A reproduction of the New Zalavruga Petroglyph from the city of Belemosk, Russia / You can see a whaling ship with several people on board and a hunted whale (State Historical Museum at Moscow)

Figure 12-16 The location of Zalavruga in the city of Belomorskiye, near the White Sea of Northwestern Russia / The image is an enlarged area of red square on the right.

troduced Russia's Zalavruga Petroglyphs to a South Korean audience for the first time through a TV documentary titled *The First Sign of Humanity, The Stones of Ancient Humankind.*

Geographically, the city of Belomorsk is located over 4,000 miles (6,700 kilometers) away from the petroglyphs in Ulsan. Despite this, scholars believe that the prehistoric people who engraved the Bangudae Petroglyphs later migrated to the White Sea in what is now Russia and took to engraving stone canvases there, too.

The next section examines the similarities between the Bangudae and the Zalavruga Petroglyphs.

The first similarity to note is the overall organization of both collections. The Zalavruga Petroglyphs group sea animals on the left and land animals on the right, an overall organizational pattern similar to the Bangudae Amgakhwa. This similarity in structure suggests that the people who engraved the Bangudae Petroglyphs and the people who engraved the Zalavruga Petroglyphs had similar worldviews. Traditional Eastern philosophy calls the left side yin and the right side yang. In accordance with yin-yang philosophy, sea animals were placed on the left and land animals on the right.

The second significant similarity is that the Zalavruga Petroglyphs also depict whales and the details of whale hunting. The rock carvings in Russia have fewer whale species than the Bangudae Amgakhwa, but they use similar styles and expressions of detail, such as the presence of fins, disproportionately large bodies and small tails, and intaglio engraving methods.* The portrayal of using boats for whale hunting is also similar.

---

* Palgwae or 8 trigrams are eight symbols that represent fundamental principles of reality, seen as a range of eight interrelated concepts. Each trigrams represent each one of the following; heaven, earth, fire, water, mountain, lake, thunder, and wind.

Figure 12-17 Shaman with a bird's head and a large foot expressed on a petroglyph from Zalavruga

Figure 12-18 This is an enlarged photograph of the Shaman who has the head of bird and a huge hands and feet found in the Bangudae Petroglyph/The picture is an enlarged version of National Museum of Korea.

The third important parallel between these collections is that both contain elements of shamanism and totemism in their depictions of numerous people among the animals that dominate the scene. While most of these figures are engaged in hunting-related activities, other images appear to be unrelated to the hunt. In the Zalavruga Petroglyphs, footprints cross from the leftmost edge of the collection to the right. Curiously, these footprints are disproportionately large to the body of a person engraved at the edge of the image — that is, this person does have abnormally large feet. In the Bangudae Amgakhwa, there is a depiction of a person with slightly bent legs and hands folded together toward the sky. Below this is another figure with a bird-shaped head and elongated arms and legs, and the feet and hands of this person are disproportionately enlarged as seen in the Zalavruga Petroglyphs. The facial features of one figure appear to include face paint or makeup, and another seems to be blowing a musical instrument. Scholars believe that these people were shamans, the leaders of Korean society at that time.

08

A shaman's hunting song

7,000 years ago, before a hunt, a shaman would pray to the heavens for a successful hunting expedition and a safe return. Once the shaman's prayer was done, brave hunters wielding bows and spears would go forth to the fields and the sea.

The shamans depicted in the Bangudae Amgakhwa and in the petroglyph collection on the coast of Russia's White Sea appear to have oversized feet and the heads of birds. The famous wall art of the Lascaux Caves in France also features a shaman with the head of a bird standing before a large ox that has been hunted down.

To the prehistoric people who lived in Ulsan, a bird was a sacred creature that delivered their wishes to the god in the heavenly realm and brought back messages for humankind. A shaman would wake the spirits of the ancestors by playing a drum with large hands and

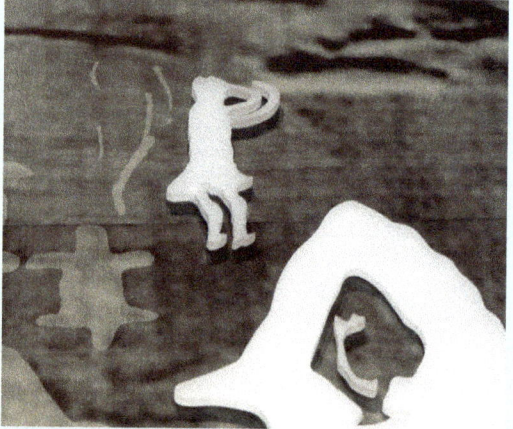

Figure 12-19 Images of people in Bangudae Petroglyph Rock / Enlarged version of the image from National Museum of Korea.

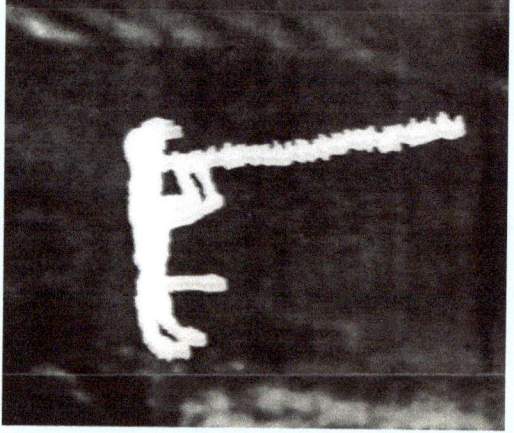

Figure 12-20 Shaman with a head of a bird and a Sotdae is standing in front of a hunted cow, a painting found in the cave in Lascaux Petroglyphs, France / reproduced at the Lascaux Cave Art Exhibition in Gwangmyeong, Gyeonggi-do Province

wake the spirits of nature by stomping on the ground to deliver the prayers of human society to the spirits of heaven and earth. This is why shamans were depicted with such distinctive hands and feet. In later generations, it became common to wear feathered headgear (or headgear with feather-shaped ornaments) as a status symbol. Such depictions can be seen in the ancient Muyongchong tomb mural in Goguryeo-era tombs. Even today, shamans still occasionally wear feathers as headgear.

The Korean phrase Jae Jeong Il Chi refers to theocracy, or the unity of church and state, which describes society in ancient Korea. Shamans were the leaders of society, ruling as supreme officiants who made ritual offerings to the heavens. The depictions in the Bangudae Amgakhwa, which include a person with the head of a bird and disproportionately large hands and feet, as well as a person with their hands held skyward in prayer, portray shamans—the ultimate rulers and religious leaders of their people. It was believed that only a person chosen by divine power to serve as the divine representative could rule a village, tribe, or state. Prosperity in life and victory in battle could be achieved only by following the will of the divine.

During this time, the shaman was referred to as "the king of the hunt." Because the king of the hunt ruled the people by divine will, it was thought that he could control animals by borrowing divine power, and so he was expected to pray and make ritual offerings to the heavens. The people's earnest wish was that this divine power would protect them, ensuring not only a successful hunt but also survival and safety from the threat of wild animals. Under the shaman's direction, they performed grand hunting rituals, which were essentially ritual offerings to the spirits to beseech them for a successful hunt.

The prehistoric people who made the petroglyphs must have wanted to memorialize the animals that they targeted in their hunts and the details of their hunting rituals. Upon a successful hunt, they took delight in engraving a record of their trophies. The petroglyphs therefore are a record of the hunting rituals of a prehistoric people who long ago dreamed of leading happy and bountiful lives.

Defining "shaman"

- The etymology of the word shaman is often linked to a word from the Siberian Tungusic language, saman, meaning religious leader, but shaman actually comes from a word that combines the characters of Sam (three) and Ahn (heaven or god). The modern formulation of this Korean word is Samshin (Triune Spirit). Samshin is a famous grandmother figure in Korean culture, a triple goddess whose name literally means "Three Spirits." The word shaman originated from the same "saman" or "samshin" used to describe this grandmother goddess. The word "saman" has been in use throughout East Asia since antiquity. When Western scholars learned of this word, they pronounced it as "shaman." The religious activities and rituals through which people communicate with the divine through a shaman are called shamanism. The reason Koreans refer to Buddhist monks as "samun" can also be traced to the history of the spiritual authority of shamans.

Figure 12-21 A procession of whale hunting ship and reindeers (left), leaving for whale hunting after a hunting ritual / This image was restored and recreated at the State Historical Museum in Moscow, Russia

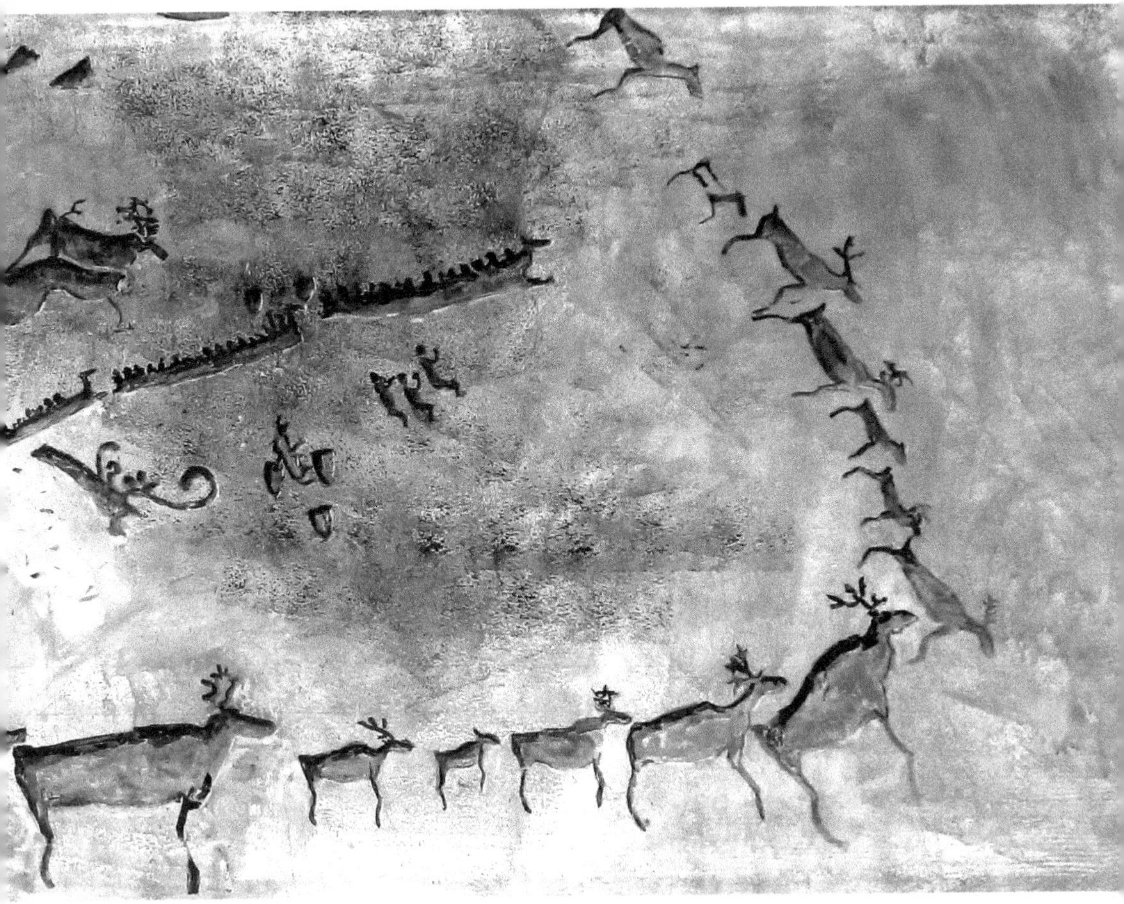

Figure 12-22 Partial Enlargement of 12-21 / A scene of three Shaman wishing the fleet to return safely from the whale hunting.

12・Whale Hunting 7,000 Years Ago, Bangudae Amgakwha

PART 13

A Trip to the Museums in Korea

Rice, The Oldest Farming Culture in the World

01 Why prehistoric people began settling down
02 Ancient agricultural remains in Goseong-gun County
03 A 5,000-year-old diet
04 Growing rice 5,000 years ago
05 17,000-year-old rice seeds

01

Why prehistoric people began settling down

Resources in the modern world are abundant, making it easy for us to forget the humble beginnings of this prosperity: grain. Humankind could not have reached this level of abundance without the rise of a culture of cultivating grain as a food source. Prior to developing agriculture, humans gathered wild crops and fruit in hunter-gatherer societies. Economic anthropologist Marshall Sahlins describes this in his book *Stone Age Economics*, maintaining that people worked just four to five hours a day and spent the remaining time resting and sleeping. Given they did not suffer from a scarcity of food sources, and as long as they could survive in a rough natural environment, their standard of living was better than in an agricultural society. They managed to achieve a level of food intake comparable to modern society even though they had not yet developed the concept of food storage. Because these hunter-gatherers were nutritionally advantaged, they were healthier and taller than people in agricultural

Figure 13-1 Rice plant brings its head down, signaling that it has ripen in the autumn season/ Our ancestors have farmed for thousands of years.

societies. Their social and family solidarity was also strengthened by the necessity of hunting and fighting wild animals for survival. The modern misperception that hunter-gatherer societies were savage while agricultural and livestock farming societies were advanced and civilized is based on an egocentric way of thinking.

For this reason, Israeli historian and author of *Sapiens: A Brief History of Humankind*, Yuval Noah Harari, insists that the concept of the Agricultural Revolution was history's biggest fraud. As human civilization took to the plow, we suffered from hard work and malnutrition, which resulted in not only shorter people, but shorter lifespans.

In *The Fall: The Insanity of the Ego in Human History and the Dawning of a New Era*, British psychologist Steve Taylor discusses an era of humankind he describes as a Golden Age without war, a period between six to ten thousand years ago. This is because no trace of weaponry or evidence of war has been discovered among the remains left behind from that period. According to Taylor, society then was egalitarian, without patriarchy or social class.

However, due to an increasing human population and dramatic climate change, people began to migrate to other places where they could secure food. For example, the Sahara Desert was fertile land until around 10,000 years ago, but as the climate changed, people had no choice but to migrate to the region around the Nile, where food was abundant. Approximately 6,000 years ago in Siberia, people migrating due to climate change (then a cold wave) conflicted with societies that already existed in those lands, which resulted in bloody conflict in some areas. The regions of modern Iran and Turkey became a war zone. Social classes appeared, weapons were developed, and food storage became a necessity.

In *Guns, Germs, and Steel: The Fates of Human Societies*, UCLA professor of geography and physiology Jared Diamond outlines four reasons ancient civilizations began choosing farming over hunting starting about 10,000 years ago:

1. Wild food sources decreased.
2. Wild crops that could be domesticated and cultivated increased due to climate change.
3. The development of technology for processing and storing wild food allowed the cultivation of grain.
4. Increased food production due to an increased population further increased population density, which required even more food.

Of course, the transition from gathering to cultivation took several thousand years. This was followed by the revolution of the Neolithic Age, when earthenware was invented and agriculture spread.

02

Ancient agricultural remains in Goseong-gun County

When did early Korean civilization begin engaging in agriculture? A clear answer to this is still under examination, as scholars continue to sift through the evidence left behind.

Ancient agricultural remains were excavated in a hilly coastal area near Munam-li Village in Goseong-gun County, Gangwon-do Province. This discovery attracted international attention when it was identified as the oldest agricultural remains in East Asia. This find is between 5,000 to 6,000 years old and dates to the Stone Age, making it a priceless discovery for scholars and a notable addition to Korea's cultural heritage. Japan has yet to make such an ancient agricultural discovery, and even China, which has been prematurely lauded by some as the origin of agriculture, does not have any known agricultural remains that date to the Neolithic Age.

Evidence of ancient farming activity was not the only Munam-li finding. Excavations also revealed a residential structure and outdoor workspace for building fires for cooking and other work. Prior to the Munam-li discoveries, the leading theory was that Korean agriculture began during the Bronze Age, but the unearthing of the Munam-li remains proved that crop cultivation had already begun in Neolithic Korea.

Stoneware, stone arrowheads, and comb-pattern pottery pieces were discovered at the site of the residential remains. The shapes and comb patterns of these artifacts resemble earthenware excavated from the former territory of Ancient Joseon (including the entire Korean Peninsula, the Dongbei region of modern China, and an additional region including the Amur River that borders Russia and China).

As the remains of Munam-li have been estimated at about 5,000 to 6,000 years old, it appears that they belonged to Baedal, which preceded Ancient Joseon. In the Baedal state era, a cultural icon named Shennong figured prominently in the history of agriculture. Shennong, also known as the Divine Farmer, is a person introduced in several places throughout this book. He was an official of the state of Baedal during the reign of Anburyeon, the eighth Heavenly Emperor Hwanung. Born in the Gahngsu River region, Shennong became the progenitor of the Kang family. His status as a cultural icon came about in large part due to the story that he tasted one hundred types of herbs to distinguish which were beneficial and which were toxic for human consumption. As this legend maintains that agriculture developed from Shennong's classifications of different herbs, it appears that the people who lived in Munam-li applied Shennong's teachings to the cultivation of their crops.

Figure 13-2 The Bronze Age relic on the Nong-gyeong-mun Bronze Relic, depicting a farmer plowing a field / One of the oldest relics excavated in Korea that depicts an ancient form of agriculture, the artifact is believed to have been produced around the 4th century BCE. A man with feathers on his head is plowing a field with a Tta-bi(a plowing tool), and underneath it is a figure holding a hoe. (National Museum of Korea)

Figure 13-3 A bird is seated at the tip of a branch that stretches from side to side of a tree, depicted on the back of the bronze relic. It is presumed to be a Sotdae. Sotdae is another form of Shindansu and Korean people held various festivals under the Sotdae on every Lunar Janurary 15th, asking for a year of abundant harvest.(National Museum of Korea)

03

A 5,000-year-old diet

Evidence of intact furrows are among the findings of the Munam-li agricultural remains. These furrows were formed when the land was plowed, a method that piled soil in long and narrow strips to make the irang (ridges) where the crops were planted. The soil between the irang was removed to make a depression called the gorang (furrow), which gave the crops room to flourish. Because crops planted in high density have to compete with each other for nutrients found in the dirt, the existence of the gorang allowed each plant to absorb enough nutrients. The gorang also facilitated water drainage, which prevented the submersion of crops in standing water. The key feature of this irang and gorang system was separation. Compared to remains from the Bronze Age, the pattern of the Munam-li remains has unevenly wide gorang and irang that are not completely parallel.

The system of gorang and irang was an agricultural method developed through trial-and-error; furrows like these do not occur naturally. The excavation of the Munam-li agricultural remains also unearthed human footprints, traces of crop cultivation, and traces of the stalks of planted crops.

But what exactly was the diet of the people of ancient Munam-li? Archaeologists discovered the answer to this in the soil of these agricultural remains. A range of experiments on the excavated hulls, pollen, and stems from crops found in Munam-li have shed light on this varied diet.

The key crop among these findings was the rice plant, which can be cultivated in paddies as well as dry fields. Prior to the development of paddy cultivation, rice plants were cultivated solely in dry fields. Wild rice plants do not grow naturally in Munam-li, meaning that the excavated rice grains were seeded and cultivated by the people who settled the region millennia ago. Along with rice, fragments of ancient strains of wheat, millet, proso millet, barley, ginger, goosefoot, and perilla were also excavated, but beans were the most surprising discovery of all. The beans found in Munam-li were a wild species, but it is speculated that they were cultivated as a cover crop to restore soil fertility. The fact that beans were cultivated here strengthened the theory that agriculture was more advanced during this time period than previously believed.

In Yangyang County, not far from Munam-li Village, lies a small village named Osan-li. Excavations here unearthed Neolithic Age earthenware with traces of adzuki beans. This suggests that the crops cultivated several thousand years ago were not that different from modern crops. The combination of discoveries painted a new picture of the people who once lived here—people who cooked multigrain rice with a mixture of various crops, such as rice, wheat, millet, proso millet, barley, and adzuki beans.

04

Growing rice 5,000 years ago

In 1991, a broad range of relics from the Paleolithic Age to the Iron Age were excavated from Gawaji Village (Goyang-si City, Gyeonggi-do Province) during the local development of Ilsan New Town, a planned South Korean city. A total of 107 rice seeds were identified from these remains. The rice seeds at this site, which included rice pollen, traces of rice, and carbonized rice hulls, were discovered intact and in even better condition than the Munam-li findings.

Analysis by the U.S. Beta Analytic Testing Laboratory revealed that the rice seeds from Gawaji were about 5,000 years old. Prior to this discovery, the leading but incomplete theory maintained that rice cultivation had been transmitted to Korea from Japan, rather than the other way around.

Many museums inaccurately claim that ancient Korean civilization started cultivating rice between the twelfth to tenth centuries BCE

Figure 13-4 Gawaji Rice Seeds Museum in Goyang City, Gyeonggi-do Province

(just over 3,000 years ago). This underdeveloped theory attempts to fit the start of rice cultivation into a period around the Bronze Age. With the excavation of the Gawaji rice seeds, the historical record should be corrected to acknowledge that Korean civilization began rice cultivation at least 5,000 years ago.

In reality, rice farming is not significantly related to bronzeware. During the Neolithic Age, there was agricultural activity, and during the Iron Age, stoneware was used for farming, not just weapons, ritual tools, and accessories. The Munam-li and Gawaji findings have shown that tools of stone and wood were more than sufficient for the cultivation of rice without bronzeware.

An agricultural site abroad has further validated this argument. In the Peruvian Andes, there are numerous terraced fields called andenes that have been in use since prior to the Incan civilization. Even today, it is incredible that people engage in agriculture 2,000 to 4,000 meters above sea level.

Figure 13-5 Moray, an Inca-era agricultural test site in the Andean alpine region of Peru / Andeanes, where the terraced agricultural land in the Inca era creates a spectacular scenery, has a temperature difference of about 5 degrees from the top of the field to the bottom.

Table 3-1. Rice found in Neolithic Age sites
(explanation from the Gawaji Rice Seed Museum in Goyang-si City)

Location	Era	Finding
Gahyeon-li Village, Gimpo-gun County, Gyeonggi-do Province	4,000 years ago	Unhulled rice (hull)
Gawaji Village, Ilsan City, Gyeonggi-do Province	5,020 years ago	Unhulled rice (hull), rice (carbonized rice), rice hull silicates
Jodong-li Village, Chungju-si City, Chungcheongbuk-do Province	6,200 years ago	Unhulled rice (hull), rice hull silicates
Residential site in Daecheon-li Village, Okcheon-gun County, Chungcheongbuk-do Province	5,000 years ago	Unhulled rice (hull), rice (carbonized rice)
Shell mound in Nongso-ri Village, Gimhae City, Gyeongsangnam-do Province	End of Neolithic Age	Unhulled rice (hull), rice hull silicates

Currently, Peru and Bolivia, where the Andes civilization prospered as a result of agriculture, cultivate about seventy percent of the crop species consumed by modern civilization. This includes hundreds of species of potatoes, cassava (a root crop of the cassava tree that is shaped like a sweet potato), tomatoes, chili, quinoa (a crop that grows mainly in the Andes), peanuts, and more. The total number of plant species grown in this area stands at about 20,000, four times that of South Korea.

Today, highland people in the Andes continue to forego the use of machinery and livestock in their agriculture. In some places, they even grow crops with wooden sticks. Outside Peru, people throughout Asia and Africa sow seeds and cultivate crops by using wooden sticks the same way their ancestors did.

Early agriculture required a copious amount of human labor, making the development of social groups inevitable. While agriculture made it easier to survive, it also resulted in a new set of problems.

After a successful harvest, surplus products needed to be stored. This triggered the Neolithic Revolution: the invention of earthenware. In addition to food storage, these agricultural societies needed to be stronger in order to guard their surplus products from other groups. These complex problems naturally led to the development of a state system. While it is estimated that Dangun Wanggeom founded Ancient Joseon in 2333 BCE, the Gawaji and Munam-li discoveries suggest that people settled and began farming there significantly earlier, predating the foundation of Ancient Joseon. People practiced agriculture during the time of the Hwanung's rule of Baedal.

---

* Warring States period of Korea. (Buyeo, Goguryeo, Baekjae, Dongye, Okjeo, Jinhan, Mahan, and Byeonhan) - Just before Ancient Joseon(Dangun Joseon) came to an end, Northern Buyeo established itself and conquered all the old lands of Joseon. Northern Buyeo later changes its name to Goguryeo. Then the migrants of the Three Han States came to the Southern part of Korean peninsula to establish Jinhan, Mahan, and Byeonhan. Okjeo and Dongye are micro nations located in the Northern Parts of the Korean peninsula. These two nations was eventually absorbed in to the surrounding nations.

05

17,000-year-old rice seeds

Though the Gawaji rice seeds paint a surprising picture of early agriculture, ancient history even more amazing than this was unearthed in another Korean village. A Paleolithic Age stratum was excavated at a field preparation site for the Ochang Scientific Industrial Complex in Soro-li Village, Chungcheonbuk-do Province. During the excavation, ancient rice and similar-rice (which appears to be rice) were discovered alongside Paleolithic cultural artifacts. The remains were sent to Seoul National University in South Korea and to the Geochron Laboratory in the U.S. for radiocarbon dating, where they were dated as 13,000 to 15,000 years old and became known as the famous Soro-li rice seeds.

Ancient rice and similar-rice can only be distinguished with an electron microscope. The hull of an ancient rice seed is uneven like that of a modern rice seed, whereas the surface of a similar-rice seed is even. The much higher proportion of similar-rice than ancient rice in this finding led to speculation that similar-rice was the main food source at the time. In the fall of 2003, the BBC introduced the Soro-li rice seeds as the oldest rice seeds in the world even though some scholars insisted that the climate of 15,000 years ago (at the end of the Paleolithic Age and near the end of the last glacial epoch) was unfavorable for subtropical plants like rice. This argument was largely based on the fact that the minimum sprout temperature for rice in natural conditions is established to be 68 degrees Fahrenheit (20 degrees Celsius). Additionally, it was unclear whether the Soro-li rice seeds were wild or cultivated. To answer this question, a team from the South Korean Cheongju Muhwa Broadcasting Corporation (MBC) reported on an experiment performed at the National Institute of Crop Science (NICS). They found that seventy percent of rice seeds were able to sprout in temperatures as low as around 55 degrees Fahrenheit (13 degrees Celsius). This cold tolerance test revealed that rice can adapt well even in relatively cold environments, strengthening the finding that Soro-li rice seeds are at least 15,000 years old.

In response, some scholars posed a problem with the credibility of the results of the age-dating technique and requested a radiocarbon dating of the Soro-li rice seed sample from the Accelerator Mass Spectrometry Laboratory at the University of Arizona in the U.S., which estimated the age of the rice seeds to be 12,520 years old. This put to rest the conflicting theories by providing results that were nearly identical to the previous dating process performed in 2001.

Scientists have since determined that the Soro-li rice seeds are an intermediate species between wild rice and cultivated rice; this species is called sunwha rice (according to the Chungbuk University Museum in South Korea). The existence of sunwha rice means that people selected for certain types of wild rice.

Furthermore, it is believed that the Gawaji rice seeds were selectively bred from the cultivation of Soro-li rice seeds because the Soro-li rice seeds are genetic predecessors of the Gawaji rice seeds.

The discovery of the Soro-li rice seeds was scientific proof that ancient Korean civilization independently pioneered its own agriculture. These findings refuted previous claims that the cultivation of rice was transmitted to Korea from either China or Japan. The Soro-li, Gawaji, and Munam-li discoveries confirm that early Korean civilization developed agriculture. Additionally, these discoveries are a valuable addition to Korea's cultural heritage because they reveal that the settlement and the development of farming culture is what enabled the founding of Baedal and Ancient Joseon.

Soro-li rice seeds predate Chinese rice

- Prior to the discovery of rice seeds in Soro-li, 11,000-year-old rice seeds discovered in Hunan Province, China were regarded as the oldest in the world. However, the Soro-li rice seeds gained recognition when they were established to be as at least 4,000 years older than their Chinese counterparts, which resulted in a reversal of the previous theory that China transmitted rice cultivation to the Korean Peninsula.

Previously, farming culture was theorized to have first originated around 7,000 BCE from Mesopotamia, which is in southwest Asia. However, the alternative theory in which northeast Asia was the origin of the farming culture that reigned during the Neolithic Age gained persuasive power after the Soro-li rice seed findings were presented at a 2004 research symposium in Paris.

According to the calculation method for carbon dating more recently developed by Cambridge University in England, the estimated age of the Soro-li rice seeds has increased to 17,000 years. As a result, the Soro-li rice seeds have been given the new nomenclature of "oryza sativa coreca," meaning "rice cultivated in Korea."

PART 14

A Trip to the Museums in Korea

A Beginning of Korean Wave, Comb-Pattern Pottery

01 Korea's Oldest Earthenware: Gosan-li pottery from Jeju Island
02 Osan-li's comb-pattern pottery predates Siberian ware
03 Comb-pattern pottery spreads through East Asia and Europe
04 The anti-breakage science of comb-pattern pottery
05 A better name for comb-pattern: sunshine-pattern pottery

01

Korea's Oldest Earthenware:
Gosan-li pottery from Jeju Island

Every year, about 10 million domestic and international travelers visit the tourist heaven of Jeju Island. Despite the constant waves of tourists, few are aware that Jeju Island is home to the oldest prehistoric artifacts in Korea. In Gosan-li Village, located on the western edge of Jeju Island, excavations have unearthed an impressive collection of artifacts that are approximately 10,000 years old.

Gosan-li is a beautiful place where tourists can view Suwolbong Peak from an outlook along the Jeju Olle Trail and take in the sight of the volcanic islands of Chaguido in the sea in front of the peak. But Gosan-li is also home to the site where 10,000-year-old earthenware—some of the oldest pottery in the world—was excavated. This earthenware is a plant-based pottery that was made by mixing earth with plant fiber. Different types of pottery have been discovered in Jeju Island, including types with or without plant fiber and types with

Figure 14-1 Chagwido Island off Gosan-ri, Jeju Island. Legend has it that during the reign of King Yejong, the 16th King of Goryeo Dynasty, Ho Jongdan(a man from Northern Zhou. A Fengshui master) came to cut off the energy stream of Jeju Island, but could not disconnect all of them. On his way back, he met a great storm and was lost at sea. It also means Chagwido is a place Hojongdan could not reach.

Figure 14-2 The Gosan-ri excavation site located near a beach in Jeju Island. 1,000 pieces of reddish brown fiber earthenware and other pieces of earthenware, 99,000 stone tools, and living grounds from this Early Neolithic site of Korea.

or without engraved patterns. The Gosan-li type of pottery is known to contain plant fiber, to have no pattern, and to be excavated solely in Gosan-li, Jeju Island.

It is speculated that Gosan-li pottery was produced in a period that predates the pottery of the Neolithic Age. In addition, it is believed to be the original form of Korean earthenware and Korea's oldest pottery. Because Jeju is an island, some have argued that its earthenware was developed independent of mainland influence, but this is incorrect. 10,000 years ago, sea levels were lower, and Jeju Island was connected to the peninsula. Back then, the peninsula and Jeju Island were geographically linked as one extended cultural area, meaning that this cultural heritage represents the unique style of the Korean people as a whole; it is not a piece of history that belongs to Jeju Island alone. Though the idea that Korean earthenware originated from Siberia was once the leading theory, the excavation of the Gosan-li pottery on Jeju Island has revealed that Korean pottery was a home-grown invention.

Figure 14-3 Gosan-ri style earthenware from Jeju Island, which is estimated to have been made about 10,000 years ago. It is one of the oldest earthenware in the world. It was made by grinding organic matter and soil, but during the baking process, the organic matter gets burned and dissolved, leaving only its trace on the surface. It was displayed at the special exhibition of the National Museum of Korea.

02

Osan-li's comb-pattern pottery predates Siberian ware

The ancestors of modern Korea produced and utilized a variety of pottery shapes. Compared to modern bowls, these look primitive, but they were produced through a systematic process. A base of mostly mud, sometimes combined with sand, was mixed with water to make a paste that was then molded into a bowl shape and fired at a temperature of over 932 degrees Fahrenheit (500 degrees Celsius). It is unclear whether this early pottery was fired in a kiln. The shape and hardness of the pottery was determined based on the kiln technique that was used. As various techniques were developed, pottery began to be produced in a range of firmness and colors such as brown, black, or gray. Pottery produced during the initial stage of production was consistently a reddish-brown hue.

When these early Korean potters made their wares, they did not limit themselves to functional products and began adding patterns to create aesthetically pleasing bowls. The artisanry that began with the raised-clay Yunggimun pottery (where lumps of clay were attached in bands on the surface of the bowl to form raised patterns) eventually gave birth to bitsal-muni pottery, known in English as comb-pattern pottery. Both types of pottery are typical of the Neolithic Age in Korea.

Comb-pattern pottery is the umbrella term for pottery engraved with comb-like geometric designs. This includes comb-dot pottery, also called pit-comb ware, the surface of which is imprinted with dots that look like they were made by the teeth of a comb. Finnish archeologist Julius Ailio coined the German term "kammkeramik" to describe comb-pattern pottery, and a Japanese archeologist translated this into Japanese as "jeulmun." Korean scientists translated the name literally to "bitsal-muni" (comb-pattern) pottery.

Until recently, comb-pattern pottery production was believed to date back about 5,000 years, but this estimate was adjusted to about 8,000 years. The adjustment was due to the excavation of 8,000-year-old comb-pattern pottery from the Bohai Bay (Liao River) civilization, which was established by the ancestors of modern Korea.

As described earlier in this book, the oldest comb-pattern pottery in Korea was excavated in Osan-li Village (Yangyang-gun County, Gangwon-do Province) and found to be approximately 7,500 to 8,000 years old. This is at least 500 years earlier than pottery found in Siberia and Eastern Europe. Osan-li comb-pattern pottery also differs from Siberian pottery in terms of production method and design. The Osan-li discovery, along with the Gosan-li and the Bohai Bay (Liao River) civilization pottery, overturned the once-dominant theory that comb-pattern pottery was transmitted from Siberia to Korea. Out of all the comb-pattern pottery found in the world today, the ancient pottery of Korea predates pottery produced by other groups.

Figure 14-4 Comb-patterned earthenware excavated from Amsa-dong, Seoul. It is estimated to have been produced around 5,000 BCE (National Museum of Korea)

03

Comb-pattern pottery spreads through East Asia and Europe

Sites with comb-pattern pottery are distributed throughout the Eurasian continent and found in places that include Siberia, Estonia, Sweden, and Finland. The world's oldest comb-pattern pottery was excavated in the Liao River region (coastal area of the Bohai Bay and cradle of the Bohai Bay civilization), which includes Liaodong Peninsula, Hebei Province, Liaoning Province, and the Shandong Peninsula; all of these were part of the territory where the early Korean people, the Dongyi, once ranged. Both the geography of the Liaodong Peninsula and the Korean Peninsula and the components of the types of soil used for making comb-pattern pottery in these two regions are similar. Notably, chipped stone tools (made by chipping flakes from a stone), ground stone tools (made by grinding a stone), and microliths (small, usually geometric stone tools often used for hafted weapons) collocated with the comb-pattern pottery were also excavated.

The oldest comb-pattern pottery was excavated in the former territory of the early Korean people, its production period predating all pottery made by other prehistoric tribes around the world. This makes it reasonable to infer that the prehistoric Korean people were the first to make comb-pattern pottery. The comb-pattern (bitsal-muni) pottery then spread slowly toward Western civilization, passing through Siberia to northern Europe.

The types of comb-pattern pottery that spread throughout the Eurasian continent took similar shapes and had similar designs. The most common shared features were a conical bottom, a surface pattern, and a few holes, the purpose of which is still unknown.

If this type of pottery was transmitted from ancient Korean civilization to eventually reach northern Europe, it begs the question: What enabled this transmission? Did East Asians carrying comb-pattern pottery traverse the entire continent? The cultural technology to make the Bangudae Amgakhwa took approximately 1,000 years to be transmitted to Russia where the Zalavruga Petroglyphs were created, so it stands to reason that the cimb-pattern pottery design was shared and transmitted over the course of a thousand years, too. The Eurasian Route, a road that reached from Asia to Europe that has seen recent and frequent mention in scholarly discourse, may have already existed when comb-pattern pottery was transmitted.

Figure 14-5 Distribution diagram of comb-patterned pottery. It runs through Mongolia and Siberia to northern Germany, Estonia and Sweden on the Scandinavian peninsula.

Figure 14-6 (left) A comb-pattern pottery housed in the Siberian branch museum of the Russian Academy of Sciences in Novosibirsk, Russia.

Figure 14-7 (right) A comb-patterned earthenware displayed at the State Historical Museum in Moscow / 3500 to 3000 years ago in Siberia

Figure 14-8 A comb-pattern pottery at the National museum in Stockholm, Sweden. An image of the sun is also painted on the pottery, so we could call it a sunshine-patterned earthenware.

04

The anti-breakage science of comb-pattern pottery

When I first saw a piece of comb-pattern pottery with my own eyes, I was amazed to see that its surface was covered with geometrical patterns. Engraving such a pattern to cover the entire surface of a piece of pottery would have been an intensive task. Why, then, would anyone have invested their time, energy, and resources in crafting comb-pattern pottery?

A likely answer to this question actually comes from a theory proposed by a pair of South Korean high school students, named Lee Seon-young and Jeong Yu-jin. Their project "Why did Neolithic Age people engrave comb-pattern on pottery?" was submitted to the 2013 National Science Exhibition for High School Students. Their science-backed theory was the astounding result of over 10 months of research.

According to their theory, comb-pattern was scientifically

designed to overcome various limitations of the process of pottery production. At the time, pottery was made with mud that contained a significant proportion of impure substances and fired at relatively low temperatures. As mentioned previously in this chapter, it is still uncertain whether kilns were used in the firing process. Firing a piece of pottery requires a temperature of at least 932 degrees Fahrenheit (over 500 degrees Celsius), so a potter without a kiln to concentrate and distribute the heat evenly would have had to rely on a woodfire. Heating from a woodfire is uneven, and the moisture evaporates rapidly, resulting in cracked pottery. But if the potter pressed comb-like patterns into the mud paste before it was fired, this reduced the chance of hollow spaces forming within the mud and helped harden the pottery, preventing thin cracks and splits from spreading from a single flaw to affect the entire piece. On the other hand, patterns made by scraping at the surface instead of pressing the patterns in resulted in weakened pottery, potentially even undermining the benefits of the crack-prevention effect. The two high school students who researched this scientific reason for early Korean potters' use of comb-pattern on their pottery deserve sincere praise for their research.

05

A better name for comb-pattern: sunshine-pattern pottery

The functional application of comb-pattern as a method of structural reinforcement is not the only theory that has gained traction. Keimyung University professor Kim Yangdong suggests a different purpose for comb-pattern, which has long been considered to be patterns formed by comb impressions. In his theory, Professor Kim refers to *Shuowen Jiezi* (*An Explication of Written Characters*), a work compiled by Later Han in the early second century CE and the oldest comprehensive Chinese character dictionary.* The dictionary explains the meaning and pronunciation of about 10,000 Chinese characters, including the explanation that " ⌡ " in the 神 character means sunshine. This is significant because 神 taken as a whole is pronounced "shin"

---

* Intaglio engraving is where an image is engraved into the surface, forming concave or depressed areas. It is considered the opposite of relief engraving, where the image is carved to protrude from the surface.

and means god or spirit.* According to Professor Kim, the line patterns on ancient pottery were intended to portray the rays of the sun, like a pattern of light engraved on bowls. Given that this pattern is not simply repeated here and there but entirely covers the pottery's surface, it is believed to symbolize the sun and sunshine, which were deeply revered.

When a piece of this type of pottery is placed upside down, it becomes easy to understand Professor Kim's insistence that comb-pattern symbolizes sunshine. The following figure is a computer simulation of four different types of comb-pattern pottery viewed from the bottom.

Do you see the patterns? As Professor Kim noted, they look remarkably like rays of sunlight spreading outward. The reason for choosing this particular symbolism can be attributed to a particular aspect of ancient Korean culture in which the sun and moon, which illuminate the entire world, are regarded with reverence. This concept of revering brilliance and brightness is foundational to Korean culture. It is possible that these cultural values were engraved as comb-pattern on pottery and transmitted from ancient Korea to northern Europe through the Eurasian continent.

The Korean cultural value of revering brilliance has been passed down through countless generations, taking a variety of forms along the way.

For example, the celebration of the first day of each year, when Koreans make an effort to watch the first sunrise, is rooted in a culture that has long valued brilliance. A description of how Korean people worshipped the sun many millennia ago can even be found in *Jo Dae Gi*, a record of the ancient history of Korea:

---

* Dangun Wanggeom - The very first emperor of Dangun Joseon also known as Ancient Joseon (2,333-239 BCE).

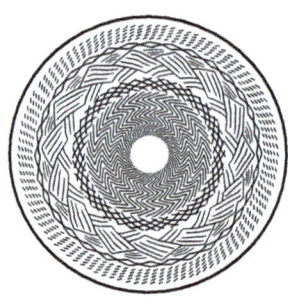

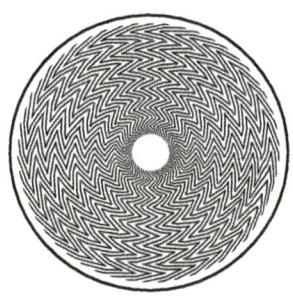

Figure 14-9 The comb-pattern pottery found in South Korea and the sunlight pattern shown at the bottom of the earthenware are recovered though computer graphics.

"According to our customs, we worshipped brilliance, considering the sun to be our god, and the heavens, our ancestor. The whole nation was united in this belief, worshipping the sun each morning and evening in a routine ceremony.

The sun is attributed as the place where the Triune Spirit (Samsin) resides. As it has been said that one's every wish can be realized without fail as long as one lives in the brilliance of the sun, people would climb a mountain in the east each morning to bow low to the sun, and they would go to a river in the west each evening to prostrate themselves before the moon."

Naturally, the religious concept described in the text, in which the Triune Spirit (Samsin) resides in the brilliance of the sun, influenced artistic expression. It was then handed down through many generations to today, making its appearance in the names of places, states, and even nations, and throughout daily life in Korea.

There are many theories as to the origin of the name Baedal, which is used when referring to the ancient Korean people of the Baedal civilization or the state of Baedal. One theory is that the word combines bae, meaning brilliance, and dal, meaning land, to mean "the brilliant land in the East." Joseon, the name of the kingdom that was founded in 1392 and lasted for five centuries, means "the place first touched by sunlight." The origin of this name is explained in a Joseon Dynasty-era book on geography, *Shin Dongguk Ryuji Seungram* (*Augmented Survey of the Geography of Korea*), which states, "Because the state is located at the edge of the East where the sun rises, people named the state Joseon."

After the name of Ancient Joseon was changed to Northern Buyeo at the end of its era, the name Buyeo saw widespread use in the names of various Korean states. For example, the Baekjae Dynasty used Southern Buyeo as its state name. Among the theories on the origins of the name Buyeo is one that says Buyeo came from the natural Korean word bul, which means light or fire. The founding monarch of the Silla Dynasty, Park Hyeokgeose (69 BCE-4 CE), used Park (bright) as his surname and included the character Hyeok (shine) in his first name.

More evidence of comb-pattern's roots in sun symbolism can be found in the sun and moon engravings on Myeongdojeon knife money, an ancient form of knife-shaped metal currency. The first character in its name, Myeong (明), is a combination of sun (日) and moon (月). This form of commodity currency was originally believed to be a currency used by the Yan Dynasty (1100-222 BCE). But more recently, persuasive arguments have been made that Myeongdojeon was a currency of the state of Ancient Joseon. The same sun and moon also make appearances in many other Korean legends and cultural artifacts such as the myth of Hae Mosu of Northern Buyeo, the Three-Legged Crow (the sun bird beloved by the people of Goguryeo), Bicheon (an image that appears in Goguryeo's tomb murals of an immortal being who carries the sun and moon in his hands as he flies through the heavens), Daylight Bodhisattva and Moonlight Bodhisattva (figuring in the shamanistic worship of the Seven Stars of the Northern Dipper, derived from traditional Korean beliefs), and Irworobongdo (a traditional Korean folding screen that was a permanent fixture behind the king's royal throne during the Joseon Dynasty). These and numerous other cultural relics feature the sun and moon as well as the Korean people's tradition of revering brilliance.

Comb-pattern pottery is another aspect of this culture that embodies the principles of revering the brightness of the sun. As reasoned in Professor Kim's book *Original Symbols and Explanations of Ancient Korea*, it would be better to change the official name to "sunshine-pattern" pottery in place of comb-pattern pottery, as this better captures the symbolic importance of the pattern. Its name notwithstanding, comb-pattern pottery was the height of art in the Neolithic Age—it took science into account in its production process, spread across the land as a design popular throughout the Eurasian continent, and paid homage to brilliance itself in the patterns marked on its surface.

Winter solstice celebrations as a vestige of sun worship

- The winter solstice occurs once a year on the shortest day and the longest night. The days grow longer again after the winter solstice, which is why people around the world began celebrating it as the day when the sun was born again. In Rome, where the invincible sun god Mithras was worshipped, people held a festival for their sun god on their winter solstice, December 25. The Christian holy day of Christmas only became December 25 in 350 CE, when Pope Julius I (337-352) declared Jesus's birthday as December 25. Jesus's real birth date was unknown and remains a mystery even today. Meanwhile, the Korean people continue to celebrate winter solstice as a New Year's Day because it is the day when yang energy, a symbol of life, begins to stir. In other words, it is the first day of preparing for spring. The most famous festival in South America, the Incan Sun Festival (Inti Raymi), is held on June 24 every year. Although this falls during the summer solstice by the Korean calendar, it is the winter solstice for Peru because it is located in the southern hemisphere.

Key similarities between the Bohai Bay (Liao River) civilization and Korean culture

Although artifacts excavated from the Bohai Bay (Liao River) civilization area appear similar to ones from the Korean Peninsula, findings of this type were not discovered in central China. Liaodong, Liaoning, Manchuria, and the Korean Peninsula were a cultural area led by the Woongjok (a Korean clan that used a bear totem), where four different Neolithic civilizations overlapped. Megalith, color-pattern pottery, comb-pattern pottery, and microlith cultural areas all have been discovered in the former stomping grounds of the Bohai Bay civilization.

Relics from the Bohai Bay (Liao River) civilization introduced in this book are summarized chronologically in the table below.

Some of the cultural remains described above are considered typical of ancient Korean civilization and have not been excavated in China. These are described in greater detail below.

Stone Mound Tombs

Excavations in the Niuheliang ruins of the Hongsan culture discovered a pyramid well over 300 feet (100 meters) in length on a single side. This pyramid predates Egyptian pyramids by about 1,000 years. The custom of building a stone mound tomb (also called jeokseokchong) was transmitted from the Hongsan culture to Goguryeo, Baekjae, and Japan respectively.

Chronological Index Of Bohai Bay (Liao River) Civilization

Order	Period	Cultural Classification	Date	Features
1	Neolithic Age	Sohhaseo culture	8,500-9,000 years ago	· Human face-shaped pottery
2		Xinglongwa culture	7,200-8,200 years ago	· world's oldest jade earrings; jade bowl · oldest dragon · oldest comb-pattern pottery · teeth with holes (evidence of dental treatment) · grouped residential sites (120-150 houses)
3		Sahe culture	since 7,200 years ago	· dragon formed by piled stones
4		Fuhe culture	7,000-7,200 years ago	· phoenix design usage · colored pottery · microliths
5		Zhao Bogo culture	6,400-7,000 years ago	—
6	Chalcolithic Age (transition period at end of Stone Age when bronze and stone tools were used contemporaneously)	Hongshan culture	5,000-6,500 years ago	· elementary-level civilization: stone mound tomb(pyramid), shrine, altar, goddess statue, jade dragon, patternless pottery, pottery for ritual use
7		Sohhayeon culture	4,000-5,000 years ago	· pottery engraved with script, stoneware, microliths
8	Early Bronze Age	Lower Xiajiadian culture	3,500-4,000 years ago	· high-level civilization: Ancient Joseon bronze sword

Suam-ok, a special kind of jade

The oldest jade earrings in the world were excavated from a Xinglongwa cultural site (dated to approximately 8,200 years ago). The earrings were made from suam-ok, a type of jade gathered from the northern part of the Amnokgang River (also called the Yalu River, this river runs along the modern border between China and North Korea), which was the same material as the jade earrings excavated in Goseong in Gangwon-do Province, South Korea. This suggests that people from the Bohai Bay civilization engaged in a cultural exchange that stretched down the east coast of the Korean Peninsula to Goseong, Busan, and Japan. Significantly, half of the numerous excavated jade pieces were made of suam-ok jade, twenty to thirty percent were from baikal-ok jade, and another twenty to thirty percent were made from locally sourced jade.* This indicates that the Korean Peninsula belonged to the same cultural area.

Bitsal-muni (comb- or sunshine-pattern) pottery

The earliest comb-pattern pottery in the world (about 8,000 years old) was excavated from a Xinglongwa cultural site. In Xinglongwa culture, dental treatments were performed by drilling holes into teeth.

Color-pattern pottery

This type of pottery has not been excavated in central China.

---

* Ok is prounced like Oak, just like an oak tree. Baikal Ok here is referring to jade that was found near the Lake Baikal region.

Ancient Joseon (Liaoning) bronze daggers

This type of bronze artifact has not been excavated in central China, but it has been discovered throughout the Korean Peninsula.

Chee structure of ancient fortresses.

A chee was a defensive structure where multiple sections along the front edge of the fortress protruded toward the enemy. It earned the character Chee (pheasant) as its name because the chee structure looked like a pheasant in hiding that would only expose its head to scan its surroundings. This design can be seen in structures from throughout Korean history, especially during the period when Goguryeo was in power; all fortresses built then had the chee structure. Suwon's Hwaseong Fortress (built in 1796 during the Joseon Dynasty) also has the same structure.

During the Bohai Bay civilization period (8,000-3,000 years ago), the Liao River area was warmer than modern day, the temperature annually averaging just over 50 degrees Fahrenheit (10-12 degrees Celsius). This is like the average annual temperature of the central region of modern South Korea, which enables agriculture to flourish and people to prosper. During the peak of Hongshan culture, which was the golden age of the Bohai Bay civilization, the sea level was 30 feet (10 meters) higher than today, submerging the downstream regions of the Yellow and Yangtze rivers in the sea. Obviously, no human civilization was able to settle in a region that was underwater. It is speculated that as the climate of the Hongshan culture area grew colder and the average temperature dropped, exposing the downstream regions of the Yellow and Yangtze rivers, the Han Chinese tribe migrated there and cultivated what is known as the Yellow River civilization. Consequently, the Hongshan culture predated the Yellow River civilization.

慈壼尚感翟褕之舊貯肆欽遵
於 遺旨乃亟舉於舞華
咨爾金氏稟姿幽閒襲訓
詩禮璜聲靚穆動合坤元

PART 15

A Trip to the Museums in Korea

The Ancient Fashion "It-Item", Jade

01 A people bedecked with precious jade

02 A jewel guiding the way to heaven

03 "Ok" as a modifier of beauty and greatness

04 Reconstructing ancient jade accessories

05 Banishing ghosts and bolstering health:
    the mystical powers of jade

06 Embracing divine vitality and bestowing virtue

07 The ancient state system evidenced by jade artifacts

01

A people bedecked with precious jade

The use of hard minerals—diamonds, rubies, sapphires, and emeralds—as jewels is not as ancient a practice as you might think. Several millennia ago, people did not even know that these stones existed, and processing them was out of the question, but they still found ways to adorn themselves and their belongings with precious materials. In the prehistoric era, animal bones, teeth, and shells were used for ornamentation. Later, materials such as jade, turquoise, gold, silver, and copper came into popular use. Of these, jade became the most desirable precious stone among Koreans, enjoying a long-lasting popularity that left behind numerous jade artifacts for us to excavate in the modern era.

Jade is known for its soft color, fine luster, and hardness. The purer the quality of the mineral, the stronger the gloss of the jade, and polished soft jade in particular exhibits a gentle sheen, as if it has been oiled. It is smooth and cool to the touch, which adds to its appeal,

Figure 15-1 Necklace made by the Triphylians of the Northwestern Peloponnesian Peninsula in southern Greece about 4,000 years ago (National Museum of History of Ukraine)

and the sound it emits when struck is remarkably bright and cheerful. It appears that jade garnered many fans among the Korean people of long ago for precisely these reasons.

The oldest jade earrings in the world (excavated from the remains of the Xinglongwa culture from the Bohai Bay civilization) are also the oldest known jewelry in the world. Notably, the 8,000-year-old jade earrings excavated in Munam-ri Village (Goseong-gun County, Gangwon-do Province) were discovered to be of the same shape, production period, and even material (suam-ok jade). The site where suam-ok jade was produced is not far from the Amnokgang River.

This suggests that the Korean Peninsula and the Liao River area belonged to the same sphere of cultural influence around 8,000 years ago.

The Hongshan culture was the crowning achievement of the Bohai Bay (Liao River) civilization, and many of its jade burial goods were excavated from the Niuheliang ruins. 26 of the Niuheliang tombs had

Figure 15-2 Gold earrings with curved jade (Shillla Exhibition of the National Museum of Korea)

Figure 15-3 Jade bracelet excavated from the Hongsan Culture Excavation Site in Niuheliang/ The picture is a reference from the book <Niuheliang Yizhi>

jade burial goods only, without the stone or earthen pottery that is commonly found in tombs from the Neolithic Age. Excavations at Niuheliang have turned up body ornaments like jade necklaces, jade bracelets, and jade earrings, as well as jade totems (figurines in the shape of symbolic and religiously revered animals and plants). Dragons, birds, and bears are the most typical totem animals, although the jade carving of a silkworm has also been discovered. As mentioned in the chapter on Korean silk and sil-kkury, this is evidence that the people who cultivated the Hongshan culture also engaged in silkworm farming and used silk.

The sheer number of jade artifacts from the Hongshan cultural era is enough to dub it the Jade Age. Accordingly, some scholars insist that the classification of time periods should be the Stone Age – Jade Age – Bronze Age – Iron Age. This chronology even has precedent, as a 2,000-year-old history book from the Han Dynasty, *Yue Jue Shu* (*The Glory of Yue*), describes those time periods in the same way.

As discussed throughout this book, it is believed that the people who cultivated the Bohai Bay civilization and Hongshan culture were the early ancestors of the Korean people, the Dongyi. In other words, the Bohai Bay (Liao River) civilization region was the foundation for the successive states of Baedal, Ancient Joseon, Northern Buyeo, and Goguryeo. Their sphere of activity covered a sizable region northeast of the Great Wall of China and geographically far from the civilization of central China. Nevertheless, China has been persistent in its claim that the Bohai Bay civilization was the origin of Chinese civilization. To this end, China has extensively fabricated a version of the ancient history of East Asia through amendments to China's national history through a governmental project, the "National History Correction Process" (2005-2015), which stretches from the ancient Yellow Emperor (2697-2598 BCE) to the medieval Ming Dynasty (1368-1644).

Figure 15-4 A jade ring disk from early Iron Age was found in Jeju Island, where no natural jade is found./ The disk is very similar to the one made in the Qinhuangdo, Hebei, China (National Jeju Museum)

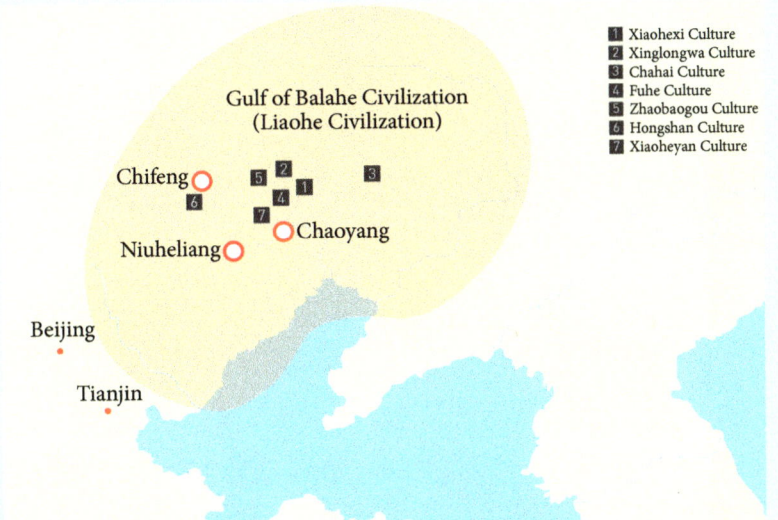

Figure 15-5 Gulf of Balhae Civilization of Hongshan Culture. Modern day Chaoyang, Niuheliang, and Chifeng. And Xinlongwa Culture, where the oldest jade relic was found.

02

A jewel guiding the way to heaven

For those new to Korean television, it might be surprising to see men wearing ornaments and accessories in historical dramas set during the Three Kingdoms period or Goryeo era of Korea. But throughout Korean history, makeup and accessories were not exclusively used by women; Korean men also used cosmetics and wore accessories like rings, earrings, and necklaces. In fact, men wore earrings until the early years of the Joseon Dynasty, which was founded in 1392, and the Eunpyeong History & Hanok Museum in Seoul has a collection of this jewelry on exhibit. Back then, men wore earrings regardless of social position, but the size and shape of a man's earrings varied based on his status.

Traditions of men engaged in self-adornment with cosmetics and accessories were once common worldwide. For example, soldiers in ancient Egypt, Greece, and Rome applied cosmetics and had their nails manicured prior to war, and varying traditions of self-adorn-

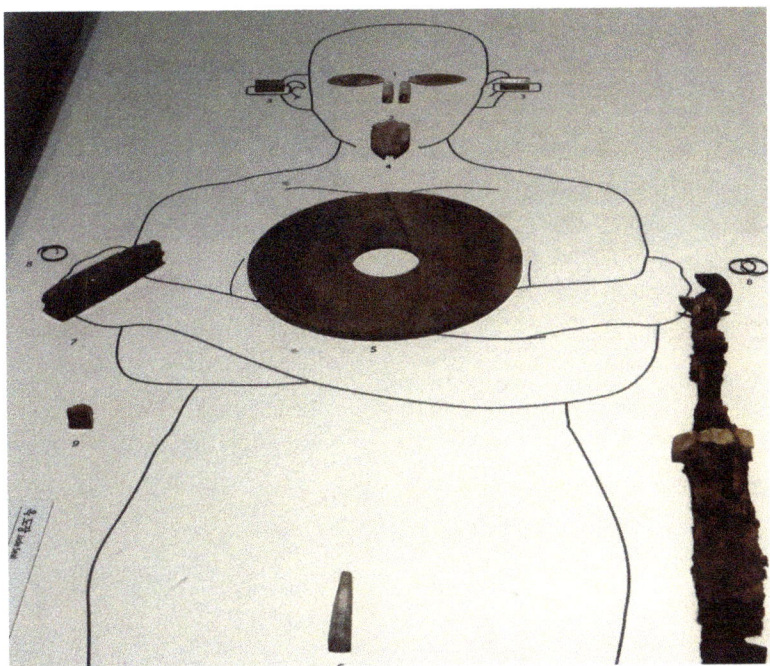

Figure 15-6 The burial jade of the Nang-nang-guk Tomb displayed at the National Museum of Korea / They covered all the holes in the body with the jade.

ment that were developed long ago are still retained by the male warriors of some tribes in Africa.

Adornment traditions begun in ancient eras also extended to dead people, which explains why the people of the Hongshan culture who lived in Niuheliang honored their dead with jade. This use of jade ornaments even after death was symbolic, with the unchanging characteristics of jade representing eternal life and immortality.

Jade used in funerary rites is called jang-ok (tomb jade). Jang-ok artifacts excavated from the Niuheliang tombs include turtles, pillows, cloud-shaped plates, circular plates placed on the chest of the dead, bracelets, and okgo, which were used for securing hair in a top-

Figure 15-7 A jade disk placed on the chest for burial.

Figure 15-8 A sacred animal, jade boar (Donok), that leads the dead to the underworld (National Museum of Korea)

Figure 15-9 The cicada-shaped jade known as ham-ok which is placed inside the mouth of the dead in hopes of reincarnation. (National Museum of Korea)

knot with binyeo (traditional ornamental hairpins). The old Korean word for this type of topknot was sangdu, meaning the Seven Stars of the Northern Dipper, and the circular jade plate placed on the chest of the dead body symbolized the sun and the veneration of brilliance and light.

The Hongshan culture tradition of using jade as a burial good was once popular in Ancient Joseon and throughout East Asia, and many of these jang-ok (tomb jade) artifacts are now on exhibit at the National Museum of Korea. Each piece had significance. For example, jang-ok shaped like a molting cicada and placed in the mouth of the dead signified a wish for resurrection. Jade pig figurines were also placed in the hands of the dead, because the pig was a water deity and a sacred beast that led the dead to the underworld. Colored jade for plugging the ears, nostrils, and anus expressed an effort to prevent the leakage of vital energy. Although entombing the dead with jade may seem curious to modern people, there were clear reasons for this ancient custom. The Jin Dynasty scholar Ge Hong (283-343 CE) wrote on this subject in his canonical Daoist scripture Baopuzi (Master Who Embraces Simplicity), which compiled theories on immortality through the Warring States Period (770-221 BCE).

According to the "Inner Chapter" of Baopuzi, inserting or placing jade on the "nine body openings" of the dead prevents the corpse from decaying.* Also, in I Ching, the chapter titled "An Explanation of Divination Signs" compares the characteristics of Geon—one of the eight trigrams and which symbolizes the sky—to jade. The custom of using jade in burial therefore can be attributed to the wish that jade, which symbolized the sky and is sky-colored itself, would grant its powers to the dead for a safe ascent to the heavens or a return to the immortal realm.

---

* All human beings have 9 holes in their body. Two the ear, two from the nostrils, one from the mouth, one from the anus, one from urethra, and the two holes (blocked with eyeballs) from the two eyes.

03

"Ok" as a modifier of beauty and greatness

Another jade-related relic can be found in the Korean language itself. Long ago, Koreans began affixing the single-syllable character "ok," meaning jade, as a modifier to terms for very precious or beautiful things. There are numerous examples, such as how a noblewoman's delicate hands were called "seom-seom-ok-soo" and her delicate skin was described as white jade and given the name "ok-gi," meaning soft skin like jade. A pavilion built in beautiful surroundings was called an "ok-ru," and a male baby born in a noble family was called "ok-dongja." A person of noble character and angelic appearance (like a divine immortal) was praised with the term "ok-gol-seon-pung," while a very expensive and delicious side dish was called "ok-chan."

In particular, ok was frequently used in reference to the king. The king's body was called "ok-che," and the king's chair was "ok-jwa." The "ok-se" was a stamp made of jade that was used for royal commands.

There is even such a thing as an "ok-chaek"—literally a book made of jade. One such example is the *Sutra of Filial Piety* ok-chaek (a Buddhist scripture on repaying the deep kindness of one's parents) that was produced during the reign of Gwangjong (925-975), the fourth king of the Goryeo Dynasty. Another example is the *Weolinseokbo** ok-chaek, which appears to have been produced during the reign of King Sejong the Great (r. 1418-1450), the fourth king of the Joseon Dynasty. Records of eulogistic posthumous titles that were given to deceased kings, queens, queen dowagers, queen mothers, and grand queen dowagers were also called ok-chaek, and these titles were written in golden letters in a book made of jade. The National Palace Museum of Korea displays the ok-chaek of "Queen Jeongsun of Danjong" with important words inlaid in gold on jade plates.

A variety of terms and names for heavenly bodies and deities are also associated with jade. For example, a moon rabbit is called ok-tokki; a moon toad is ok-seom. The capital of the universe, where the supreme divine ruler resides, is called Ok-gyeong, and the greatest god in Ok-gyeong is called Ok-hwang Sang-je (Jade Emperor).

As described in the examples above, jade was an accessory that connoted a noble or exalted status, and it also served as a medium for communicating with the divine. At one point, even the utensils that were used in ancestral rites were made of jade. The importance of jade can also be seen in the character Ye (禮),

---

* Weol-in-seok-bo is a combination of Seok-bo-sang-jeol, a book of Shakamuni Buddha's life, and Wol-in-Cheon-gang--ji-gok, which is King Sejong's praise for every 2 verses of Seok-bo-sang-jeol. King Sejo combined the two books in to Weolinseokbo for the bleesings of his late father Great King Sejong and his dead son, Crown Prince Ui-gyeong.

which is used in Korean words related to manners and courteousness. This complex character places Ok (珏), meaning two jades, above Du (豆), meaning utensils for ancestral rites. The combination of these two characters can be interpreted to mean "to worship the deity by offering jade." In this same manner, there are numerous other expressions in the Korean language that offer high praise or magnify the meaning by adding "ok" (玉).

Figure 15-10 A jade waistband inscribed with a dragon, worn by the king during the Joseon Dynasty (National Palace Museum of Gyeongbokgung Palace)

Figure 15-11 The Jade Book of Queen Jeongsun, the wife of Danjong, displayed at the National Palace Museum of Korea in Gyeongbokgung Palace

04

Reconstructing ancient jade accessories

Figure 15-12 is a 6,000-year-old impression of a lady ornamented with jade. Although viewers today will probably critique it with the filter of modern aesthetics, it was considered impressive in its own time. The Ung Empress* herself surely would have adorned herself in this magnificent manner during her wedding ceremony with Heavenly Emperor Hwanung. When that divine ritual was held, the entire nation would have participated in an exuberant festival, and men and women would have celebrated while bedecked with this type of ornamentation.

It is speculated that the Korean people's long-lasting love for and cultural incorporation of jade began with the Bohai Bay civilization. From there, it suffused the Korean Peninsula's cultural sphere,

---

* Also known as Woongnyeoh. The first empress and consort of the first Heavenly Emperor of Baedal dyansty. She meditated in a cave by only feeding on garlic and mugwort for 21 days.

spreading south along the east coast before crossing the sea to Japan. Although most accessories during the Four Kingdoms Period (42-562CE) were made of gold, jade continued to reign as one of the most prized materials. Curved jade pieces called gok-ok were even used as ornaments on the king's crown, earrings, and necklaces. Although gok-ok has not yet been excavated in the former Goguryeo region, its discovery is only a matter of time, as Goguryeo shared the same cultural heritage of Silla and Baekjae.

Even when compared to other gok-ok artifacts from Baekjae, Silla, and Gaya, the jade pieces attached to the gold crowns of the Silla Dynasty are second to none. Dozens of gok-ok are attached to the gold crown discovered in the Northern mound of Hwangnam DaeChong, Gyeongju, and over 130 gok-ok were excavated with the crown discovered in the Geumgwanchong Ancient Tomb Gok-ok diversified as its use spread across the land, developing into a variety of forms on the Korean Peninsula and the Japanese Archipelago. Among the later and more advanced forms of gok-ok is a shape called Moja Gok-Ok. This name originated from the presence of a couple of smaller gok-ok attached to the main gok-ok's surface, like a jade mother with her jade children gathered around her.[*]

The dominant theory is that gok-ok was shaped to imitate a dragon, the symbol of the ruler. Evidence for this comes from the discovery of dragon-shaped jade artifacts from the Bohai Bay (Liao River) civilization, including a C-shaped jade dragon called Ok-Jo-Ryong.[**] Scholars speculate that this was an early version of gok-ok. This means that the gok-ok attached to golden crowns were intended as dragons that embodied the ruler and the status of ultimate authority.

---

* Moja means "mother and son."
** Ok-jo-ryong - Dragon Sculpture made from Ok (jade).

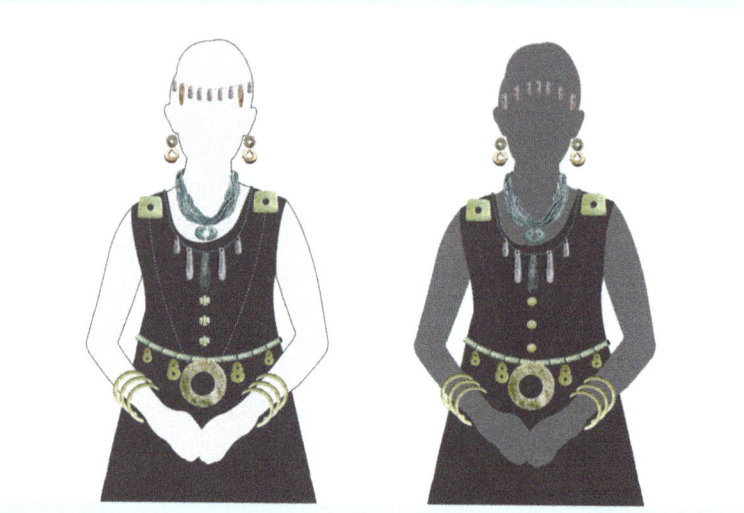

Figure 15-12 Imagined re-creation of a Lady Dressed in excavated jade artifacts

Figure 15-13 Hongsan Culture C-shaped Ok Jo-ryong (5,000 years ago), unearthed from Chifeng City, Inner Mongolia / The sourece of the photo is the book [Hongsan Culture]

Figure 15-14 Deteriorated Jade-bear-dragon unearthed from Hongshan Culture. The bear clan who honored the bear totem made the curved jade in the shape of a bear's face. (personal collection)

Figure 15-15 Gold crowns unearthed from the northern tombs of the Hwangnamdaechong Tomb / It is heavily laden with curved jades.(National Museum of Korea)

Figure 15-16 Golden pendant found in the the tomb of King Michu in Hwangnamdong, Gyeongju. / It's the most splendid pendant among all pendants and ornaments that trace back to Shilla dynasty. (National Gyeongju Museum)

05

Banishing ghosts and bolstering health: the mystical powers of jade

Although jade has been recognized as a valuable mineral for millennia, it was not until recent years that scientists found evidence of its health benefits. People in ancient times believed that it not only bolstered their health, but that it also warded off evil. The Chinese mythological book *Classic of Mountains and Seas* and many other classic texts describe the mystical powers of jade, some of which are introduced in this section.

It is said that ghosts of both heaven and earth consume five colors. In this context, color means a visualized form of energy, called "qi." As jade comes in five different colors, it is believed that the jade energy has the ability to inhibit spiritual beings, preventing them from causing unlucky events. Another ancient myth related to jade is associated with the goddess Queen Mother of the West (Seowangmo in Korean, Xiwangmu in Chinese). In the *Classic of Mountains and Seas*, Seowangmo was a frightening goddess who lived on Ok-San (Jade Mountain), administered the five punishments (including plague), and decided matters of life and death. Her appearance was mostly human, but she had the tail of a leopard and the teeth of a tiger—teeth that did not prevent her from whistling, because she was regarded as a skilled whistler. In particular, she was known for wearing a special ornament in her bushy hair. This hair ornament was made of jade and called Ok-Seung. As a result, people began to imitate her by wearing jade hair ornaments as amulets to repel evil forces. From this story and its impact on ancient society, we know that jade was believed to have the power to exorcise evil energy. This can be compared to how people today believe that they can protect themselves from evil by wearing a charm, cross, or another warding symbol.

In addition to warding off evil, jade has long been lauded for its health benefits. "The Royal Health Secret," an oral tradition passed down through the eunuchs of the Joseon Dynasty, references the use of jade for health purposes. The practice of using a jade pot when rice was cooked for the king was one of these many customs. Jade even figured in prenatal care, where it was used for its calming effect on women who had conceived a baby by the king. A woman who was pregnant with a royal child would stay in a separate palace once she finished her first trimester, cultivating a calm and healthy pregnancy by viewing jasper (green jade) and pine trees. The queen's ornaments always included jade. Her rings, binyeo (ornamental hairpins), hair bands, and norigae (trinkets) were decorated with jade because people believed that wearing jade instilled a feeling of refreshment and stability. Overweight eunuchs and court ladies sought to lose weight by standing on a jade stone for 20 to 30 minutes every day.

Another long-lasting belief maintains that kidney stone (the literal name for a soft type of jade) in particular grants health benefits. The *Dongui Bogam*, a famous classic text on traditional medicine written by Heo Jun (1539-1619) during the Joseon Dynasty, recommends ingesting jade powder for medicinal purposes.* The *Bencao Gangmu*, written by Li Shizhen (completed in 1578, published 1596) during the Ming Dynasty in China, and the *Shennong Bencao Scripture*, which is presumed to have been published between the Later Han Dynasty (25-220) and the Three Kingdoms Period of China (220-280), both describe the potency of jade and similar medicinal practices of its ingestion. Through legends and texts like these, we can see how firmly jade gained people's trust in its ability to drive away evil spirits and offer health benefits, winning popularity throughout the majority of East Asia.

---

* Heo Jun - Court physician of during the reign of King Seonjo of the Joseon Dynasty in Korea. He is known for his work, Dongui Bogam.

06

Embracing divine vitality and bestowing virtue

508   The section "An Explanation of Divination Signs" of *I Ching* links Geon, the first of the Eight Trigrams for divination and a symbol of the heavens, with jade, an association connected to the belief that the vitality of heaven and earth was concentrated into the form of jade, which the Heavenly Emperor then gave to humankind. In Xu Shen's second-century Chinese dictionary *Shuowen Jiezi* (*An Explication of Written Characters*), he describes jade as having five virtues: benevolence, genuineness, wisdom, righteousness, and justice. Benevolence is symbolized by jade's tempered, glossy brightness, while genuineness is seen in its pellucid qualities, which expose jade's internal patterns to the naked eye. Wisdom is symbolized by the sound that jade emanates when struck; it emits a sonorous sound that can be heard from a distance. Righteousness is embodied in its trait of breaking or crumbling rather than bending. Jade's final attribute, that it looks sharp when cut in two but does not harm human skin, symbolizes justice. In this vein, Xu Shen's text explains that we must adopt

the qualities of jade to combine a noble mindset, purity, beauty, and constancy; by doing so, we will be able to lead a good life in our society. The Confucian scripture *Book of Rites* explains that, "A noble man does not let go of jade from himself without a reason, he patterns his virtues by looking upon the jade as a mirror." In both life and death, people used jade in an effort to obtain the powers of the heavens and earth. This love and praise for jade and its lustrous color continues to today. In the Korean language, sights like the "ok-bit" sky and the "ok-bit" sea compare the fine, clear colors of these natural wonders to those of jade.*

---

* "Bit" (빛), pronounced like the vegetable beet, can be translated to mean tint, color, or light.

07

The ancient state system evidenced by jade artifacts

As a symbol of divine authority, jade was a means of displaying one's constancy and noble status, making it a prized possession regardless of status or gender. Jade's popularity made it a product that was coveted by many, but how did people in ancient times produce jade ornaments to meet this demand? Today, processing jade is straightforward. However, the lengthy undertaking of mining, transporting, and processing the prized stone was fraught with difficulties thousands of years ago.

Professional mining workers, transportation workers, and jadeware producing workers existed as far back as 6,000 to 8,000 years ago. Considering the number of jade artifacts excavated from all over Korea, it is speculated that the number of people who worked in jade-related jobs was quite high. Jadeite is a mineral found only in specific regions. Because there was only a limited number of possible

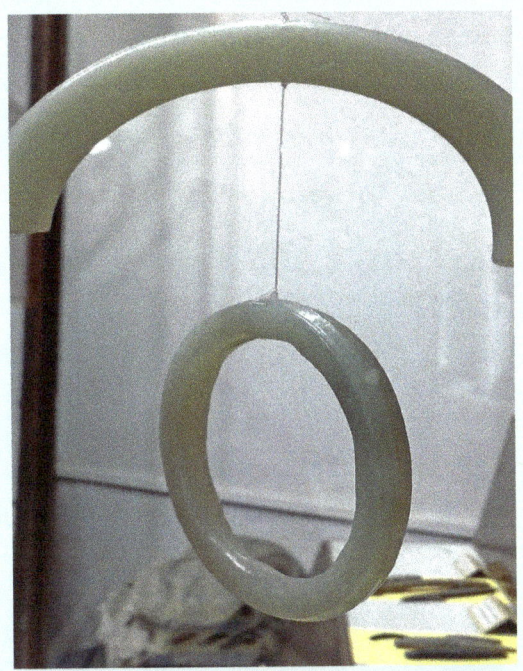

Figure 15-17
A jade bracelet made of Baikal jade displayed at the Museum of History of Irkutsk, Russia / When we visit the museums around the world, it is rare to see jade artifacts in display. In ancient times, jade relics were so valuable that they were worn by people of high standing.

mining sites, locating a new jadeite mining sites took a significant amount of time. Considerable economic power and reliable military force would have been necessary to obtain jade as a proper precious stone after its extraction, transportation, and processing. This resulted in the saying: "The value of gold can be converted into money, but you cannot put a price on the value of jade."

Expert archeologist and Sunmoon University professor Lee Hyeong-goo says that the emergence of jade ware is evidence of a theocracy. In other words, it was the birth of a state system. The monopoly of jade processing led to the emergence of social classes and professional jade technicians, which resulted in further role specialization. This implies that a theocratic society emerged in which a religious leader held rituals for the heavens, carried out the divine will, and governed the state.

As previously mentioned, jade artifacts from the Hongshan culture have been excavated in the Bohai Bay area, along with stone mound tombs, comb-pattern pottery, and Ancient Joseon bronze daggers that are representative of ancient Korean culture. This is in stark opposition to the previous leading theory on Neolithic culture. These unique relics and remains have not been discovered in other early archeological sites in central China, suggesting that this ancient Korean civilization began developing more advanced states (Baedal and Ancient Joseon) earlier than other tribes.

In my travels exploring the cultures of different countries around the world, I have come to recognize that Korea's ancestors were truly a versatile and talented people. It is sad that so little about the brilliant achievements of this early Korean civilization has made it into common knowledge. Fortunately, interest in Korean history is growing, but there are still many who consider history a dull topic. For those people, I highly recommend touring a museum. If you go to a museum, you can put yourself into the shoes of people who lived long ago and better understand how their lifestyles and beliefs evolved over millennia to how we live and interact with the world today. It is my hope that Korea's museums become a place not only for special events, but a cultural space where daily life takes place alongside the great tales of the past.

PART  16

A Trip to the Museums in Korea

The God of War, Dokkaebi

01 A familiar god passed down in folktale and legend
02 Ttukseom Island, Emperor Chi-u's former shrine in Seoul
03 Dukje rites for the god of war
04 The Dokkaebi as a symbol of Emperor Chi-u
05 Emperor Chi-u: ancestor of the Korean Dongyi or Chinese Zhonghua?
06 The power of the Dokkaebi design
07 The Dokkaebi's journey to Europe and America

01

A familiar god passed down in folktale and legend

Recently, when a South Korean TV drama based on the Dokkaebi (goblin) became a global sensation, the character of this traditional Korean goblin drew considerable public attention. While successfully capturing traditional features of the goblin's behavior that are familiar to Koreans, the drama also presented the Dokkaebi with a sophisticated and modern twist.

There are numerous manifestations of the Dokkaebi that have been passed down in folktales and legends. The many faces of this legendary goblin include the Dokkaebi as the god of war, an immortal being, or a figure that is capable of exorcising ghosts and demons. Many iterations of the Dokkaebi are known for a love of singing and wrestling, and for craving buckwheat and sorghum rice cakes with adzuki bean paste. The Dokkaebi also appears in stories as a character (sometimes multiple characters) who is jealous, skilled at metamorphosis, or even stupid, often lusting after beautiful women. In some tales, it appears as a man, and in others, it takes the form of an elderly person or a robust youth. The Dokkaebi is like a god in some ways, but at the same time, the goblin is not that different from a human. Perhaps these relatable, humanlike characteristics are the reason the persona of the Dokkaebi has survived and even thrived for millennia, taking on a variety of folktale roles as it was passed down through the ages to become a protagonist enjoyed by modern society.

Figure 16-1 Dokkaebi tiles from the Unified Shilla dynasty on display at the National Museum of Korea

The Dokkaebi's tale is old enough that goblin symbols can be found on a range of ancient Korean artifacts and remains from dynasties like Goguryeo, Baekjae, and Unified Silla. The oldest known Dokkaebi symbols are found in the ancient mural of Anak Tomb No. 3 of Goguryeo (located in South Hwanghae, North Korea) and on a roof tile from Goguryeo (exhibited at the National Museum of Korea). The Dokkaebi also turns up on Baekjae artifacts like the famous gilt-bronze incense burner of Baekjae and another roof tile; the United Silla era also boasts the Dokkaebi on one of its own delicate roof tiles, as well as on a doorknob and three-legged earthenware.

These are the oldest artifacts known to feature Dokkaebi patterns, but there are Dokkaebi patterns on many other cultural assets, such as the Geumcheongyo Bridge post (the stone pier used as structural support) in Changdeokgung Palace, the Okcheongyo Bridge post in

Figure 16-2 (left) The tomb owner of In the Goguryeo dynasty tomb known as Anak Tomb No. 3 on Hwanghae Island, is holding a fan with a painting of dokaaebi on it. (Woo) Fully extended fan with the painting of a dokkaebi / Both pictures are replicas from the special exhibition on the Goguryeo tombs at the Hanseong Baekje Museum.

Figure 16-3 (Left) Goguryeo dynasty Dokkaebi roof tile (National Museum of Korea), (U) Baekje dynasty Dokkaebi brick (National Museum of Korea)

Changgyeonggung Palace, the Hongjimoon Bridge (which serves as Seoul's north gate), the door of Mahavira Hall of Bulguksa Temple in Gyeongju, as well as on the chests of the Four Devas statues (four heavenly guardians of Buddhism) that watch over the gates of many temples. To commemorate the historical significance of the Dokkaebi to the Korean people, images of Dokkaebi with two horns are featured on the walls of Anguk Station, an underground plaza on Seoul Subway Line 3.

The staggering number and range of Korean artifacts and remains that pay homage to the Dokkaebi comes from the belief that the Dokkaebi prevents misfortune. There are also rituals for exorcism associated with the Dokkaebi, which can be seen on Jindo

Figure 16-4 Reproduction of the turtle ship / There is an image of the dokkaebi on the breast side of the turtle ship.(Yongsan War Memorial)

Island, just off the southwestern coast of the peninsula. When a Korean village faces trouble that must be exorcised, the village women lead the ritual. The Dokkaebi also comes in a variety of forms on Jeju Island, appearing as the old man Dokkaebi, Dokkaebi Chambong (the lowest public office rank during the Joseon Dynasty), the guardian of the family house, and even a god who helps with catching fish. In thanksgiving for the Dokkaebi's assistance, people would make offerings of the Dokkaebi's favorite things.

In addition to its many faces, the Dokkaebi also has many names, including Dochaebi, Dokgabbi, Dotgabi, Dogakgwi, Gwitgeot, Mangryang, Mulchambong, Kim Seobang, and Heoche. The variety of names is not only the result of being a cultural icon that has dominated legends and folktales for thousands of years, but also a byproduct of the evolution of a figure that is rooted in historical fact.

The link between history and legend can be found in the story of Admiral Yi Sunshin (1545-1598). In a historical record of the Imjin War (the Japanese invasions of Korea from 1592–1598) of the Joseon Dynasty, the Korean naval commander is described as performing duk-je rites three times as an offering to the god of war, Emperor Chi-u, before combat.* This scene is depicted with the appearance of the Dokkaebi in the film *The Admiral: Roaring Currents*, in which Admiral Yi Sunshin is the hero. In this movie, the night before a crucial battle, Admiral Yi holds memorial rites in front of his deceased mother's ancestral tablet. The form of the Dokkaebi appears, symbolizing the Emperor Chi-u, along with the character Hwan, which is used in the special title of Hwanung.

---

* Read "Ch 16. Dokkaebi, the God of War, Sect 02 Ttukseom Island, Emperor Chi-u's former shrine in Seoul" of this Book.

Emperor Chi-u was worshipped as the god of war, a symbol of invincibility and victory. He was memorialized as the forefather of fighters and the inventor of martial arts and weapons. It was believed that he had the power to command the wind and clouds and to defeat all ghosts and demons. Although these aspects of his story are a mythical interpretation of the Emperor Chi-u, he was an actual person who left an indelible mark on history: the fourteenth Jaoji Heavenly Emperor Hwanung of Baedal.*

---

* Jaoji refers to the 14th heavenly emperor of Baedal popularly known as Chiwoo Read 'Ch. 16 Dokkaebi, the God of War Sect 5. Emperor Chi-u: Ancestorof the Korean Dongyi or Chinese Zhonghua?' of this book.

02

Ttukseom Island, Emperor Chi-u's former shrine in Seoul

Ttukseom (Ttuk Island) is a unique area along the Hangang River that links Ttukseom Station of Seoul Subway Line 2 and Seoul-forest Station of Line 7. In recent years, Ttukseom has been transformed into a popular attraction with its combination of resort experiences and nature in the Seongdong-gu district of Seoul, but despite the presence of the word seom (island) in its name, it is not a true island. In fact, Ttukseom only won its island title because of flooding from heavy rains. Its name also conceals an interesting tie to the Dokkaebi.

Ttukseom was originally called Duk-do. Long ago, it contained a shrine for Emperor Chi-u, and a Duk flag representing Chi-u was erected, so the place came to be called Dukseom. Duk was also pronounced as Dok, meaning that it was sometimes referred to as Dok-do. Here, "do" is a Korean suffix for island, like the word seom. Korean oral tradition tells us that a mysterious red smoke would rise

Figure 16-5 Red colored dukki flag displayed in the eight-panel folding screen of King Jeongjo's Procession to Hwaseong Tombs (National Palace Museum of Gyeongbokgung Palace)

Figure 16-6 A dukki flag displayed in front of the Ttukseom Water Museum

Figure 16-7 Ttukseom Monument in the Forest of Seoul / The bank of King Sejong Orye painted on the signpost indicating the origin of Ttukseom

during the annually-held national rites and during times of national hardship; this was named Chi-u's flag or Chi-u-gi. This is why the flag known as the Duk-gi (Chi-u-gi) is red. Dukseom, where the annual dukje (Chi-u-je) ritual was held, was later called Ttukseom.

The Duk-gi flag appears on the folding screen called "Hwaseong Neunghaengdo," which depicts the return of Joseon Dynasty's King Jeongjo (r. 1776-1800) to the capital, Hanyang, after his visit to Hwaseong. In this picture, a red Duk-gi flag is held aloft between the ssangyong-gi flag (double dragon flag) and a sedan chair carrying the king. These same ssangyong-gi and Duk-gi flags appear in another picture, which depicts an important ceremony held in the city of Hwaseong.

There was even a shrine for Emperor Chi-u on Dukseom until the 1940s, but it was swept away during a season of particularly heavy rains. This shrine featured a large picture depicting the Battle of Zhuolu, where Emperor Chi-u fought Huangdi (the Yellow Emperor) north of the Great Wall of China. Korean independence activists attempted to restore the shrine during the Japanese occupation of the Korean Peninsula in the twentieth century, but a horse stable was installed in its place as part of the Japanese colonial administration's policy to forcibly erase Korean culture. The location was a horse racecourse until recently.

During the Goryeo and Joseon dynasties, people held dukje (Chi-u-je) rites before going into combat as well as before Gyeongchip (one of the 24 seasons, which falls around March 5 on the solar calendar and signifies the end of hibernation) and Sanggang (another one of the 24 seasons, which falls around October 24 on the solar calendar). The next section will explore the history and traditions of the ritual ceremony of dukje ritual.

03

Dukje rites for the god of war

Each spring in South Korea, Jeollanam-do Province holds the Turtle Ship festival, which includes an event called the Jeollanam-do Province Naval Base Dukje ritual. The general's flag is raised aloft in this ancestral rite held before troops are dispatched; the flag is the Emperor Chi-u's flag and symbolizes the authority of military command. As mentioned earlier in this chapter, historical records show that Admiral Yi Sunshin also performed dukje rites three times during the Imjin War (Japanese invasions of Korea from 1592-1598). Dukje rite was held in the Hour of Chuk (approximately 1:00-3:00 a.m.), during which soldiers, local personages, and Admiral Yi Sunshin himself gathered together in prayer to the god of war, the Emperor Chi-u, for victory against Japanese invaders.

In general, mention of ancestral memorial rites calls to mind somber and quiet ceremonies, but in dukje, people dance to music. Soldiers wield axes, shields, spears, swords, and arrows, and move as if in combat, and the event proceeds like a drill in combat position. Another ancestral ritual performed with dancing is the famous Ancestral Ritual held in the Jongmyo Shrine, but this is an elaborate ceremony with solemn and intricate steps. In contrast, dukje is a simple ritual without ancestral tablets that instead raises aloft a Duk-gi flag made from luxuriant red hair. This red hair is fashioned from a bull's tail, which is a nod to how Emperor Chi-u is depicted wearing a helmet with the horns of a bull.

The Miao people, a minority group in China, honor Emperor Chi-u as their ancestor and observe their own annual holiday for him during the tenth month of the lunar calendar. For this festival, women wear bull horns made of splendid silver to celebrate Emperor

Chi-u, who wore a helmet with bull horns. When the festival marches through the streets, people carry along a massive drum decorated with a picture of a bull's head with huge horns.

Not unlike the Korean Duk-gi flag of red hair, the Mongols historically erected nine flags made of white hair in front of Genghis Khan's ger (also known as a yurt). Later in the history of the Ottoman Empire, the Cossacks (Slavic cavalry) and people in Poland also used hair flags. Traces of this tradition can still be seen today, as the Mongolian government keeps its modern Nine White Banners in the Government Palace in the capital, Ulaanbaatar, and hair flags are still in use in some Polish military units. Traditionally, Mongolians have used white flags during peacetime and black flags in times of war.

Does the Dokkaebi have horns?

The figure of the Dokkaebi that appears in children's fairy tale books is somewhat different from that of Korea's traditional Dokkaebi. The Dokkaebi of fairy tale books is much closer to the Oni, a traditional Japanese depiction of the Dokkaebi. This shift came about when Japanese used the figure of their Oni to replace the Korean Dokkaebi. As explained previously in this chapter, the Korean Dokkaebi appears in a wide range of shapes, including as a child or woman, or as an elderly person or youth, rather than taking a fixed form. The Korean Dokkaebi also can transform into inanimate objects such as pots, brooms, wood fire pokers, and more. It plays tricks, but it is foolish enough that it can easily be fooled by a smart person. The many forms of the Dokkaebi in Korean legends are both marvelous and heartwarming to those who grew up hearing about them.

This gave rise to the misperception that the traditional Korean Dokkaebi does not have horns. In reality, the aspects of the Dokkaebi engraved on ancient artifacts and remains are widely depicted with horns. Even though the appearance of a Korean Dokkaebi clearly differs from the Japanese Oni's fearsome visage, both do have horns. The mistaken portrayal of the Dokkaebi without horns is the result of the attempt at erasure of the Japanese depiction of the Dokkaebi, Oni. Still, it cannot be denied that the Korean and Japanese interpretations of this cultural icon look similar. These similarities came about because the tradition of the Korean Dokkaebi was transmitted to Japan through cultural exchange, giving birth to the Oni.

04

The Dokkaebi as a symbol of Emperor Chi-u

References to Emperor Chi-u can be found on numerous Korean cultural artifacts, and various modern sites pay homage to him as well. For example, the front steps of the War Memorial of Korea in Yongsan, Seoul, are guarded by a brave Dokkaebi engraved overhead in a blaze of fire. Considering its frequent use as a symbol of war, the Dokkaebi is a fitting feature at this War Memorial. In addition to the Dokkaebi at the entrance, the museum has numerous shields with Dokkaebi motifs on display.

To better understand why Emperor Chi-u was worshipped as the god of war and depicted as the Dokkaebi, we must first delve into the historical context of the widespread use of Dokkaebi symbolism.

Surviving records from the era when Emperor Chi-u played an active role in history, a period about 4,700 years ago, are exceedingly rare. Although the contents of these rare records differ slightly, their

Figure 16-8 Dokkaebi, the god of war, installed above the main entrance of the Yongsan War Memorial.

Figure 16-9 The Joseon dynasty long shield displayed at the Yongsan War Memorial./ The image of the Dokkaebi is painted

Figure 16-10 (Right) Circular plate with an image of the dokkaebi.

depictions of the power wielded by Emperor Chi-u remain consistent. The emperor is described with the phrase Dong-Du-Cheol-Aek, which means "a head of bronze with a forehead of steel," which sounds like the description of a superhuman being. This phrase is actually an allusion to the fact that he made and wore such a helmet.

Emperor Chi-u, the fourteenth ruler of the state of Baedal, possessed considerable military power predicated on the use of metal weapons made by extracting and smithing ores. This is how Emperor Chi-u came to be attributed as the inventor of metal weaponry like swords, spears, and longbows. Because an active munitions industry would have required a strong economic foundation, it is thought that the Emperor Chi-u's reign was abundant in food and supplies. The establishment of a legal system and a governing state organization in the Neolithic Age is a colossal feat achived by Emperor Chi-u.

Approximately 4,700 years ago, during the reign of Emperor Chi-u, multiple ethnic groups in East Asia were competing for regional domination. Emperor Chi-u's military, the army of Baedal, advanced from the east toward central China (the territory of the Yellow River and the Yangtze River) and established control. In another region of China, Huangdi, who aspired to be an emperor, raised his own army and fought Emperor Chi-u. The Battle of Zhuolu took place beyond the Great Wall in its namesake county, which lies north of modern-day Beijing. The two rulers met in battle 73 times over a decade, Huangdi losing every encounter. Eventually, Emperor Chi-u captured Huangdi and made him a retainer, which enabled the transmission of the Baedal people's culture. Huangdi is both a cultural icon and a historical figure acknowledged as one of the ancestors of the Han Chinese people (Zhonghua minzu), which is China's largest ethnic group.

Emperor Chi-u's instrumental role in ancient East Asia is reaffirmed by a particular image that was passed down in China. This hua-xiang-shi engraving (a stone relief sculpture set in front of a tomb) from the Northern and Southern dynasties of China in Jiangsu Province portrays the figure of Emperor Chi-u with the head of a bird, holding a sword in one hand and a bow in the other hand. On the hua-xiang-shi of the Mu Family shrine wall painting in Shandong Province, Emperor Chi-u is depicted as a bear wielding a variety of weapons with both his hands and feet. There are portrayals even more frightening than these, where Emperor Chi-u has two sets of arms and legs, two heads, and four eyes; his feet are the hooves of a bull, and there are horns on his head. In these images of Chinese origin, he is portrayed much like how a modern horror movie would imagine a ferocious monster. In this way, the ancient Han Chinese tribe habitually described the heroes of the Dongyi people not as humans but as monsters. For example, they illustrated Taeho Bokhee (Fu-shi) and Yeowa (Wahuang) as half human and half beast, with the lower body of a snake; like Emperor Chi-u, Shennong was shown with horns on his head. Even among these frightening depictions, Emperor Chi-u's altered image stands out as particularly bizarre.

According to the tales of his many great feats, Emperor Chi-u produced metal weapons and helmets earlier than his contemporaries, generated thick fog, and at times even used gusty rains and raging fires in combat, making him an invincible opponent to the Han Chinese. His 73 victories against Huangdi (the Yellow Emperor) over a ten-year period established him as a war deity in East Asia and won him fame as "the God of War." However, in the *Shiji*, a compilation of ancient history by the historian Sima Qian, Huangdi seized victory at the end of the war and killed the Emperor Chi-u. If Huangdi truly did kill Emperor Chi-u, it stands to reason that he would have been worshipped as the winner of the war and been elevated to Emperor Chi-u's stead. Despite the assertions in *Shiji*, Emperor Chi-u is the figure who became memorialized as a war god by the generations that followed—even by the Han Chinese. The reason for the type of

---

* Shiji (Records of the Grand Historian) - Written by Sima Qian around 94 BCE.

Figure 16-11 A relief sculpture at the Muryangsa Temple in Shandong Province, China / This image is believed to be depicting the Great Battle of Taklok /
It describes the Emperor Chi-u as a bear-shaped animal, indicating that he is a descendant of the bear tribe. Chi-u is dancing with his brothers holding his invention of the great bow (the dae-no),
Gojoseon style (mandoline type) daggar, a branched spear, a trident, and a club.

historical contradiction found in the *Shiji* stems from China's distortion of the history of the war between the Emperor Chi-u and the Yellow Emperor Huangdi.

Historical records of Emperor Chi-u

Guanzi, An Ancient Chinese Text

According to *Guanzi*, as water gushed forth from Mount Gallo, iron came with it. Emperor Chi-u collected this iron and made swords, armor, spears, branched spears, and so on.* When iron and water also gushed forth from Mount Ongho, Emperor Chi-u smelted this iron and made a spear called Onghogeuk and a spear called Yegwa. The historical evidence for this record is further illustrated by the old character for iron, which was Cheol, a combination of the characters Geum and Yi, meaning "iron of the Dongyi people."

Taiping Yulan from the Song Dynasty of China

Taiping Yulan describes how Emperor Chi-u smelted iron to make weapons, cut leather to make armor, and started a military system with five types of soldiers. This record identifies the originator of metallurgy as Emperor Chi-u.

Chinese Confucian classic *Zhou Li Zhu Shu*

This record explains that ancestral rites held for Emperor Chi-u were intended to honor him as the inventor of these weapons: the Mo, Geuk, Geom, Sun, and Gung. It also states that the emperor was the strongest person among the foreigners, able to make any weapon with ease, which earned him praise as "the best weapons-maker."

One of Four Books and Three Classics of Confucianism, the *Book of Documents*

This record describes how Emperor Chi-u ruled the Miao people with a legislative system.

---

* Korean branched spear is a spear with many sharp metal branches on it. It is very useful in protecting against enemy weapon and it is also effective in blocking arrows.

05

Emperor Chi-u: ancestor of the Korean Dongyi or Chinese Zhonghua?

A variety of Chinese historical records offer us glimpses into the power of Emperor Chi-u's legacy. For example, Emperor Gaozu Liu Bang, the founder of the Han Dynasty (202 BCE-220 CE) prayed for victory by offering memorial rites for Emperor Chi-u. Qin Shi Huang (259-210 BCE), the founder of the Qin Dynasty and the first emperor of a united China, also offered memorial rites to the Emperor Chi-u, stopping at Mount Tai during his royal tour to the east.

The story of Emperor Chi-u might sound like pure legend, but there is a real person behind the legend. He was the fourteenth Jaoji Heavenly Emperor Hwanung of Baedal (3897-2333 BCE), a state that was established earlier than Ancient Joseon (2,333-239 BCE), and he made Baedal strong in both military and economic power. Given that the Miao people, a minority group in

China, continue to venerate Emperor Chi-u as their progenitor even today, it appears that Emperor Chi-u has been regarded as a respectable ruler for thousands of years. The Korean word wu-du-meo-ree, meaning leader or chief, originated from Emperor Chi-u's helmet with bull horns, while bull-horned helmets that were worn by Goguryeo generals are among the many excavated artifacts that allude to his long-lasting cultural impact.*

However, in 1995, China revised its original version of ancient history and began insisting that Emperor Chi-u was an ancestor of the Han Chinese. As part of this, China built a temple for the Chinese Three Ancestors at Zhuolu that featured statues of the Dongyi Korean people's ancestors Shennong and Emperor Chi-u alongside an established Han Chinese ancestor, the Yellow Emperor Huangdi. Zhuolu is where Emperor Chi-u and the Yellow Emperor Huangdi battled for a decade. The mural in this temple depicts a battle between Emperor Chi-u and Yellow Emperor Huangdi, but the original monstrous portrayal of the historical figure of Emperor Chi-u has been replaced with a human form.

Why would China abruptly change its negative stance, to favor an emperor that it historically depicted as a monster? The answer to this question is rooted in the Bohai Bay (Liao River) Hongshan civilization described throughout this book. With the discovery of this ancient civilization, China changed its stance. The Bohai Bay civilization is older than the previously established cradle of civilization and dates anywhere between 2,000 to 3,000 years earlier than the Yellow River civilization. Links to this civilization have not been discovered in the traditional ancient Chinese regions that are located inside the Great Wall of China. To weave the significance of this ancient civilization into China's history, China had to rapidly change its official stance and claim the long-scorned Dongyi Korean people as an early

---

* Wudu-meori: Wu-du is head of a bull, and meo-ri is the head.

Chinese people.

To make this change, China has significantly reconstructed its ancient history. These government-led revisionist history projects include the Xia-Shang-Zhou Chronology Project, the Northeast Project, the Origin of Chinese Civilization Exploration Project, and the Historical Records Revision Project. But why would China want to subsume ancient Korean history under its own at the cost of distorting Chinese history?

China's United Multi-Ethnic Country theory asserts that all ethnic groups living in the contemporary territory of the People's Republic of China are part of the Chinese people, and the histories of all these groups are a part of Chinese history. According to China's new theory, the ethnic group that cultivated the Bohai Bay (Liao River) civilization and led Hongshan culture was the Huangdi tribe, and this has been accepted as a doctrine. This revises history so that even the vast territory that Emperor Chi-u once ruled might be considered a part of China. It is China's overall plan so places like Tibet, Manchuria, Xinjiang and other ethnic minority places cannot claim independence.

According to China's new theory, Emperor Chi-u's area of control included Shandong Peninsula, Liaodong Peninsula, Manchuria, and the Korean Peninsula as well. In this version of the past, the Dongyi Korean become Chinese, and ancient Korean history becomes a part of Chinese history.

Dokkaebi and ssireum (traditional Korean wrestling)

- The Dokkaebi's love for ssireum is a characteristic that comes directly from Emperor Chi-u, who was ascribed as the inventor of ssireum. In China, ssireum is called gakjeohee or chiuhee. This nomenclature suggests that the origin of ssireum was indeed connected to Emperor Chi-u, and it is further supported by a Goguryeo tomb mural that depicts Emperor Chi-u's relationship with ssireum. In the past, victors in traditional Korean ssireum were given a bull in commemoration of Emperor Chi-u. In Chinese ssireum, competitors traditionally wore horned helmets.

06

The power of the Dokkaebi design

538

Emperor Chi-u's ten years and 73 victories in battle against China's Yellow Emperor Huangdi are an obvious justification for his elevation as a symbol of victory in East Asia. There is even a persuasive argument that the Korean word ji-wee (status), meaning "a powerful and brave person," can be etymologically traced to his name: Chi-u. The Dokkaebi design, which is a symbol for Emperor Chi-u, was widely used throughout the Three Kingdoms of Korea, the Goryeo Dynasty, and the Joseon Dynasty. But the widespread use of the Dokkaebi design among commoners was not actually related to its function as a symbol of victory; for many people, it was primarily used to suppress bad energy and prevent the intrusion of evil spirits.

With so many versions of the Dokkaebi to choose from, you might wonder which aspect of the Dokkaebi scares away evil spirits. The answer to this can be found in legends about Huangdi, who battled

Figure 16-12 Doorknob in the shape of a dokkaebi / Excavated from Eastern Palace of Gyeongju and Wolji, the site of a royal villa of the Shilla dynasty Royal Palace (National Gyeongju Museum)

against Emperor Chi-u. According to some of these stories, Huangdi had an unusual ability that he learned from an encounter with a peculiar creature known as the Baí Zé. This creature lived in the immortal world, eating tigers and speaking human language, and it taught Huangdi how to drive out 11,530 types of ghosts, monsters and evil spirits that appeared in ancient legends; this is how he gained power over them. Essentially, the tale maintains, Huangdi became the king of eveil spirits.

But despite his powers over otherworldly beings, Huangdi was unable to win against Emperor Chi-u, who mobilized an army of Dokkaebi to overpower Huangdi's spectral troops. Some of the names of the Dokkaebi from this story, such as Imae, Mangryang, Sindo, and Ulru, have been passed down in oral tradition. In the legends of battles between the king of ghosts, Huangdi, and the Dokkaebi king, Emperor Chi-u, Emperor Chi-u always won. This provided the foundation for later generations to use the Dokkaebi as not only a symbol for Emperor Chi-u, but as an amulet to expel ghosts and evil spirits as well.

The traditional door handles of Korean gates are emblazoned with the face of the Dokkaebi and carry the same meaning. Two Dokkaebi named Imae and Mangryang are mentioned in *Seongho's Editorial Articles*, a text written by Joseon scholar Lee Ik on a wide range of topics, including astronomy, geography, history, government institutions, the military, customs, and literature. Some people even replace the common phrase Ib-Chun-Dae-Gil, which expresses a wish for spring to bring good fortune and which may be used on the doors of traditional houses, with the Dokkaebi names Sindo and Ulru. Sindo and Ulru are Dokkaebi brothers believed to block evil spirits that attempt to enter a household through one of its gates. In fact, even the

Figure 16-13 Bronze pots dating back to the Zhou Dynasty, part of a special exhibition at the National Museum of Korea. / It is engraved with a do-cheol-moon which symbolizes the face of the dokkaebi.

gate to the main building of the old house of Yi Hwang* (1501-1570), one of the most prominent Korean Confucian scholars of the Joseon Dynasty, references this. Sindo and Ulru, as well as the phrases "Ga-Emu-Bul-Sang" and "Mun-Sin-Ho-Ryeong," are written on Yi's gate as a warning that the spirit of the house will prevent anything inauspicious from entering. Similarly, the names of Sindo and Ulru were written in red and attached to the doorpost of the palace building that held Joseon Dynasty government offices of astronomy, geography, and weather. This, too, was done to repel and expel ghosts.

Notably, there are impressive taotie (legendary voracious beasts that drive away evil creatures in Chinese mythology) with Dokkaebi-like faces inlaid on bronze vessels from the Shang (1600-1046 BCE) and Zhou dynasties (1046-256 BCE) of China. As such, it is speculated that the Dokkaebi was a historically significant symbol for many other groups in East Asia beside the Korean people.

---

* One of the most widely known Joseon dynasty Neo-Confucian scholar. His work on Neo-Confucianism was taken by Japan during the Imjin Wars and made a huge impact in the progress of the Japanese Neo-Confucianism.

Figure 16-14 Dokkaebi-patterned roof tiles of the Unified Shilla dynasty on display at the Gyeongju National Museum.

Figure 16-15 Dokkaebi carved on the feet of the three-legged Pottery of the Unified Shilla dynasty on display at the National Museum of Korea.

Figure 16-16 Dokkaebi-patterned brazier of the Koryo dynasty (National Museum of Korea)

07

The Dokkaebi's journey to Europe and America

As with other elements of their culture, the horse-riding people of the east spread the symbol of their god of war to their neighbors and on to the rest of the world. Deities with striking similarities to Emperor Chi-u also appear in Western mythology, such as the northern European Nordic deity Tyr (Ziu), who is known as a war or fire god. In Old High German, Tyr was called Ziu. Ziu was the highest god of heaven, and he wore a horned helmet.

In northern European Celtic mythology, the war god was called Tiw, a name that sounds considerably similar to Chi-u. Some theories also posit that Zeus in Greek mythology is related to Emperor Chi-u. The book *Black Athena*, by American author Martin Bernal (1937-2013), theorizes that the ancestors of the Greeks were of the mixed blood of Semites and Asians. It might

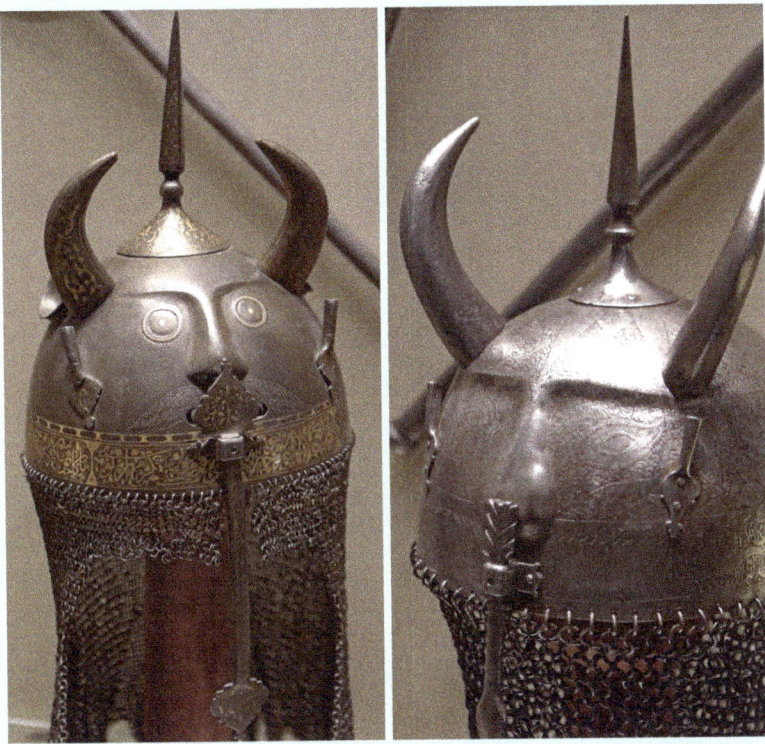

Figure 16-17 Turkish soldier's helmet on display at the Hermitage Museum in St. Petersburg, Russia. / Bull's horn attached to the helmet resembles the dokkaebi helmet.

Figure 16-18 The Court Church (Hofkirche) at Innsbruck, Austria. Also known as the Black Cathedral, it has a belt style ornament on the bronze statues of the ancestors of Habsburg lineage. / The pattern looks very similar to Korean Dokkaebi.

Figure 16-19 (left) Bronze vessels bearing the dokkaebi patterns of ancient Bulgaria (National Archaeological Museum, Bulgaria)

Figure 16-20 (right) The front gate decoration of the birthplace Mozart in Salzburg, The figure of a dokkaebi is biting the snake.

not be such a coincidence after all that there are features of the European pantheon that resemble Korean culture.

In my travels through Europe and many other parts of the world, I have been pleasantly surprised to encounter the familiar figure of the Dokkaebi in new and different aspects. Although it has not been proved beyond a shadow of a doubt that these are foreign interpretations of the Korean Dokkaebi, it is not impossible that the Korean Dokkaebi migrated to Europe and the Americas over generations of vigorous exchange between the East and the West, evolving over thousands of years into new aspects and acquiring new names.

The Dokkaebi aspect of Emperor Chi-u — the god of war, a symbol of victory, an invincible legend, the creator of martial arts who also invented weapons, the one who could command

Figure 16-21 Goblin engraved on stonework erected at the entrance of the Winter Palace in Ulaanbaatar, Mongolia

Figure 16-22 The Dokkaebi of the Andean Civilization / The people who developed Andean Civilization were those who crossed from the Far East to South America through the Aleutian Islands. They have a cultural similarity to our ancestors, and their traditional language, Quechua, is an agglutinative language which has the same word order as the Korean language. The culture created along the Andes Mountain Range is characterized by pyramids, sotdae culture, dragon culture, shamanism, and the sun god culture.

Figure 16-23 The dokkaebi of the Moche culture, a civilization that was a part of the broader Andean civilizations.

the wind and clouds, who could transform at will using Dao mastery, who made ghosts and demons surrender — this historical figure-turned-legend was eventually transmitted beyond Asia to other parts of the world. Recently, the Emperor Chi-u who lived thousands of years ago was revived as the mascot of the Red Devils of the Korean national soccer team (Red Devils is the name of the official fan club for the Korean national soccer team) in the 2002 FIFA World Cup, and he even made its red carpet debut as a character in film and TV.

This same Dokkaebi, a cultural icon and historical figure who was long ago seen as an object of both fear and respect by neighboring tribes and states, has been appropriated as an ancestor of the Han Chinese through the revision and fabrication of the Korean Dongyi people's history. It is incumbent on us to restore and protect Emperor Chi-u's rightful and original place in history. This is precisely why the facts of ancient history must be made clear. If we disregard the great cultural footprints of those who came before us as outdated and unimportant, our own future will ultimately come under threat.